THE KING OF SPAIN AND I

Surviving cricket, depression and the greatest ever Ashes

THE KING OF SPAIN AND I

Surviving cricket, depression and the greatest ever Ashes

ASHLEY GILES

fairfield books

First published by Fairfield Books in 2025

fairfield books

Fairfield Books
Bedser Stand
Kia Oval
London
SE11 5SS

A CIP catalogue record for this title is available from the British Library

Printed by CPI Group (UK) Ltd

For Mum and Dad, Stine, Anders & Tilly

Contents

Foreword

As a captain you want different characters and personalities in your team. You need not only *cricketers* you can rely on, but dependable human beings. In that sense, Ashley Giles was right at the top of the list.

Gilo's career wasn't always an easy ride. Like all of us, he had his ups and downs, but he cared so much and was so desperate to do well for the team that sometimes it became a burden for him.

I remember after the first Test of the '05 Ashes he felt lost and thought we were going to drop him from the side. I had a heart to heart with him before that famous match at Edgbaston, where Gilo ended up taking five crucial wickets, to try and relieve some of the pressure he was putting on himself. Never in a million years were we going to drop him in that series. He'd done such a good job for us as a player, and perhaps even more so as a character. We had a five-man leadership group within the team and he was one of the first names I wanted in there.

He didn't grab the headlines like a Pietersen or Flintoff, but Gilo was an integral member of the England team that had so much success and went on to win the Ashes after such a long wait. Our four seamers were delighted to have him in the team. He very rarely got hit out of the attack so that allowed me to rotate the quicks and give them a bit more rest. His over-the-wicket angle created the opportunity for him to play an important role in the first innings, holding up an end, but people forget that he was capable of bowling teams out from around the wicket when conditions were conducive to spin.

As a player he'll be remembered as a dependable left-arm spinner and a punchy No.8 who used to get the ball through backward point, not to mention a very safe pair of hands at gully. People would have been less aware of the warrior spirit that he brought to the side. If Shoaib Akhtar, Brett Lee or Dale Steyn were bowling the quickest spell of the match, he'd walk out there and face the music and never take a backward step.

He's needed that spirit as he's faced family health issues in recent years, and also during his time as England's director of cricket.

He had that role in an extremely difficult period, negotiating the challenges that came with the Covid pandemic, and I thought he was treated unfairly at the time. The finger was pointed at him but many of the circumstances were out of his control.

Seeing him so emotional at the SCG in the midst of a very challenging Ashes series was hard to watch, but it just tells you how much it means to him. He has always cared passionately about English cricket and has done whatever is in his power to make it as strong as possible. I'm delighted to see him doing such a good job at Worcestershire now.

Mental health and wellbeing is still something which isn't often talked about. I wasn't always aware of Gilo's struggles during his playing career, although I could see his desperation to do well led to anxiety at times, and sometimes he took criticism too personally. I'm glad he's been open and honest enough to speak up and share his story.

We had some great times together as England teammates, playing PlayStation together on long, lonely tours with our late, great mate, Graham Thorpe. Gilo's not only a former teammate, he's a great friend too. He's one of those people you know you can always ring and he'll be there to help. He never goes missing.

Michael Vaughan, June 2025

Introduction

The King of Spain tale began around 2001 with a simple printing error. The club shop at Edgbaston had arranged for sample mugs to be produced to celebrate my performances with England. They were meant to feature my image and the words 'The King of Spin'. What came back from the printers, however, was something very different. Instead of 'Spin' the mugs proudly declared me 'The King of Spain'. Just two misprinted mugs in that first batch—but enough to spark something none of us expected. We had a good laugh about it at the time. One mug stayed with me in the dressing room for my coffee; the other remained in the club shop as a bit of a novelty.

Then, friend, local TV legend and news anchor Nick Owen happened to mention the mug during a broadcast – and that's when things began to take off. The story made the papers soon after. Still, it wasn't until 2004 – after what turned out to be my most successful cricketing summer at home – that King of Spain mania really took hold. More mugs were printed (with the same glorious error), and before long, the Spanish flag was spotted waving proudly in the stands during Test matches. By the winter tours of 2004/05 and the unforgettable Ashes summer of 2005, it had all gone into overdrive.

Since my retirement from playing in 2007, I have remained in the game through a number of different roles across coaching, leadership and administration. That's almost 18 years now, far longer than my playing career. But if there's one thing that's stuck with me, beyond any of the cricketing moments or the leadership achievements, it's that nickname. Whether at the cricket, or if I am recognised in a shop or pub, it's always the King of Spain that comes up. In fact, if I walk past someone and they do a double-take, I know that I will only have to wait a few seconds before they shout after me, "King of Spain!". I honestly love it, it's always done in good spirit, and it connects me again to that special time in my career.

My cricket journey began about 20 years before anyone had thought of printing a mug with my name on it. I watched in awe as an eight-year-old when Ian Botham almost single-handedly won the Ashes, and I dreamed of experiencing the same thing one day.

Without Mum and Dad, I certainly wouldn't have had the opportunities or experiences I have enjoyed – to be part of such incredible moments, to see the world, or to play the cricket I have played. I will always be grateful for the wonderful environment in which I was raised, full of love, support and encouragement. I'm also thankful to my siblings Andrew, Carrie, and Tracy, for their love and support.

Likewise, without the unconditional love of Stine and our children, Anders and Tilly, I am quite certain there would have been times when I may have found it easier to walk away from everything. They have supported me through some of the darkest moments and somehow always manage to lift my spirits, mostly by making me laugh. Even if, as in Stine's case, it is often unintentional. I love them more than they could ever know.

There have been countless coaches, colleagues, teammates and friends who have shaped both me and my career over the last four decades. Some of them continue to do so, and I thank each and every one of them.

This book has been a work in progress for nearly 20 years. I first began writing at the start of 2007, while Stine was recovering from brain surgery. I managed to write about 50,000 words in those early months, much of it centred on the Ashes series of 2005 and my struggles with the game. Over the past decade, I have revisited those words many times, editing and refining as I went, wondering if I would ever finish telling the story of my journey and whether anyone would want to read it.

Thanks to encouragement from George Dobell and an introduction to Matt Thacker from Fairfield Books towards the end of the 2024 season, I found the motivation to complete my story. And without the excellent editing support and advice from Matt, Phil Walker and Jo Harman-McGowan, this may simply not have happened. Thank you.

1

That will be England gone

On February 2, 2022, I lost my job as managing director of England men's cricket. Called into Lord's that day to see my boss, Tom Harrison, our conversation quickly moved to the terms of my exit, and that was it. It hadn't been a surprise to me, and I don't remember much of it. I was in a bad place by then. For months, in reality, I'd been a shadow of myself.

A disastrous Ashes tour of Australia had capped off two incredibly tough years managing our men's teams while trying to keep the game on during the Covid pandemic. For much of the previous 10 months I'd felt myself starting to deteriorate, and by the time I left the ECB I was a mess. I was burnt out and broken.

For the previous couple of months, I'd not slept at all well. Regularly I would wake up in the night having what I can only describe as anxiety attacks. I had struggled to concentrate because my head just felt so full of rubbish and my decision-making and communication since that Christmas had been erratic.

Being sacked, in truth, had lifted a huge weight from my shoulders. Reaching what I thought was the pinnacle of my profession had now become a millstone around my neck and being relieved of my responsibilities was a relief. That only confirmed how far I'd fallen over the previous few months. I do remember how sad that felt; in many ways, it still does.

The 4-0 Ashes defeat had indeed been a disaster, and I'd witnessed all but nine days of it first-hand with the team. Those nine days were spent with my family over Christmas at home in Droitwich. I had been due to spend at least 12 days at home, but when a Covid outbreak hit our management team, including our head coach Chris Silverwood, I made the decision to return to Australia earlier than planned, on New Year's Eve.

In hindsight I probably shouldn't have come home at all. Don't get me wrong, I was desperate to see my family after spending so much time away, and I really did need the break. But nine days was too short. I was jetlagged, became ill when I got home, and my mental health was really beginning to suffer. I'd had a breakdown in front of my wife, Stine, when I got home. She only asked me how I was doing and I burst into tears. Between Christmas and New Year I reached out to our team psychologist. It was more of a cry for help, and he came round to our house to see me. I knew I really had no choice but to return to Australia; after all, it was my job and the whole squad was having an awful time out there.

My personal situation wasn't helped at all when Mum and Dad came up to visit us for a couple of days. I hadn't seem Mum for months and I was shocked when she got out of the car. She was incredibly thin and frail, I couldn't believe my eyes. Mum had been suffering with dementia for some time and had slowly been weakening. She was finding it more and more difficult to recall anything that was said five minutes before and she repeated herself a lot, yet she could recall the finest detail of things from our past and her childhood. The problem by then was that she'd almost completely stopped eating. Previously, she was still happy, laughing and joking with us, and she loved her food. This time, she was completely different. When she was with us for those two days she only ate a few scraps during the whole time, and we tried her with everything. Unsurprisingly, she had hardly any energy and just sat watching the TV, falling off to sleep regularly. It was agonising to watch.

A couple of days after saying goodbye to her, on New Year's Eve morning, I left for Heathrow to return to the tour. I had been home barely enough time to get over my jetlag. Seeing Mum so ill was horrible and left me with feelings of guilt and anger that I hadn't been around more for her and Dad. When I arrived at the check-in desk and was told I didn't have all the right passenger locator documentation for Australia – a simple form that takes five minutes to fill in – I had an anxiety attack. I remember sitting and looking at my phone for what seemed an age, seriously contemplating getting a taxi to take me home. I was in a really bad place when I boarded the plane back to Sydney.

In hindsight, from the perspective of my own mental health, I probably shouldn't have gone. My situation wasn't helped by having to spend another five days in isolation when I arrived at the team hotel. I wasn't allowed to see anyone (apart from the nurse once a day to take my Covid test) and all of my meals were delivered to my door. The unhealthy mix of jetlag and my mental state left me clawing at the walls night and day.

That Australia tour was a nightmare from start to finish. We were two years into living in bio-secure bubbles and the toll was heavy on all of us. At one stage, in the build-up, the question we faced as a management team was who, of the playing staff, was even *willing* to go. Everyone in the end signed up, we did enough to convince them, with me negotiating with both sides – trying to persuade the players to play, and trying to get Cricket Australia to give us enough assurances that it would be workable. Ultimately, it didn't matter what they gave us. As soon as we got on that plane, we were never going to win the Ashes.

We were broken, and we just became more broken. We wanted to honour our commitments to Australian cricket because it was crucial for them, but our people were at breaking point. Personally, I was going from 7:30am to 8pm at night on Teams calls. And it wasn't just the volume, it was the intensity of those conversations.

Joe Root, Silverwood and I wore a lot of it. We were close, but I was trying to allow them to concentrate on the series, and I would act as a buffer. Still, some of our behaviours as a team weren't ideal. Protocols were quite clear about how many people you should have in one place, and we weren't always getting that right. So I'd have to step in and be the ogre. I was cast as the bouncer, the doorman. My job was to protect them, but also to protect the series. What was most worrying was the sense that some players had run their race, that they just couldn't summon the will to care any more. And once you're there in that state, it's a long way down the road, but a long way back.

No one really understood what the players were going through, and that was quite isolating. The perception was that everything was normal in Australia, but the levels of anxiety when we stepped onto that plane were already high. People thought that life had returned to normal; well, it hadn't for us. We still had to abide by certain rules to keep the series safe.

The results on the field were predictably bad. Although the team battled hard at Sydney for a well-fought and deserved draw, a capitulation at Hobart in our second innings was the final nail in the coffin of the tour and probably for my position. I felt there were a number of bad actors behind the scenes, people coming after me, looking to stick the knife in. There were some personal attacks. And again, I shouldn't have read it. But when you're in the heat of it, and you're in a bad spot, you start to.

I returned home with the team after the fifth Test at the end of the third week in January. By that time I'd pretty much finished a review I'd been asked to complete for the ECB board, covering all aspects of the Ashes tour. It was close to 12,000 words in all. The reality was that we'd probably had no chance of winning the Ashes when we arrived at the beginning of November.

Many of the players and management were already running on fumes by the time we landed on the Gold Coast. Having played considerably more cricket than any other team during Covid, operating in bio-secure environments and having been through multiple quarantines in all parts of the cricketing world, the Ashes felt like a bridge too far.

A series in Australia is hard enough at the best of times, even when you have a group full of confidence and fully fit, physically as well as mentally. At the time, we had only won there once in 35 years, and that was with arguably our best batting line-up in all that time – against arguably Australia's worst bowling attack.

A week after arriving home I delivered my Ashes review to Andrew Strauss, Tom Harrison and other members of the ECB board. I doubted that any of it was going to make a difference. This feeling wasn't helped by the fact that I didn't hear anything from anyone at the ECB from the point of filing the report on the Thursday evening. On the Sunday night, I began to feel anxious again, knowing that, as we stood, I needed to get back to work soon.

I emailed Tom and the ECB's people director explaining where I was and that I really needed more time off to try to get my head straight. Monday morning, I had a message from Tom saying he was sorry to hear how I was feeling but needed to see me face to face by the end of the week. I could have resisted that meeting given where I was, but I wanted to know where I stood, which was now becoming obvious, and my anxiety wasn't going to get any better by not knowing. Wednesday we met, and that was that.

It's a strange thing losing your job in front of the world. It's spread across the media, everyone with a view on where you got it wrong, and why you had to go. One minute you are the ringmaster, with a handle on everything. The next day you wake up in the middle of a field, the circus has moved on and no one is looking back.

That is the reality of professional sport. The show has to move on and there are countless bodies left in its wake. In some respects, it was hard to say goodbye to something that now appeared to be in such a bad state. Legacy has always been important to me – leaving something behind in better shape than when you took it on. In this instance, while we'd had some big wins during my three years in charge – particularly in how we'd kept the game on during the pandemic, and of course winning the World Cup – I can honestly say that at that point I reflected on it with no fondness whatsoever.

Some of the weight lifted immediately from my shoulders as I made my way by train back to the Midlands. Relief was the most immediate feeling. But then, as some of my anxiety lifted, it was replaced by shame, and the question, 'Well, what *do* people think of me?'. I was like that for quite a long time. I don't think many people in the game really knew where I was. I got some messages from the players. Not all of them. A couple of senior guys didn't message me, which I was disappointed by, considering how hard I'd fought for them over the previous two years.

Over the next couple of weeks I spent most of my time in Ripley at my mum and dad's house. Mum was now in a really bad way and not eating at all. Trying to get her to take even the smallest amount of water was difficult and could make her sick. It seemed as if something had switched off in her brain, through her dementia, that controlled her eating, hunger and swallowing functions. She faded away in front of us. We spoke to the doctors and they came to visit, but there was little they could do. I wanted to spend as much time as I could with her and be around to support Dad. My three siblings were all brilliant, and during that period we spent more time together than we had since we were very young. We sat and talked to Mum as much as we could, we played her favourite music and tried to keep her hydrated. She was bed-ridden at this point, but we still tried to tempt her with some of her favourite foods and snacks. None of it worked. Within a few days she was barely awake at all.

On the morning of January 23, Dad walked across the landing and knocked on my door. He told me that he thought Mum's condition had worsened and asked me to come and see her. He was not wrong. I texted my brother and sisters and told them that they should come to the house as soon as they could. By this time Mum was barely communicating. She would lift a hand in reply to questions about whether she was comfortable or needed some water on her lips, but that was it. Up to a couple of days before, Mum had still been trying to get out of bed which, given she hadn't eaten anything for weeks, was extraordinary. Just two days before, as my brother and I sat with Mum and recalled our favourite memories of holidays and trips abroad, she started humming the tune from the 'It's a small world' ride in Disney World, the place we'd both taken Mum and Dad with our kids over the years. She loved that bloody ride. Given her condition it was remarkable that she'd managed to make a sound.

Later that morning my brother and sisters arrived, as did the district nurse. Mum had been slightly more agitated and her breathing was just different. She was barely responsive. The nurse gave her some medication and she settled. In fact for the next few hours she seemed to sleep like a baby. I remember heading down to the bakers in the village to get some lunch and when I came back my brother and I sat with Mum and just chatted. For some time all was calm and she continued to sleep soundly. Then, suddenly, her breathing started to change, from normal to much deeper and faster. It came in waves, slowly at first, getting more regular and more pronounced. We called down to my sisters and Dad. We also called the nurse, as she'd asked us to do if there was any significant change in Mum's condition.

Her breathing was now deep and rasping, like she was struggling for air, loud and terrifying. Her eyes were wide open and watery. We had in the space of an hour gone from relative calm to a state of chaotic desperation. We knew what was happening. We sat close to Mum and talked to her, held her hand and head and cried our eyes out. This seemed to go on for an age and was the most awful thing I have ever witnessed. The nurse eventually arrived and was able to administer something to help her settle. Her breathing began to slow and the noise eased. It became apparent that Mum was drifting away, her breaths less and less frequent. Our mum, the love of our dad's life, took her last breath and was still. We'd lost the most wonderful, strong and loving woman in the world. Life could never be the same again.

That final hour stays with me until this day – the noise, the emotion and the pain. I pray that she didn't feel anything in those final moments. There are very few days since when I haven't thought about it, the five of us there with her at the end, just as she would have wanted it. Family was everything to her, and she was fiercely protective of all of us and our own little families.

The next morning I woke once more in the spare room. This time it was the rain that woke me up, and it was so hard it felt like the heavens were crying. The reality of losing Mum hit me again and I cried my eyes out as I lay there.

Mum had been a rock for all of us, her love unconditional. I never did tell her that I'd lost my job. She didn't need to know that at that point. She had been dying – it simply wasn't important. I also didn't want to hurt her any more. Nothing else had mattered for the last few weeks, and now she was gone.

The only saving grace of that period was that I'd been able to spend the last three weeks of her life by her side. She died in Ripley Village, Surrey, where she was born and married, the place she loved more than any other on earth on February 23, 2022 at around 3.40pm. It's a beautiful place, and it's also where my journey started. It's where my education in cricket began almost as soon as I could walk. It's a journey my parents had been on with me throughout. From a Surrey junior cricketer to a Test player, and from a wet-behind-the-ears head coach at Warwickshire to managing director of England men's teams.

A large part of this book is focused on the best and hardest part of that ride, the Ashes in 2005. A remarkable series of legendary players, great cricket and staggering moments. It was a privilege to be part of that team and that story. I can't believe it's been 20 years.

But it's also about where I came from, how I got to 2005, how I almost didn't, and how my journey ended. It's about the great highs that come with professional sport and the incredible lows along the way. Some of the darkest days of my life, and some of the very best.

These days I am back in cricket, and loving working with some great people at a great club as CEO at Worcestershire. I have more energy, and I'm certainly more present as a father, husband and friend than I've been for a long time. My mental health is in a good place, and I'm happier. I miss Mum terribly, of course. As I expect to forever.

Sowing the seeds

Up to the age of 12 we lived in a small semi-detached house in a cul-de-sac in Kingfield, near Woking in Surrey, which was around 10 miles away from where I was born at St Peter's Hospital in Chertsey. On one side as you entered Trentham Crescent was a retirement home which was separated from our road by a fence, and on the other was a modern Baptist church. Our house was number 2, opposite a small grassy area behind the church. It was a relatively small neighbourhood with only 16 houses, and everyone on the road knew everyone else. There was generally a good community spirit and it felt a very safe place to grow up. So much so that the key to the house would remain in the front door so that anyone could pop round and see us. Even when we were out, the key would be left under a piece of slate by the front door.

Our house backed onto a stream which separated us from a large area of farmers' fields. We had a plank that straddled the stream and enabled us to get to the other side, and we could spend the whole day out there playing games, catching frogs or building hides in the hedgerows and swings in the trees. We would always return when we were hungry or thirsty and, in those days, Mum didn't have to worry much about us.

We would go fishing in tributaries of the River Wey, down towards Unwins Mill, in Old Woking, which was originally a Victorian printing mill. We didn't catch much apart from the odd minnow and stickleback, but it was a nice way to spend a few hours. During periods of heavy rain the fields also served as a flood plain, and the water would often come right up to the back of the house.

We always had animals at home when I was young. We had a cat called Pepe who lived until he was around 18 – he wandered across to the fields behind our house one day, made a nest in the long grass and died. I also had a hamster, although it would perhaps be more accurate to say hamsters. I now know that hamsters don't live particularly long, and on one occasion when we were away my hamster died, but rather than give me the bad news my mum thought it would be better to buy a replacement. Unfortunately they couldn't get one that was the same colour, which I did question, but it was passed off as a reaction to the change in seasons. Poor old Herbie.

Mum and Dad had five children. Sadly they lost a child at the age of two before I was born. Stuart would have been my older brother by seven years. But I do have an older brother, Andrew, who is 10 years my senior and I have two older sisters, Carrie and Tracy, born in 1964 and 1970 respectively. I'm the youngest, born in 1973, and if you listened to my siblings, they'd tell you I was spoilt rotten as a child. They are probably right but, despite this, Andrew, Carrie and Tracy always took very good care of me. Our house had four bedrooms which meant that until my brother left home I shared a room for quite some time with my sister Tracy.

I remember a big love of musicals and films in the house when I was growing up. Having two older sisters I was regularly forced to play a role in a homemade production of *The Sound of Music* or *Grease*. We knew every single word. If Mum and Dad listened to anything on the record player it would be on a Sunday morning before they headed over to the Kingfield Arms for a lunchtime drink with their best friends Doris and Viv, who also lived in our road. It was usually Abba or Glen Campbell.

My auntie Jane, who was much younger than my mum, lived with us for a while when I was small and she used to spend a lot of time looking after me. She used to take me out in my push chair to the park or shops. Apparently I picked up some very colourful first words and would often share them when I was out and about!

Both Mum and Dad always worked incredibly hard and while I don't remember us having a lot of money, I don't remember us wanting for much either. When I was young Dad worked as a Maths lecturer at Westminster College in London and Mum worked as a dinner lady at a Catholic school about a mile from home. We used to love it when Mum brought back leftover doughnuts or hot cross buns. We used to go and visit her in the kitchens sometimes and, although she had the benefit of long school holidays, I remember it seemed really hard work, particularly with us to look after at home as well. Mum would come home from work and cook every night for the family. She was a great cook, although I was a very picky eater when I was young. On Sundays we'd always have a family roast and Mum and Dad would open a bottle of Lambrusco. Us kids would argue about who was going to get 'scrapesies' of the pudding bowl.

Mum's first love was gardening and although she had a number of very happy years at St John the Baptist School, she was thrilled when she secured a job at a nearby garden centre, Jackman's, in the house plant section. Dad didn't really seem to enjoy his work at all at Westminster College and when I was about 11 he started working weekends as a driver for a data collection and delivery firm, Data Express. He'd work incredibly long hours when he was doing both jobs and often get very little, if any, sleep. He eventually gave up his job at the college and went full time with Data Express as their weekend operations manager. We used to worry about him when he was driving at night, but he enjoyed it far more than teaching and it gave him a certain amount of freedom. Unfortunately, one weekend, while Dad was at the depot on a Saturday night, there was an armed robbery and he was tied up and had a gun held to his head. This was a terrifying experience for him and it took him years to get over it.

We always seemed to be playing sport of some sort in our road. Everyone would get involved, boys and girls, but I'd also regularly play with just my brother and his mates. I'm sure when I was very little they used to go easy on me, but I was always allowed to play. We used to play cricket and football on the grass area behind the church. For cricket we used a tree near the pavement as the stumps at the bowler's end, and at the batter's end we used a metal heating grate as the wicket. The pitch was probably only about 15 yards long, but we had some great matches out there, and by playing against my brother and his mates my cricket seemed to develop quite quickly. We'd occasionally play in the road but that brought cars, houses and windows into play, which was a recipe for disaster. Playing behind the church also wasn't totally without its risks, and on a couple of occasions Dad had to go round to the retirement home or speak to people from the church about windows I'd broken and offer to replace them. But Mum and Dad were never too hard on me about this, and they never stopped us going out and playing.

We also used to play a game called pom-pom, which would involve most of the kids in the road, and was basically a giant game of hide-and-seek. There was a telephone pole about half-way up the road, which acted as home, and one person would have to wait here and count to 30, while everyone else would hide. The aim for those hiding was for one of them to get back to home, touch the pole, and shout 'pom-pom all saved' before they were seen. Once you were found you joined the hunt for everyone else. Games could go on for hours.

Our house was always busy with family and friends. My sister's best friend Deborah, who lived on the road, was a regular visitor. She'd just let herself in and come and join us. Tracy and I often used to get into fights when they were together. Most of it was probably my fault, and my sister says that even when I was in the wrong, I'd make sure I was the first one downstairs to tell Mum that they'd been horrible to me and Deb would get sent home. They got their own back one day when they set up a ghost house in Tracy's bedroom. I was scared senseless and ran out crying. Generally though we did get on. We are the closest in age, and Tracy and Deb would both play football and cricket with us in the street. They were both pretty good.

At Christmas the house always seemed to be full. I don't think Mum ever turned anyone away and she loved having the house packed with family, friends and children. We loved a board game at Christmas, and Trivial Pursuit was a particular favourite. It was also the source of quite a few arguments. Dad stopped playing after a while because he'd swear that some of the answers on the cards were wrong – which, given we didn't have the internet in those days, was a difficult argument to win. When he wasn't playing, he had a horrible habit of shouting out answers from his chair in front of the TV. He still does it today. At Christmas, Tracy and I were allowed to drink a port and lemon as a treat – a mix of cheap port with lemonade.

I went to the first and middle school almost directly across the main road at the end of Trentham Crescent. Kingfield School was just a five-minute walk door to door. It was so close that during my time at middle school I would walk home at lunchtime and make myself soup or beans on toast. I was a slow learner at first and struggled with reading. Mum and Dad never pushed me to do extra work at home and if I wasn't at school I was free to do as I pleased. At school we generally played football but we'd play cricket at lunchtime in the summer, and there was a set of stumps painted on the wall outside the school hall. I often used to bat through a whole lunch period, which made it increasingly difficult to find people to play with. I also enjoyed the school shows and played lead roles in both *The Lion, the Witch and the Wardrobe* and *The Wizard of Oz*.

When it was time to leave Kingfield School I wanted to follow my mates and look at local secondary school options around the Woking area. However, around the same time Mum and Dad were planning to move back near Ripley, where they had both grown up, and where much of our wider family lived. The village of Ripley fell into a different catchment area and I ended up being accepted at George Abbot School in Burpham, near Guildford. I had also taken the entrance exam for the Royal Grammar School in Guildford, which is where Dad went to school. My cricket was beginning to show some real promise, and that was appealing to the RGS, but I was simply not strong enough academically at the time to get a place.

I found George Abbot hard work at first. I didn't know anyone at the school when I started, and was pretty miserable for a while. I also had to walk a couple of miles to get the school bus before we moved to Ripley. However, George Abbot turned out to be a fantastic comprehensive school and after I'd made new friends I was very happy there. It took some time for me to catch up academically, and early on I had some very average reports. But eventually I managed to get myself a decent set of GCSE results.

We didn't play much cricket at school, probably two or three matches a year. We, like most state schools, were primarily a football school. We were pretty good as well. I played in the school football team and also captained the basketball team. I did score my first hundred at George Abbot – I can't remember the opposition but the school bought me a new bat, a Gunn & Moore Striker, as a reward for my efforts.

There was a lot of work to do on our new home just outside Ripley and it took some time to get everything straight, but once it was done we were left with a wonderful home. By that time both Andrew and Carrie had got married and moved out, but while I'd lost a brother and sister, we gained a lodger. Richard worked with my mum at Jackman's and settled in well with the family. He lived with us for a while in Trentham Crescent and then moved with us to Ripley. Richard has since become a much bigger part of our family. He and Carrie became an item soon after Carrie's first marriage broke down and they have two girls, Jessica and Hannah. Mum and Dad loved being back in Ripley where they were close to my grandparents and the rest of the family.

During the winter I started some part-time work with Mum at Jackman's to earn a bit of spending money. I didn't make much, but it allowed me to buy a new album if I wanted one and have some extra money in my pocket during the week. The work was pretty bland, and involved stacking shelves, tidying and helping with deliveries. The best times of year were the build-up to Guy Fawkes night, when I helped out in the fireworks department and Christmas when the centre came to life. There was a Santa's grotto built on site every year and a short train ride around the grounds to entertain the children on their way there. At Christmas I worked there and the atmosphere for customers and staff was fantastic. Jackman's wasn't a small garden centre, but it was family-owned and had a great feel to it.

Generally my childhood was very happy, and I feel extremely fortunate to have had such a large and close group of family and friends. The family home always seemed to be full of people and laughter. During the holidays, if we did go away, it would be within the UK, often camping or a visit to the coast. I didn't go abroad until I was 10, when Mum, Dad, Tracy and I went on a driving holiday to Austria, travelling through Belgium and Germany. It was a great adventure. Our Austin Princess got a puncture on the motorway in Belgium and I can still remember Dad trying to communicate with their equivalent of an AA man, who wanted to change a tyre for an extortionate price. We stayed in a couple of hotels on our way to Austria, which was a real novelty for Tracy and me. We'd scoop up all the freebies in the room and at breakfast Mum would get my sister and I to smuggle out enough food to get us through the day.

Our summers on the whole though were dominated by one thing. Cricket.

Life in the fast lane

I feel extremely privileged to have played cricket in some of the biggest matches, against some of the best players, in the greatest grounds in the world. Yet, many of my fondest and purest memories of cricket are those of long summers as a young boy on the green in Ripley.

Ripley is a small village on the old Portsmouth Road, just outside the M25. Mum and Dad both grew up there and, during the late seventies and eighties, much of my family lived in or around the village. The green in the village incorporated a large open space, woods, a playground and the cricket club. We used to spend hours exploring the woods and the scruffy green areas that bordered the cricket pitch, nicknamed the fuzzies, riding our bikes or climbing trees. It isn't much different today to what it was then. It has a newer playground, and the clubhouse has had several coats of brilliant white paint, but otherwise very little has changed.

When I wasn't exploring I was playing cricket in the nets or on the outfield with anyone who would let me bowl at them, hit me a few catches or, if I was lucky, bowl at me. It felt like we would spend the whole summer at the cricket club. Dad, my brother, uncles, and cousins all played cricket at the weekends. Mum would prepare a picnic to keep us going through the day, unless it was her turn to make the cricket teas for the teams. As the youngest in the family, I spent most of the time watching from the sidelines or in the nets, and I just loved it. I remember Dad scoring a hundred on one occasion and feeling so proud and excited. I would always have my kit with me in the car, and I'd occasionally be called onto to the field to substitute for an injury or a late arrival.

We'd enjoy long nights up at the club, particularly on Saturdays, and Ripley was famous for its hospitality. The club is one of the oldest in the country, over 270 years old. The changing rooms and toilets were downstairs, with the bar, kitchen and lounge area upstairs, reached via a very narrow and steep set of steps. Inside were a number of exposed beams and original features. The central beam in the bar area was a large block of wood, around 18 inches thick, that ran from one side of the club to the other. It stood at about 7 feet, with one end slightly lower than the other. After a few pints members of the opposition team were challenged to compete against our lads in going over the beam. It was trickier than it looked, but we had two or three specialists who could go up and over the beam with ease. Fuelled by a couple of pints the opposition often fancied themselves but it was about technique as much as strength, and many of them failed. The beam was also rough and could rip your arms to shreds if you got it wrong. I went over it as a child, but only with the help of Dad and my brother-in-law. I'd have no chance nowadays.

There was a piano and we'd have regular singalongs late into the evening. We also had the occasional famous guest appearance, including Eric Clapton and Phil Collins. Clapton grew up in Ripley and was a regular visitor to the village green and the cricket club. I remember many fun evenings of music and games at the club during the summer and it really was a fantastic environment to grow up in.

Both my sisters also played, mostly for the colts teams, and they could both bowl. I remember a few matches where their presence on the field caused some sniggering from the opposition but they'd often have the last laugh by bowling very tidily and picking up wickets.

At the age of nine, when I was playing for the colts, I also played my first match for the men's second team on a Sunday. I played alongside Dad, my brother, cousin and godfather at Merrow, near Guildford. I didn't do much, but it was brilliant. I do remember hitting a four, which I think wound the bowler up because the next delivery was a lot quicker and bowled me. After that I began to play more and more regularly, and would take every opportunity I had, even if that meant just fielding.

It was around this time that I remember Dad coming home one evening and telling me that he'd arranged for me to have some coaching at Guildford leisure centre during the winter. Dad sat on almost every cricket committee you could imagine when I was growing up and at one of these meetings he met a coach by the name of Brian Ruby. Up to this point I hadn't had any real technical coaching at all, I just loved bowling and would run in all day practising my left-arm seamers. I remember being very nervous about going to these coaching sessions. I'd never really had anything to compare myself against and was worried that these other boys would be at a far higher level than this lanky left-armer from village cricket. I loved playing, but I didn't really know if I was any good.

Brian was a player and coach at Guildford Cricket Club and a hard taskmaster. His language could be described as colourful at best, particularly for a group of 10-year-olds, but he was also a fantastic coach and my cricket developed quickly from our weekly sessions. There were only about six or seven boys on the course and his sessions had a strong technical element to them. Brian was keen on teaching us the fundamentals that underpinned the game. Up until that point I'd been pretty much self-taught and worked things out for myself. Under Brian's guidance, my cricket went from strength to strength.

Brian did have particular 'fun' with my batting. My bowling had always been my stronger skill, probably because I was able to practise it much more easily on my own, either at a set of stumps or against a wall. There were a couple of sharper bowlers in our group and I had a tendency to move towards square-leg as they ran in to bowl (some would say I retained that ability later in my career…). To stop me doing this Brian put a cricket bag behind my legs and told me in no uncertain terms to "stand fucking still". I hopped over it a couple of times but the message eventually got through.

It was at these sessions that I first met Ian Ward, who also went on to play for England and now does a brilliant job as one of Sky Cricket's anchors. We became very good friends, and remain so to this day. At the time Wardy was a right-arm fast bowler who batted, rather than the left-handed opening batter he became. That probably had something to do with the fact that he was probably the same height at 10 as he is now! He was quick for his age and swung the ball away from right-handers. He was a naturally gifted all-round sportsman and, unlike me, ate up the ground when he moved across it. Soon after we met, Wardy's parents separated and when he was home from Millfield School in Somerset, he would spend more and more time with us. He became part of our extended family and I think he loved how busy our house always seemed to be. Later, when we were about 16, we'd go down the pub and order Malibu and pineapple, come home and have a beer and talk for hours while listening to Phil Collins. I know... what a life! Unfortunately these evenings often ended with me throwing up in the downstairs toilet, as my ability to consume alcohol wasn't quite what Wardy's was. The same probably still applies today, to be honest.

After our first winter of coaching, Brian informed Wardy and I that we were being put forward for trials for the county under-11 squad. I can still remember that trial and the nerves I felt. None of that ever changed for me. At every level I felt incredibly anxious about changing environments and moving up levels. It was never that I lacked the ambition or dedication to progress and push myself. In fact, I would say I've always been incredibly ambitious. However, I've always considered myself something of an introvert. New groups or environments that I'm not familiar with frighten me, and it takes me time to settle. A room full of strangers is my worst nightmare, and I'll often head for a corner to hide or gravitate straight to a familiar face. I think some people can read this behaviour as rude, when it's anything but. I think that's why when I've gone up a level, I've often quickly come back down again, taking time to work it out before going back in. When I'm happy in an environment, well, I hope I'm quite good fun.

The trial was short. We all bowled a couple of overs and I batted in a pair for four overs with Wardy, but it went well and both of us made the squad. In that first season we were all tried in different batting and bowling roles. Everything settled a bit more in the following years as we found our feet. From 12 to 16 years old Wardy and I opened the bowling together and for our age group, at 12 and 13 particularly, we were pretty quick. Aged 13 we bowled out Berkshire for 9, taking five wickets each, and later in the same year we did something similar against the Wirral. That victory in particular was one I remember well and it taught me a couple of important lessons. Firstly, don't take the piss out of the game, as there is generally someone better than you, and secondly, the match is never over until it's over. Let me explain. The match was part of a Surrey under-13 tour to the north-west, our first as a team. This was scheduled to be an all-day match starting at 11am, with breaks for lunch and tea. Most of our cricket up to this point was afternoon only. Well, we won the toss and elected to bat. Everyone was excited about playing an all-day match, and we hoped to put a good score on the board. Just after midday we were bowled out for 45. It was decided that we'd take an early lunch before Wirral started their innings. I still remember to this day how full of it they were at lunch. They were laughing and joking about how bad we were, how they'd be home soon and made no effort at all to hide their amusement at our batting display. It was embarrassing.

Our batting hadn't been great, but the pitch was a little bit damp and they had a decent fast bowler who took six or seven wickets. My decision, as captain, to bat first was looking a pretty poor one at this point. However, Wardy and I had been bowling well and their arrogant behaviour at lunch got us really fired up. The ball swung around corners and we bowled them out for 17! They never even looked like getting to 45, with Wardy taking six wickets and me getting four. I hope that was a lesson learnt for everyone in that Wirral team. It certainly was for me.

By the age of 14 my cricket had outgrown the village green. I don't mean that arrogantly, but it was clear at this point that if I wanted to progress my cricket I had to move up a level. Guildford was the obvious progression given my relationship with Brian Ruby and the fact I was already playing in their colts section. I was also playing in the age-group above at county level with Surrey, a team that had Mark Butcher and Adam Hollioake in its ranks. I was playing everywhere and anywhere I could. I just wanted to play as much cricket as possible.

Guildford played in division one of the Surrey Championship and at 14 I was a regular member of the first team. Having never had the opportunity to play much at school, I played the majority of my cricket at club level when I was growing up, and I have always seen this as an advantage. I was playing with adults from a very early age and although it was tough at times, I was never a big fish. I was always trying to prove myself and get better. From an early age I wanted to play at the highest level, to play for England, and I dreamed of representing Surrey as a 'brown hatter' at The Oval. By the age of 14 I was already receiving extra attention from the senior coaches at Surrey, including Geoff Arnold and Chris Waller. I would attend winter nets at least twice at the weekend, with a session either at East Molesey or West Horsley during the week with the Surrey coaches. I loved it.

At that point I was on track, I thought, to go on and fulfil my dreams of playing senior cricket for Surrey as a left-arm fast bowler. Little did I know that over the next two years the direction of my cricket and my career – indeed, my life – was to change forever.

An unexpected turn

By the time I was 14 I was playing as much cricket as I possibly could: senior men's cricket at the weekends, colts cricket for Guildford (often on a Sunday morning before the men's game) and representative cricket for Surrey at my age group and the age group above. I'd take every opportunity offered to me. Then, in the winter months, I'd start indoor practice as soon as possible and play right through until the new season.

In hindsight, I bowled far too much as a 15-year-old and, unsurprisingly, near the start of the 1988 season I got injured. I started to get stiffness in my lower back, which gradually got worse and worse. At first I tried to bowl through it but after a while I had to take a break. We didn't have any guidance on workloads back then and no one really paid attention to how much we were playing. I'd estimate that in the previous year I played around 70 matches. That would never happen for a 14-year-old these days. But I wasn't complaining. I loved my cricket and was doing well – I didn't want to take a break.

However, after seeking physiotherapy advice from Surrey I was advised to stop bowling for a while and given a back-strengthening programme. I had grown a fair bit over the previous two years and my muscles probably hadn't caught up, but my back pain was most likely down to over-bowling. These days I would probably have been diagnosed with a stress fracture.

At Guildford the decision was made to move me down from the first team to the third team so I could develop my batting against weaker opposition. I could see that it would help my batting, and overall game, develop. I missed bowling though. As a bowler you always feel like you've got a chance of being in the game but being only a batter was pretty boring, particularly if you didn't get many runs, and I didn't like it.

So one day, when we were practising midweek at Guildford and were short on bowlers, I picked up a ball, walked in off a few paces and bowled a few left-arm spinners. It was more to help out than anything else, but they landed OK and it didn't hurt my back. It was great for me as it kept me busy while I was waiting to bat. That weekend, playing at Bannister's Field near the Royal Surrey Hospital in Guildford, our third-team captain turned to me and asked whether I was able to bowl "some of that stuff you bowled in the nets". I didn't need to be asked twice. It was far better than standing around in the field watching us get hit to all parts.

I didn't really have a run-up, and wasn't sure what I was doing, but loved it. I also landed it well for my first attempt. So well, in fact, that I picked up five wickets. I can't remember my exact figures, but I was chuffed to pieces. I also felt no pain in my back at all. Well, that was that: my journey towards becoming an England spin bowler had begun. At that moment I had no idea, of course. It just seemed like a good way to get me in the game more. The following week the captain brought me on earlier, and I got five wickets again. In the space of four weeks I took 21 wickets bowling left-arm spin. Given my somewhat surprising success, the decision was made to play me in the second team as a frontline spinner and middle-order batter. I did OK, holding my own while not getting quite the same success that I'd enjoyed in the third team.

Once I'd been given the green light to return to bowling pace, I was back in the first team. Word had got around the club about my left-arm spin and I was soon opening the bowling and then bowling spin later in the innings, sometimes without even taking a break. The captain, Tim Walter, would often just come to me and say, "Time to change now, what field do you want?" Unfortunately, the coaching staff at Surrey had also got wind of my spin-bowling exploits and weren't impressed. They had consistently backed me, with extra coaching and support, as a seam bowler and weren't impressed that I was now spending a lot of time bowling spin rather than pace. They asked me to stop bowling spin and, given that I hoped to play for them professionally, I did as they wished.

While we understood the reasoning, the situation became frustrating for everyone. Guildford were suddenly down a bowler, and I was far less involved in matches than I had been. I also wasn't bowling that well and found myself struggling to get rhythm and control. My pace was down and I felt like I might even get dropped from the team.

Then came a moment that would alter the course of my career. We were playing at home and Chris Waller, the Surrey second-team coach, had come to watch me bowl. He was sat in the Guildford pavilion, right behind the bowler's arm. I opened the bowling and bowled poorly. I was taken out of the attack and not long after Tim Walter asked me whether I would bowl some spin. We were light on bowling and the opposition were scoring with ease. It was a huge call for me given that Surrey had told me not to bowl spin, and Chris Waller was sitting in the ground. My ambition since I was a small boy was to play professional cricket for Surrey. I left the field to speak to Dad, who always came to watch, and Brian Ruby, my coach since I was 10. I needed to know what they thought, particularly as my decision could have huge ramifications. Dad was very much of the mind that I had to do what I wanted to do, and he would back me all the way. Brian said something along the lines of, "Just get on with it, I've been saying for ages that you're a better spin bowler and better than most of what Surrey have got". There were probably a few expletives in that sentence as well.

So I went back out and told Tim that I would bowl spin. It felt the right thing to do, and more important than anything, the team needed me to bowl. I was on almost immediately and bowled for the rest of the innings while Chris Waller sat and watched me. He didn't move until the game was over. I think I understood that my decision could have a really negative impact on my relationship with Surrey, but no one said anything to me directly and I carried on playing representative cricket for the county as a seamer. For Guildford, my game went from strength to strength. I continued to bowl some seam, but I was primarily used as a spinner. My batting also started to improve with more exposure further up the order.

Over the 1990 and 1991 summers I played more and more cricket. Given how much spin I was bowling for Guildford the high workload didn't seem to be a major issue for me physically. In 1990 I played 73 matches in total. I played for Guildford at the weekend, Surrey representative sides, the occasional match for Surrey second XI, and pretty much any other team that wanted me to play. I also had my first little taste of what County Championship cricket was like when I was asked to do 12th man for Surrey at Woodbridge Road, Guildford's home ground, for their festival match against Sussex. I got on the field for part of the last innings in a run-chase. I remember fielding at mid-off for a young and extremely quick Waqar Younis as the match started to really heat up. I'd never seen anything that quick, that close-up. I found it really difficult to know where to stand at mid-off when everything was happening so quickly. It was a real eye-opener.

My results on the field started to improve. In 1990, as a 17-year-old, I took 48 Surrey Premier League wickets at an average of 18, primarily with spin, making me the sixth-highest wicket-taker in the league. I also continued to impress for Surrey but never bowled spin in any of their representative teams. Part of that was probably down to my decision to ignore their earlier directive, but it was also due to the fact that our age group had two of the best left-arm spinners in the country. One of them, a close friend of mine named Mark Bainbridge, was the England under-19 spinner.

In 1991 I had an even better year in the league, taking 56 wickets at 19 and scoring 324 runs at an average of 27. For Surrey Young Cricketers I had a really strong year which was rewarded with the Young Cricketer of the Year award, something I was incredibly proud to win. In all I played 77 matches in 1991, taking a total of 138 wickets at 19. I also scored 1,116 runs. I bowled almost one thousand overs that year and it was my strongest all-round season by far.

Given how well my year had gone, I held out hope that Surrey might offer me a professional contract. Perhaps that was naive given their reaction to me bowling spin most of the time for Guildford, but no one could argue with my performances. Also working against me was the fact that Surrey were very likely to offer Bainbridge a contract. He'd also had a strong year at age-group level, and Surrey already had two left-arm spinners, Neil Kendrick and Keith Medlycott, in their professional ranks.

In September I was asked to travel to The Oval for a meeting with Mike Edwards, my Young Cricketers manager and head of the Surrey youth system. It was quite a long trip from our home in Ripley and we had no indication as to what the outcome of the meeting would be. I hoped for the best but it was the worst possible news. In the short time we were in his office, Mike told me that in the opinion of the Surrey hierarchy I wouldn't make it as a seamer and they wouldn't be signing me as a spinner given their current resources. I understood they were well-stocked in the left-arm spin department, but I do remember thinking that this was something to hide behind. I don't think they were happy that I'd ignored their request to stop bowling spin, and I also think they believed that I wouldn't make it as a professional spinner.

That was a long, quiet journey home. I can recall being very upset, as was Dad. All I'd ever wanted to do was play professional cricket and play for Surrey. It now looked like that dream was over. I felt like I'd let everyone down.

Bear necessities

My conversation with Mike Edwards at The Oval left me devastated. As far as I could see, my dreams were up in smoke. I'd only ever imagined wearing the brown cap and the three feathers of Surrey. I'd never even thought of representing anyone else. Also, cricket was literally everything for me: the amount of school I'd missed over the previous two summers had seen me record a very average set of A-Level results. I was working as a cashier at a Shell service station in Burnt Common. It was a great little job and put money in my pocket, but it certainly wasn't what I had planned as a career.

Thankfully my brother, Andrew, and my dad had other ideas about where I could play my cricket. They helped me put together a letter and CV to send to the other first-class counties asking for a trial. My CV was pretty good: I'd played at every age group for Surrey, often above my age group, also played for Surrey second XI and that year, 1991, I'd been named as Surrey's young cricketer of the year. Most of this, however, had been as a seam bowler and I was now asking to trial as a left-arm spinner.

I did have some positive news. I was awarded a place on the MCC's school of merit at Lord's for that winter, which basically meant me going to the indoor school at Lord's every Saturday morning for nets and coaching. It was also a potential route into joining the Lord's groundstaff for the following year, which acted as a half-way house for those on the cusp of playing professionally who hadn't yet been awarded county contracts. They were good shop windows, and county coaches would often turn up to Lord's to have a look at the talent on show.

I began to get a few replies from counties. Most were of the 'thanks but no thanks' variety, and some didn't bother replying at all, but some were positive, either asking for more detail, or offering me trial dates. This was progress. One of the few to offer me a trial was Warwickshire. I knew nothing about them as a club – their players and coaching staff were a mystery to me. I could have told you everything about the Surrey staff at the time and how they had fared over the last few years, but I had no idea about anyone else.

On January 7, 1992, my stomach full of nerves, I made my first visit to Edgbaston. I couldn't drive, so Dad picked me up from work to make our way up the M40. I'd never been to Birmingham before. Edgbaston back then was very different from the ultra-modern stadium we see today. The old indoor school was a tired, grey building that sat right next to the main gates, and this was where I was told to report. There were quite a lot of players around and some, I thought, must be club pros, with their bear and ragged staff emblems slapped on tracksuits, jumpers and shirts. I had no idea who any of them were. I just kept my head down and did what I was told. The indoor school was relatively small, with only three lanes and not long enough to get a full run-up in for the quick bowlers. This was no bad thing, given that the surface, a green rubber floor, was like glass and absolutely rapid. Behind the end where the batters stood were a few elevated wooden benches from where, on that day, my dad could sit and watch.

I introduced myself to Neal Abberley, the then second team coach, and he put me in the first net. I was actually pretty happy with how I bowled. I was never going to spin many on that surface but I was accurate and consistent. I would learn later that two of the players I bowled to that day were Jason Ratcliffe and Asif Din, both Warwickshire pros and two players I'd go on to play a lot of cricket with. Later, I had a bat and found out just how quick the surface was. I must have got cleaned up several times by the quick bowlers and the pace shocked me. When the nets ended and Abbers wandered over to speak to me, I expected a 'Don't call us, we'll call you' and was amazed and delighted when he asked me to come back for a second trial.

Two weeks later, on the date set for my second visit, we were working our way up the motorway when Dad's car broke down near Oxford. I was absolutely gutted and convinced that I'd missed my opportunity. Dad was even more upset than me and thought he'd let me down, but he wasn't to blame, it was just bad luck. We got hold of Abbers, he told us not to worry and said we'd reschedule. This time we got to Edgbaston well before time. The session was uneventful and, again, I thought I'd bowled pretty well. I wasn't aware at the time but Dennis Amiss, who was then chairman of the cricket committee, and MJK Smith, chairman of the club, were sitting behind the nets watching me. Dad told me later how starstruck he was at seeing these two Warwickshire and England legends. I didn't know either of them at that time, but both men would be instrumental in my development as a cricketer and man. Andy Lloyd, the then club captain, was also at the session and I bowled to him for a while.

Towards the back end of the session I got a tap on the shoulder from Abbers and was asked to come out the back into the coaches' office. Fearing the worst, I was shocked when the door opened and in the room already were Andy, Dennis and MJK.

After introductions Andy got to the point pretty quickly. They had liked what they'd seen and wanted to offer me a two-year professional contract. It was a moment that will stay with me forever, and one that changed the whole course of my life. They told me and Dad to go away and think about it, but we didn't need to do much of that. I couldn't get the grin off my face as we got in the car. What I didn't know was that Warwickshire had sent a scout to look at me at Lord's at one of my Saturday morning sessions and because of this I was already on their radar. Additionally, the chairman of Guildford CC at the time, Charles Woodhouse, had written a glowing reference for me and sent it to Abberley. Abbers would later tell me that both of these things played a big part in their thinking.

The decision was one of the easiest of my career. Warwickshire had treated me well, they wanted me so I wanted to play for them. At that point I didn't even know the terms of the contract but I wanted to accept just in case they changed their minds. I was pleasantly surprised a couple of days later when an official offer letter landed on the doormat. I was to be paid a sum of £6,500 in my first year, or six months, as contracts were back then. That was decent money for a first-year pro, though to be honest I would have signed for anything. The whole family was delighted for me and the feeling was mutual. They had all supported me to this point, and I've always remained grateful for that. I wouldn't have been there without them. On February 19, 1992, I signed my first contract for Warwickshire with the club secretary, David Heath. The same day I took my first steps out onto the Edgbaston turf for a few photos.

Before my first pre-season, I made a couple more journeys up to mid-week sessions at Edgbaston with the pros, and it was during one of these visits that I first met Dougie Brown. Doug would become one of my closest mates, best man at my wedding, we'd train together, share a room on away trips and travel together to matches. This all stemmed from Doug asking whether I wanted to share a house with him in my first year. It was a no-brainer: being new to the area and my first time away from home, having a housemate made a lot of sense. For Doug, originally, I think he just wanted someone to help pay the rent, but it was the beginning of a great friendship.

Doug was a fantastic all-round cricketer and we enjoyed a lot of good times together, both on and off the field. He was, and still is, one of the most enthusiastic cricketers I've ever met. He had a very disciplined approach to fitness and nutrition, although we both enjoyed a few beers together, and he always found a positive from every performance, no matter how bad it might have been. He taught me a lot during my first couple of years and was exactly what I needed in a mentor.

My first 'official' night as a professional, the night before pre-season began, was spent in the flat above the old pavilion at Edgbaston. The first-team squad were away in Cape Town and Dougie was with that group, so I spent the whole of pre-season in the flat until Doug got back and we got the keys to the house we were sharing near Harborne. It was tough and cold. Training sessions were long and gruelling and always followed by fitness work. I'm not sure our workloads were that well managed. As a bowler, you basically bowled until you got a chance to have a bat, and when you'd finished batting you started bowling again until the session was finished.

Abbers was a hard taskmaster and his 'school' was a tough and traditional one. At the time, as a young player, it felt like I couldn't do much right and, with me being wet behind the ears, I got quite a lot of his attention. It wasn't that I was poorly behaved or disrespectful, I just didn't know what I didn't know.

While it could be tough, the intentions were always good. Abbers was trying to prepare us for playing at the highest level, against the best players in the toughest of environments. Perhaps I didn't quite understand that at the time but I certainly appreciated it later in my career. He got criticised at times for 'losing' some talented players during his time as second team coach. I'd argue that he just weeded out those that weren't up to it. If you couldn't handle Abbers shouting at you and calling you out for being sloppy and ill-disciplined, you were never going to make it in first-class cricket. It isn't the only way to manage people, but it is one way and it taught me a lot.

Much later in my career, when I became director of cricket at Edgbaston, I kept Abbers on as part of my management team. He gave me a different perspective to my other coaches and was never afraid to tell me what he thought. He was also a very good batting coach. I wanted others to experience that discipline that had helped shape me as a cricketer. He fast-tracked my development as a cricketer, even if I didn't always like to hear what he had to say to me, and I've always appreciated the major part he played in getting me to where I am today. Sadly, we lost Abbers in 2011, far too early. Right to the end, he was still doing what he loved: working for the Bears.

6

Warmer winters

Midway through my first season at Edgbaston, Bob Woolmer summoned me to his office. At first I wondered what I'd done wrong, or which of the senior players I'd upset. Those worries were quickly shelved when Bob asked me what my plans were for the winter. Stuck on our six-month contracts which only covered the summer months, we were expected to make our own way in the winter. The more senior players, who were mostly settled with families, tended to have jobs, while the younger group looked for cricket in South Africa, Australia or New Zealand.

I'd overheard some teammates talk about their previous experiences playing overseas. Dougie, Graeme Welch, Dominic Ostler and Keith Piper had all talked at length about their time in Cape Town, the cricket and the fun they'd had. Bob lived in Cape Town and at the time was also head coach of Boland, with a number of strong connections which many Warwickshire players benefitted from.

I hadn't even thought about my plans for the winter. This was by far the longest time I'd spent away from home and we were only halfway through the season. Additionally, the intensity of being a professional, the training and the life, was exhausting.

Thankfully, it wasn't much of a discussion. Bob told me he'd sorted me a club playing in the Boland league and that he wanted me to go over there for the full six months of the winter. I'd be playing at the weekends, acting as the club's overseas player and coaching during the week at schools to earn some spending money. I'd also be able to spend time with him at Boland training sessions which would give me some important time working with some of the best professionals in the area. In return the club would pay for my airfare, sort my accommodation and give me the use of a car. At the time I didn't take much notice of where the club was – I think I was in shock as I walked out of Bob's office. I'd assumed, naively as it turned out, that it would be in Cape Town where some of the other boys were heading. The other issue I had at that point was that I couldn't drive! I'd only ever been in the driving seat once when Dad had taken me out for an informal lesson. The first and last time he ever did that. Within five minutes I had almost killed both of us at least twice.

When October arrived I found it hard leaving home again, this time to a country thousands of miles away. By then I'd also discovered that Vredenburg Saldanha CC was actually located on the west coast of South Africa, about 140 kilometres out of Cape Town. This meant I'd be far from any of my Warwickshire teammates and pretty much on my own. The idea filled me with trepidation.

On arrival, I was met at the airport by Albie, the club captain; Simon, the club chairman; and Bakkies, a club sponsor whom I'd be spending my first couple of weeks with until I settled. Simon and Bakkies were brothers and along with their other two siblings, Ernst and Andrei, owned all of the car franchises in Vredenburg. Bakkies ran the Mazda franchise at the time and it was he who supplied me with my first ever sponsored car – a brand new Mazda 323.

Fortunately, though maybe not for Bakkies, I'd passed my driving test just two days before I'd left England. I think he thought I was joking when I told him that as we were driving out of Cape Town. I'd only managed that by taking an intensive driving course over the two weeks prior to my departure date. It's a miracle I passed my test, and I would have been truly stuffed if I hadn't been able to drive during my time on the West Coast. I think all three men were also surprised by how young I was. Their previous overseas player had been more experienced and much older.

Vredenburg is a relatively small Afrikaans town with a population of around 40,000, sitting 12 kilometres inland from the sea. Saldanha is smaller than Vredenburg and sits on Saldanha Bay, a natural harbour that plays a major role in the local steel business as well as the more traditional fishing and seafood industries. The two communities joined to form the local cricket club, which was based next to the rugby club in Vredenburg. Bakkies had a lovely house on Piet Retief Street in the town which he shared with his wife Alwina and three young boys, Theunis, Ernst and Christo.

It was such a relief being placed with a family. The house was always busy, bursting with people and the sounds of kids playing, shouting, crying or laughing. Clara, the maid, was also a key part of the family, as was Steffy the family dog, a Staffordshire Bull terrier. I did quite a bit of crying for the first couple of weeks. I was incredibly homesick and missed my own family. Before starting with Warwickshire I hadn't spent more than two weeks away from Ripley and my family, and it was taking its toll. Bakkies, Alwina and the boys did everything they could to make me feel at home and the boys in particular were a great distraction. If it hadn't been for the Hugo family I wouldn't have lasted more than a few weeks.

The local language, Afrikaans, was also a bit of a problem. There was a lot of time spent sat listening to conversations going on around me without a clue as to what was being said. Over time I learnt to follow a lot of what was being communicated, even if I couldn't speak it, and Bakkies and Alwina were both very good English speakers. Vredenburg was the sort of place where everyone knew your business before you did, and as an Englishman in this small Afrikaans town, I stuck out like a sore thumb.

From a cricket perspective, things were really hard. I struggled to live up to the overseas pro responsibilities off the field and performances on it. The league was tough and full of many hardened and experienced club cricketers, with most of them having little time for a 19-year-old, spotty-faced English kid who, they thought, was masquerading as a professional cricketer. It was a steep learning curve for me and one I struggled to keep pace with. Having been used to playing matches almost every day during the summer I struggled to adjust to playing just at the weekend with only practice during the week. You had to make opportunities count, and in that first winter I didn't.

The vast majority of our players were good to me, inviting me out or to their homes for food. Our team was mixed – about half white and half Cape coloured – which was fairly unusual at the time, and away from cricket some of them wouldn't even speak to each other, let alone visit each others' homes. Cricket brought them together on a Saturday and Sunday and they played as a team, shared a beer and practised hard together during the week. It was, on the whole, a great group. There were a couple who were a little disrespectful to me, laughing about my performances and my 'pro' status when they'd had a drink. I didn't enjoy that.

Aside from the cricket I really enjoyed my time on the West Coast during that first winter. I learnt a lot from leading the club's practice sessions and the coaching I was doing with local schools. Away from cricket Bakkies and Alwina looked after me like I was one of their own. I never did move out to my own place and I was delighted with that. Bakkies and I would spend many nights watching the wood burning, waiting to braai, drinking brandies and cokes while watching cricket on the telly. We'd often be half cut by the time the wood was ready to cook on, but it was great fun. At Christmas, Bakkies, his brothers and their families moved down to Langebaan for the holidays. Langebaan was a beautiful little village in a quiet bay with wonderful golden beaches about 30 minutes from Vredenburg. The family took their caravans and tents down to the camp site in Langebaan and set up their own area right next to the beach and we had some great days and nights down there.

Being able to drive was not only important from a cricket and coaching point of view but it also gave me a freedom that I'd never experienced before. To be able to get into the car and go to the beach, the golf course or the pub was brilliant. The roads on the West Coast were, on the whole, long and very straight and it was a great place to hone my driving skills. I did have a couple of close calls that first few months but my driving improved dramatically during that period. Having my own car also enabled me to occasionally travel to Cape Town or Stellenbosch to see Bob and the Warwickshire players to practise. It was great to see some friendly faces from home even if just for a short time.

Despite how much I'd enjoyed the West Coast, and how close I'd felt to Bakkies, Alwina and the kids, I held out little hope of being asked to return the following winter given my frankly average performances on the field. I'd learnt a huge amount but I hadn't been able to translate that into results and remember feeling disappointed that I'd not been able to show everyone what I was capable of. I was therefore shocked when towards the back end of my stay I was asked if I would return for the following season. Despite my previous concerns about being so far out of Cape Town and in an Afrikaans community I didn't hesitate when I was given the chance to return. I had a feeling that Bakkies and his brother Simon, both big sponsors of the club, played a part in me being asked back and I was incredibly grateful for the confidence they showed in me.

When I returned for my second season in October 1993 things were literally different from ball one. I scored a century on the first day of the season and never looked back with the bat, averaging close to a hundred by the end of the campaign. With the ball I also had success and took wickets regularly. I'm not sure what the difference was exactly, but I hit the ground running and just kept going. I'd certainly got my head around playing only two days a week and the pressure to perform that comes with that, and I also had another year of professional experience under my belt. Another big factor, which continued to be the case throughout my career, was that I knew what I was coming into. I knew the people and I was happy in the environment. The standard of cricket hadn't changed, neither had the opposition's desire to get under my skin with some pretty ordinary abuse, but I sucked it up and just got on with my game.

Another plus about that second season in Vredenburg was that Dougie came out to join me after Christmas to play and train for three months. The club was allowed to play two overseas pros and having him around was not only good for the team's performances but also mine. We trained and practised really hard during the week and played hard at the weekend. Doug was always a strong distance runner, as was I, and we used to run several times a week. In the hot African sun it was tough but it helped us become bloody fit. In those days we did little else but run to keep fit, we didn't have strength and conditioning trainers and individual programmes, and we varied between short, sharp stuff or longer runs. Doug and I were built more for endurance than speed and tended to mainly bang out the kilometres on the road or around the track.

We also got into a bit of mischief. We'd be out at least three times a week, drinking Castle or Lion lager, brandy or rum, playing pool or visiting Flamingo's nightclub. Flamingo's was the first proper nightclub in the area and it was busy Wednesday, Friday and Saturday nights. It was very popular with the locals and the new recruits from the naval academy nearby. Before Flamingo's opened the only real option at the weekend was the Paternoster, which was an old Afrikaans hotel out on the coast in a beautiful little seaside location. It was very traditional and most of the dancing was 'sokkie' or long arm, which was a style of social ballroom dance performed to literally any style of music. It was a proper local experience, but we had to be careful that we didn't upset any of the huge Afrikaaner farmers by looking at them or their partners the wrong way.

We'd occasionally meet some guys from the South African special forces in Flamingo's, known as the RECCES, who were based on an island in Langabaan Bay. They were serious operators and not to be messed with. We knew a few of them through Bakkies and the family car business as many of them were customers and would visit the house for a drink or braai. Some of the naval academy students used to say they were RECCES but the real guys never talked about what they did until you got to know them. When you first met them they'd only ever describe themselves as 'divers'. Their appearance was also very different from the clean shaven, short haired naval students. The RECCE guys used to disappear for weeks on end until we'd see them again in Flamingo's or another local bar having a blowout on their return from a mission or training.

For cricket we used to travel long distances inland from Vredenburg to places like Stellenbosch, Paarl, Malmesbury or Cape Town. One weekend we played in 44 and 46 degrees over the two days. The heat was incredibly dry and punishing. That same weekend we stayed overnight in the warden quarters at Victor Verster Prison, so we didn't have to make the long trip back to Vredenburg on the Saturday night. This was the last prison that Nelson Mandela was incarcerated in, and was the place from where he made the famous walk to freedom in 1990. One of our players worked at the prison as a guard and was able to get us a free bed there for the night. Quite an experience.

Doug and I both stayed with the Hugo family in Vredenburg and were treated like kings. We paid Alwina back by teaching the children swear words in English or Afrikaans. Alwina didn't thank us for that, but we found it hilarious of course. As well as welcoming us into their home Bakkies and Alwina also hosted a number of my family and friends over the years. Mum and Dad, my sisters, my brother and my nan and grandad all visited at different times as well as a number of friends. My grandad brought his golf clubs out with him and we used to go off and play most days. I also became chief tour guide during these visits, taking groups to Table Mountain, the Waterfront in Cape Town, the Cape of Good Hope, and the wineries in Stellenbosch.

The whole Hugo family were amazing hosts. Bakkies' elder brother owned a beautiful boat, a catamaran, and a boat house on Langabaan Bay. It was peaceful going out there for evenings braaiing, fishing, drinking and relaxing. Part of the hull on the houseboat had a glass bottom and seals would sometimes come up to it and swim around us. Doug and I had a great time that winter and the team was also successful. I went back for a third visit for the 1994/95 season, without Doug, but was joined by Graham Charlesworth, another Englishman and former Bear who had actually turned out for Vredenburg the year before I'd first arrived. It was another very enjoyable year.

After three years on the West Coast I moved to Cape Town for my fourth winter of cricket. Avendale Cricket Club was a coloured club, based in Athlone, close to a number of townships and a club that Bob Woolmer had a long and rich association with. Many of my teammates at Warwickshire had also represented them in previous years. I headed out to Cape Town that winter with a young player from the Warwickshire pathway, Chris Howell, who played and coached alongside me at Avendale, and we also shared a flat in Sea Point.

This was a totally different experience from my previous three years. Left to fend largely for ourselves, being in Cape Town was a world away from living with the family in Vredenburg in a small community that protected and looked out for you. During the day Sea Point was fine, but at night it completely changed and neither Chris nor I ventured out alone after dark. Much is said and written about crime in South Africa. My experience at that time was that you had to be careful, particularly after dark, and you just didn't go to certain parts of town. I was certainly much more aware of my personal security, locking doors and windows, being hyper vigilant at traffic lights at night and on my guard generally, far more than I'd ever been on the West Coast.

The cricket however was great and I enjoyed another strong year on the field. During the day Chris and I would train hard and three afternoons a week we coached and practised at Avendale. We certainly got well looked after and we enjoyed the sights, sounds, bars and beaches of Cape Town. We also managed to get out to the West Coast a couple of times and visit the family.

I feel so lucky to have had those experiences in South Africa and to have been able to share them with my family and friends, and to have been there at such an important time in the country's history. Taking that first leap to go to Vredenburg in 1992 was a big and challenging step for me, but one that had a massive impact on my career path. Alongside my time at Edgbaston, South Africa was a critical part of my personal and professional development and without it I'm not sure I would have achieved the things I have in the game. I will always be incredibly grateful for the kindness, love and generosity of Bakkies, Alwina, Theunis, Ernst, Christo and the rest of the Hugo family.

7

Hard yards

"Getting a contract is easy. That's when the hard work really starts." This was something I heard quite a lot as a young player, and to be honest, it was pretty close to the truth. The buzz of that first contract, with all the pats on the back and the congratulations, is soon replaced by the realisation that you are, very firmly, at the bottom of the food chain. It was a big reality check for me, having never lived away from home for more than a week and having been looked after my whole life by Mum and Dad – food, washing, driving me around, cleaning up after me – everything.

Pre-season training was hard. I was at Edgbaston with Abbers and the other young players who had been left behind while the first team jetted off to Cape Town. I wasn't prepared physically for the level of training, particularly the extra running sessions, and I was blowing out of my backside most of the time. One of Abbers' favourite sessions was to make us run up and down every aisle of the Edgbaston stands, hundreds of steps, right round the ground, possibly twice if he felt we hadn't put in enough effort the first time. The cricket sessions were long, and generally in the indoor school due to the weather.

When the first team squad arrived back from South Africa, however, everything changed again. Say there were something like 27 players on the staff. If the captain, Andy Lloyd, was No.1 on that list, then I was definitely No.27. I'd played some second XI stuff for Surrey, but only a couple of matches when they were short, and that experience was very different from being a full-time 'junior' pro. I had been far from a big fish in the teams I'd played in at home, but I was a senior and experienced player in both the Surrey youth set-up and at Guildford. The adjustment to becoming the youngest and least important player in the squad was hard.

This was the early Nineties. Back then, the longstanding hierarchies of professional cricket, with senior pros holding sway and junior players only speaking when spoken to, were alive and well. You did as you were told at all times, even if those requests were often completely obscure and borderline stupid. You'd also be the butt of jokes and piss-taking, with no comeback. Senior players made it clear that respect was earned, and it would take time or on-field performance to earn that respect.

It was all a test, to see how you react under this 'heat'. Would you crack under the pressure? Run away? Fall by the wayside? Or would you take it, suck it up, dust yourself down and crack on? With each subsequent generation these environments have probably softened; the dressing rooms of today are completely different from my early days.

The environments before I joined were even worse, apparently, than the one I came into. One of my teammates told me of one senior player who used to relentlessly pick at him all the time. Including incidents where the senior guy would summon the kid back from the nets where he was practising with the second team squad, just to make him a cup of tea in the dressing room and bring it to him. Only then would he be permitted to return to his own session.

It was often worse around the first team squad but, given I was the most junior player, I got plenty around the second team too. Over time you learnt to give back as good as you got within your peer group, but you never tried that if you were anywhere near the first team. You just had to take it. I still remember the first time I was asked to do 12th man duties for the first team at Edgbaston. This involved carrying drinks, getting cups of tea, taking equipment out on the field as required and, at times, going on as substitute fielder if someone had to come off.

Back then, if the first team had a home match, any lads from the second team would have to change in the indoor school, a short walk from the dressing rooms. This applied even if you were 12th man. On this occasion, my first, it was the lunch break and I was asked to take over duties from a player who wanted to go and practise. I ran across from the indoor school, opened the dressing room door and walked in.

Andy Lloyd, the captain, was sitting opposite from where I entered, with many of the team sat around the edge of the dressing room next to their lockers. He turned to me and said, "What the fuck do you want, you spotty c***? Get out and knock." If I had already been nervous, I was now completely knocked sideways. I went out and knocked. Nothing. I knocked again, still nothing. The third time I knocked Andy shouted "Come!" and I entered the room. "Now, what do you want?" I told him I'd been asked to come over and do 12th man duties. "OK," he said, pointing to an empty chair across the dressing room. "Go and sit over there and don't say anything." It was an embarrassing moment. Of course, as these things go, I get on very well with Andy now, and he has been extremely supportive throughout my career.

There were a lot of very good people in that team, many of them still friends to this day. I also learnt a hell of a lot from many of them. Tim Munton, Gladstone Small, Andy Moles, Dermot Reeve, Neil Smith. They are just a few from that dressing room who have positively influenced me. It was just the way things were back then, it was the path you had to walk to survive. To a degree every one of us became products of our environment and carried on the cycle as we ourselves developed and young players came through behind us.

By the turn of the century, the culture had begun to move to a place that was much more focused on making young players feel accepted and truly part of it; and not before time, as that's the best way to get the most of them. Piss-taking, as far as I'm aware, is still very much part of the culture in the dressing room, but it's certainly more laughing 'with', rather than 'at' your teammates now.

It was the same around cricket. If the first team were at home and we were also around, we were expected to serve all of their needs before getting to our own games. As a spin bowler this meant bowling for hours on end, as long as they wanted, frankly. After that, when it was time for us to practise, we'd have to bowl to the second team batters. I'd often bowl for three hours almost non-stop.

On Saturdays we'd have to go to the ground and bowl at the first teamers before their match and then go off and play club cricket all afternoon. They were long days. And of course we didn't have workloads measured, it was simply a case of getting on with it.

It was hard going on a number of fronts. My transition from seam bowler to spin bowler was a steep learning curve. 1992 was the first year in which I bowled only spin. Previously, for Surrey young cricketers and for Guildford, I'd mixed it up. In the second XI we were all still learning our game, but me more than anyone. The long hours of bowling were probably, in the end, beneficial for me, learning as I went. The coaches and players offered me advice about my action, my pace, my run-up, everything. All of it was well meant, and much of it really good and important advice, often from those who had proved themselves in first-class cricket. But this was really the start of me beginning to learn my own game. In 1992 I was way off having a solid base to work from. Professional cricket allowed me the time I needed to get where I had to be.

My batting progressed quicker than anything, just through the amount of practice we were able to do. Weekend cricket was another big reason. Young players were placed with clubs back then and Abbers had put me with Solihull CC, who played in the Willis Corroon League. The main reason that I was put with Solihull, I think, was that Steve Perryman, formerly Warwickshire and Worcestershire and by then the pathway coach at Edgbaston, was pro at the club. I think Abbers wanted him to keep an eye on me.

I loved my time at Solihull. During that first season Perrers and his wife Carol used to come and pick me up every weekend and take me to cricket, then take me home again at the end of the day. I batted in the top four and got loads of overs under my belt. The team was full of characters, as most club teams are, and we had great fun on Saturday and, sometimes, Sunday nights.

It was probably in 1992 and that winter in South Africa that I really discovered beer. I hadn't drunk much at all before that time. I'd been drunk, of course, particularly when Wardy came home from Millfield, or we had a school party. I might also have had a couple of pints after cricket at the weekend in Guildford. But it wasn't very often. I'd been so focused on playing cricket that beer and girlfriends hadn't really featured.

In professional cricket in the Nineties, drinking was just part of the culture. It was also part of the education. You were expected to go to the bar after a day's play and have a drink with the opposition and umpires. As a junior player you stood and listened to the senior players exchange views on the game, and umpires tell you who was good and who was useless. Afterwards players often went back to the bar in the hotel and carried on drinking. One of the players I really enjoyed listening to during these times was Paul Smith. Smithy was an excellent all-round cricketer and always loved the big occasion, evidenced by his performances in big cup matches and finals. He always treated us younger players with respect, and has always had a brilliantly wicked sense of humour. He looked like a rock star and lived life very much to the full.

No one really binge drank back then, as you see sometimes today; players not drinking for days and then going off the rails for a night and losing control. From my experience that's when bad things happen. When I started, if you did drink, you probably drank most nights and developed a sort of tolerance to five or six pints a night. We'd get it wrong occasionally, but you knew you had to front up the next day and do your job, because it was likely that everyone around you knew exactly what you'd been up to the night before. You'd just pop a big red tablet (600mg Ibuprofen) and have a couple of cans of 'red ambulance' (code for full fat Coke). To be honest, back then, it was unusual if you didn't drink alcohol, unless for religious reasons of course, and it was a way to fit in. Things have changed a lot now, but back then you could undoubtedly have felt on the outside if you didn't enjoy a few pints after a day's play.

Given all that, my first season for the Bears went OK. I played both one-day and three-day cricket for the second team and had a little success. I certainly hadn't felt out of place. However, I had been miles off playing first team cricket in my mind, and probably felt the same as the 1993 season began. I was, therefore, shocked when I was told around the middle of May that I would be joining the first team at Canterbury, and likely to play. The second team had been playing in Maidstone when Abbers got the call from Bob Woolmer for me to join the first team. Abbers took me across to Canterbury. I remember on that journey him trying to calm me. "If you play, it's just another game," and "Make sure you enjoy it." All that stuff. He was actually quite fatherly in that moment.

Soon after arriving in Canterbury I found out I was playing, replacing the great Allan Donald, who was struggling with a niggle. I remember thinking that must have been quite welcome news for the Kent batters, this spotty 20-year-old debutant replacing one of the world's most fearsome quicks. I only remember bits about my debut. I got a few runs in both innings, 20 and 17, out both times to West Indies legend, Carl Hooper. I picked up one wicket in each innings and was pretty economical in my 26 overs in the match. I also remember Hooper coming down the wicket to me and hitting me beautifully over extra cover, straight over the rope, the ball bouncing off a car roof behind the stand. It was a shot of real class. We won the match in the end by 110 runs. Neil Smith took six second-innings wickets and was awarded his first team cap with the white bear emblem on it. It was something that all of us young players were striving for, but were so far away from.

I played once more that year, in August, against Durham at Darlington, a match we lost by nine wickets. I took just one wicket, and the whole experience was a little more chastening. I still had so much work to do to be ready for this standard. Paul Booth, another left-arm spinner on the staff but more experienced, played much more first team cricket than I did that year. Given I'd only played two matches and certainly not set the world alight, as we came towards the end of the summer and my two-year contract, I began to worry that I might have missed my opportunity. In the end, Bob and Abbers must have seen the potential in me, and I got the nod ahead of Boothy, who left the club.

I had managed to get myself a new contract, yet my chances of playing much first team cricket in 1994 were sunk almost immediately when Richard 'Dickie' Davis was signed from Kent. Dickie was hugely experienced and built a bit like me. Tall, with quite a big presence at the crease, Dickie could also bat and had a brilliant pair of hands. He was a much more rounded and better cricketer than Boothy, and miles ahead of where I was. It looked like I would be stuck in the twos for the foreseeable.

Still, I was enjoying the challenge that was professional cricket. After all, it was everything I'd ever wanted to do. Looking back now, these years of doing the hard yards as a young pro, the 12th man humiliations, the relentless piss-taking, the never-ending hours bowling in the nets, the long nights at the bar talking cricket, alongside the experiences of getting it right as well as wrong on the pitch, it was all part of the journey. A personal journey that would have as many disappointments and dark days as good. All of this was just part of the preparation.

At the club, things were beginning to change. Dermot Reeve was now captain of the club, and he and Bob Woolmer would form a fantastic partnership. While the caste system still existed at the club, and young players certainly knew where they stood, Bob and Dermot introduced a culture of learning, skill development and personal expression around the first team. They were interested in attention to detail on the finer points of the game. It was about to become a great time to be involved with the Bears, whether in the first team or not. Bob and Dermot's methods were well ahead of the rest of the country and over the next couple of years the team would dominate county cricket.

8

Itchy feet, and finding them

By the start of the 1995 season I was getting a little frustrated with my lack of opportunities. I had no particular right to say that I should be playing first-team cricket, no evidence either to fall back on, given I'd only played two first-class matches in 1993 and nothing since. In addition, we'd broken all the records in 1994 with the treble and had just missed out on winning all four.

Dickie Davis had formed a strong spin partnership with Neil Smith and given this, as we began pre-season prep that year, my chances of playing much first-team cricket looked slim at best. So much so that as we started the season I began to think that my future may have lain elsewhere. On the whole I'd loved my time at Warwickshire to that point. They had backed me when others, including Surrey, had turned their back. I knew I also needed to do the hard yards, learning my trade as a professional cricketer and spin bowler particularly. But you can only play so much second XI cricket before you need to move up a standard.

The success the first team was enjoying only added to that desire to be part of it. When I look back now, it seems unthinkable that I could have left Edgbaston aged just 22. But that was the reality. I just wanted to play, and I was much better prepared than I had been in 1993.

As the season developed it became apparent that Dickie was falling out of favour and wasn't getting picked either. Even in situations where we should be playing two spinners, Dickie wasn't getting the nod. This should have been a boost for me, given he was my direct competition. But I still wasn't getting a chance to play and, as a result, I began to think even more that they didn't think I was good enough and I should get out.

My cricket had certainly improved, and I understood my own game a lot more. My batting was really coming on and I was now getting lots of runs at No.6 in the second XI. Early in 1995 I was steady with the ball without being spectacular, but was definitely bowling fewer bad balls. With Dickie out of favour with the first-team hierarchy, he came back to play in the twos and that added an element of competition and challenge for me. I wanted to prove that I could bowl as well, if not better, than him. Often, as the senior player, he'd get first opportunity with the ball but I continued to get on with my work and do my job.

We also had a new head coach in 1995. Bob Woolmer had left to take up the same role with South Africa and Phil Neale, the former Worcestershire legend and captain, took over as our new boss. I knew it would take time for Phil to get to know me, if that was even possible at all during what were really busy summer schedules.

Come July, I was still playing twos, scoring runs and taking wickets but with little chance, it seemed, of stepping up. Around that time I had a run in with Abbers during a match against Middlesex at Studley. Abbers believed in drilling discipline into his players on an almost daily basis. It had been no different with me. At Studley, during a match we were dominating, I felt his wrath.

It was partly my fault, admittedly. We were batting at the time, and were about 400-plus for just three wickets at lunch on day two. Studley had a snooker room and during the break Tony Frost and I decided to start a game. As the players went back out on the field after lunch we were close to finishing the frame and so continued to play. The snooker room looked out on the pitch via a huge window, so we were also still following the cricket as well. Unfortunately this huge window meant that Abbers could see us playing our match from across the other side of the ground. We had an idea that he'd seen us when he began to march purposefully around the boundary heading back towards the pavilion. He burst through the door and gave us both barrels. Something along the lines of, "If you want to be professional snooker players then you can both fuck off". We got it wrong for sure, but he really tore us to shreds.

The next morning, before play started, Abbers pulled me aside to continue the telling off. It was then that he brought up the issue of first-team cricket, how Dickie wasn't playing and that I had been talked about by Phil and the senior players. His next words cut me down. "I've told them you aren't ready," he said. Those words hurt me. For a while I resented him and avoided him as much as possible. I don't know whether he actually did say that or not, it may have been a way, he thought, to teach me a lesson after 'snooker gate' the previous day. True or not, I was really flat for a few days after that.

Given that conversation, I was amazed when a fortnight later I was picked in the County Championship team to face Glamorgan at Sophia Gardens. I acquitted myself well, taking a wicket in each innings for not many, and scoring 24 in our first innings. I remember it feeling different from the two years previous and I certainly felt better prepared for this level.

We won the match easily and suddenly I'd had an opportunity to show what I could do. Thereafter I was included in pretty much every first-team squad across all formats. I'd demonstrated at Sophia Gardens that I could hold my own now and that, in turn, brought a lot of trust from those around and above me. I'd also really enjoyed the different atmosphere you get around a first-class match. More pressure, but also more spectators and greater intensity, which I loved.

A couple of weeks after that match I was picked in the side to play a NatWest Trophy quarter-final against Derbyshire. I didn't do much with the ball but got 21 not out and we won easily. For the semi-final we returned to Sophia Gardens. Apparently the Glamorgan players were in the ground early for a prolonged team meeting to work out their strategy. By mid-afternoon we were on our way back to Birmingham having bowled them out for 86. One of the things Glamorgan had discussed, apparently, was how they wouldn't take any risks with quick runs to Trevor Penney. Trev was an incredible fielder, a true all-rounder – in my opinion the best in the country, if not the world, at the time. He ran out two of their best players, Hemp and Maynard, who were almost paralysed by fear from the Penney factor.

I had a great day, bowling 11 overs and taking 3-14. Once back in Birmingham we headed to the White Swan pub in Harborne, a regular for the Bears players at the time, to celebrate yet another Lord's final for the team. In the end I would miss out on the final, Michael Bell playing ahead of me due to conditions at Lord's that morning, which wasn't a surprise in September. However, I was with the squad that day and watched us get over the line in a tight match against Northants to add yet another trophy to the cabinet.

We were also in the hunt again for another Championship title. The intensity was a world away from that of second-team cricket and with each match we closed in on our target. Allan Donald was phenomenal that year. In 1994 Brian Lara had been the star of the show. In 1995 Allan had a point to prove.

To this day I have never played with anyone who bowled as consistently quick as AD. It was almost as though he couldn't bowl slowly. A wonderful athlete, he had incredible presence in his run-up and at the crease. Having extreme pace, like that of AD, adds a completely different dimension to your bowling attack. He's also a fantastic bloke. I've had many enjoyable nights with him over the years. He finished that year with 88 Championship scalps at just over 15 apiece.

I ended up playing eight Championship matches that year, taking 16 wickets at 22. Against Worcestershire at Edgbaston at the back end of August I took my maiden five-wicket haul, including the great Tom Moody, who left an arm ball.

My other highlight was the last match of the year, down at Canterbury. The top of the table was tight going into that match, with Middlesex in the hunt behind us. We put any nerves to bed pretty quickly by winning the toss and putting a big score on the board. I took a bit of stick with the ball in the first innings, going at sixes and taking just one wicket. In the second innings, at the start of the third day, Dermot chucked me the ball saying he fancied me against their left handers, Mark Benson and Nigel Llong. It was a good move. I picked up the first three wickets, including the two left handers – taking 3-41 in 20 overs. AD finished things off at the other end and we ended up winning by an innings and plenty. We had won the County Championship for a second year in a row, and celebrated way into the night. The next day we beat Kent in the 40-over match and only missed out on a second treble in a row by having a worse run rate in the competition.

One of the things that really sticks with me from that week was a conversation I had with Dermot in his car on the way down to Canterbury. He had asked me to drive him down which, of course, being the junior player, I agreed to. On that journey he started talking to me about my season and asking me how I thought I'd done. I was obviously pretty pleased, and said so. Derm agreed but followed up with how he thought I could do so much more the following year, how I would get over 50 wickets and should be getting important runs down the order. He predicted that I would get at least 500 Championship runs. It was an important conversation for me and by the time I got to Canterbury I felt a million dollars. Dermot wasn't everyone's cup of tea and later had a number of issues away from cricket, but the Dermot I like to remember was a brilliant captain, great motivator and tactician, and an excellent all-round cricketer.

I could still never have imagined that 1996 would go the way it did. Having enjoyed another successful winter in South Africa playing and coaching, this time at Avendale, I returned for pre-season with the Bears in a completely different head space from 12 months previous. In 1995 I had worked my way painstakingly into first-team contention. I'd managed my first half-season in first-team cricket, secured my place in the first team, and shown I was capable at that level.

Still, the 1996 summer was a different beast. It couldn't have gone any better for me. I didn't play every match, as I was still second in the pecking order behind Neil Smith at the start of the summer. However, I was picked in 15 of the 17 Championship matches, took 55 wickets at 27 apiece and scored 555 runs at an average of 34.68. It was almost as Dermot had described it a year earlier. I was the club's leading Championship wicket-taker that year, took three five-wicket hauls and scored four fifties and my first hundred, which came in the last match of the season against Lancashire. It had been a dream. I worked hard on the pitch during the day and played hard down the White Swan at night. I was young and absolutely living the life.

In early August at Edgbaston, in a match against Durham where I'd taken 6-45 in their second innings, I was presented with my county cap by Tim Munton. Things have changed a bit now as player movement has become more and more common and being a one-club man is a rarity, but that moment back then, receiving your county cap, was hugely significant. It meant you'd been accepted. It also meant you got a sponsored car and a phone, though it was the blue bear on my jumpers and the white bear on my cap and club blazer that meant the most to me. A week later I celebrated by taking another nine wickets in the match against Glamorgan.

The season also saw me make strides in white-ball cricket. I didn't start well and for several games I really struggled to make an impact. It was during a match at Lord's in June when something finally clicked. It partly came from the team being in a tricky position and me being forced to bowl later in the innings. I ended up bowling six overs at the 'death' and taking four wickets. It was one of the first times I bowled over the wicket for an entire spell in shorter-form cricket and it worked. From that angle I felt like I could shut one side of the pitch down and, given my height and angle of delivery, I also bowled a ball that got under the bat, in at the batter's toes, which was an attacking as well as defensive option.

Nowadays, with the way batters are able to score the full 360 degrees, shutting down one side would be extremely difficult. But back then, not many teams played that way. We lost the game in the end but it did my own confidence plenty of good in that match. It was the beginning of me becoming an important part of the Bears white-ball attack. By the end of the season I'd gone from being a bit-part player to a consistent and reliable part of the one-day team, often bowling death overs. We ended up fourth in the 40-over league that year and I finished the campaign with 22 wickets.

We didn't enjoy as much success as a team as we had over the previous two summers, but 1996 was a career-defining year for me personally. Just 18 months before I had thought that my professional career may have lain elsewhere. Now I was a regular member of the first team across all formats, a capped player, and had just been named player of the year. I was away.

9

Gone Walkabout

At the end of the 1996 summer I was selected for the England A team tour of Australia. Only a year and a half earlier I wasn't even playing first-team cricket and now I'd been picked for my first England representative tour. In fact, this was my first England representation at any level. As a 14- and 15-year-old I had played in two Bunbury regional festivals for the South of England but had never made it to England selection at the end of the week.

Nowadays, the Lions, as the A team is now branded, are mostly selected from younger, high-potential players around the country. In the 90s the A team was largely the next best players in the country, those most likely to be next in line for full England selection. The squad selected for that tour of Australia was a strong one, and full of players who had either already played for England or who had dominated in county cricket over the previous couple of seasons. Many would go on and enjoy very long and successful careers with England. The squad included Michael Vaughan, Mark Butcher, Peter Such, Jason Gallian, Warren Hegg, Dean Headley, Mark Ealham, Craig White, Anthony McGrath, Glen Chapple and Adam Hollioake, who was our captain. Mike Gatting was our head coach.

I didn't really know many of the players that well but two I was familiar with were Mark Butcher and Adam Hollioake, who I'd played youth cricket with at Surrey. It was great to be linked up with them again. Within days we had a great spirit in the group and it was clear it would be a work-hard, play-hard sort of tour. Smokes (Adam) led from the front. Our team manager, and chairman of selectors, David Graveney was worried about how much of the candle we were burning in the evenings and one night waited up in the hotel reception to count the players in. To be fair to Grav, it was during a match, against South Australia in Adelaide, and on the back of a batting collapse that afternoon, where we'd gone from a position of relative strength at 122-3 to 151 all out! This left South Australia needing 169 to win on the last day and Grav absolutely fuming.

He caught one of our players coming in at about 1.30am and gave him a proper rollicking. Grav then went to bed soon after. What he didn't know was that most of the squad were still out. The next morning he shared his concerns with Smokey and asked him whether he would behave the same way if he were playing for the full England team. Smokey said he would and that was the end of the conversation.

That day we played out of our skins and eventually won a nail-biter by just 12 runs. Dean Headley bowled beautifully, taking five wickets, and I took three, including the last. Grav basically threw his hands up and let us crack on. The tone was set and we had a great trip both on and off the field, making memories and friendships that lasted a lifetime. Having lost our first match of the tour we then didn't lose again, recording victories against Victoria and New South Wales, to add to wins in both formats against South Australia, and in the final match of the tour we drew with Queensland in a heavily rain-affected match at the Gabba.

In that match I received the player of the match award, but for my athletic prowess rather than my cricketing performance. During one of the longest interruptions for rain, I decided I would entertain the crowd in the main stand by performing a number of Olympic events: hurdles, long jump and boxing amongst other things, mimicking the actions and getting the crowd involved while the rain poured down. The ground announcer joined in, introducing me to the crowd for each event, and the medal ceremonies. It was a bit mad, but went down a treat. It also broke up the boredom.

It was a damp end to what was a fantastic trip, and one I will remember forever. I'd also strengthened my reputation in the game and with the selectors with some decent performances. I think I'd also demonstrated that I was a good tourist and added positively to the environment. However, despite the success I'd enjoyed on the tour, and in front of the chairman of selectors, as the 1997 season began I had no expectation that I might be in the running for senior selection that summer. So imagine my surprise when a large parcel arrived for me at Edgbaston in the middle of May and inside was an England blazer with the three lions and crown on the breast pocket. I hadn't even received a phone call at that point. It created a few laughs in the dressing room, and I put the blazer back in the box and tucked it away in my locker.

A couple of days later I got the call from Grav to tell me that I'd been selected for the Texaco Trophy squad to play Australia. I acted surprised and didn't tell him about my delivery. It was a weird feeling getting that call. Something that had felt so far away was now a reality. I was in Ripley at Mum and Dad's when I got the call and it was so nice to be able to share the news with them personally.

I didn't play in the first match of the series in Leeds, which we won comfortably. But two days later I was picked to make my England debut at The Oval. It seemed somehow fitting that I would return to The Oval to make my debut for England, the same place where I'd been told as an 18-year-old that Surrey didn't want me. That day I'd left the ground thinking my dream of playing professional cricket was over, let alone my dream of playing for England.

I bowled OK on my debut without taking a wicket, conceding 48 from nine overs. That Australian team was full of legends, players I'd watched for years on the television: Mark and Steve Waugh, Ian Healy, Shane Warne, Glenn McGrath, Adam Gilchrist, Michael Bevan. We won the match easily, chasing down 249. I got left out of the third match at Lord's, which we also won to take the series 3-0.

Ben Hollioake also debuted in that series, scoring 63 off 48 balls at Lord's. Ben was such a great talent and a great man. He was tall, athletic, handsome and extremely talented. He made moving across the ground look incredibly easy and was a brilliant fielder. He also had a wicked sense of humour and was fun to spend time with. His death, in a car crash in Australia in 2002, while we were on tour in New Zealand was tragic and a terrible loss to the game. I cried my eyes out when we got that awful news.

After the series I returned to join my Warwickshire teammates at Edgbaston. I had less success in the County Championship compared to the previous summer, taking 32 wickets at an average of 33, but I contributed with the bat, scoring 474 runs at 31, and we finished fourth in the table. It was in white-ball cricket that both the team and I had most success in 1997. In the AXA Equity & Law League I took 18 wickets at 22 and averaged 26 with the bat. We played solid, consistent cricket throughout the summer and won the league, winning 13 out of 17 matches. Another trophy for the Bears.

We missed out on completing another double when we lost to Essex in the final of the NatWest trophy at Lord's in September. Princess Diana's funeral was the same weekend and London was packed full of people. We stood out on the street outside the hotel and watched as the car carrying Diana's coffin headed back to her family home at Althorp. The final was put back to the Sunday and across the capital there was a strange atmosphere.

At the end of the season I was included in both the England one-day squad for a four-team tournament in Sharjah before Christmas and the A-team tour of Kenya and Sri Lanka after. All three squads – Test, one-day and A team – met at Gatwick in early November and headed off together to Club La Santa in Lanzarote for a fitness and bonding camp. This had never been done before and, as far as I know, has not been done since. We took part in a range of activities throughout the day, starting with aerobics first thing in the morning before breakfast, followed by a mix of running, weights, swimming and other more fun activities like mountain biking and scuba diving. It was an exhausting trip, mainly because many of us were also enjoying the night life of Club La Santa, surviving on just a couple of hours of sleep a night.

The trip ended with a mini triathlon with players put in pairs. The pairs were decided from the result of a 12-minute run around a 400m track. The person who ran the longest distance over the 12 minutes was paired with the person who ran the shortest, second with second last, etc. I came in second, finishing behind my Bears teammate Dougie Brown. For the triathlon we first had to share the swimming and then between us divide up the cycling and running laps, doing both at the same time around the same course, having to tactically decide who to use where to best complete the challenge.

Doug was paired with Phil Tufnell and at one point whilst Tuffers was going round the course on his bike, absolutely knackered, Doug actually ran past him. It was very funny.

I was paired with David Sales from Northants, but we didn't make the podium. Swimming was a bad start for me and I've never been a fan. I was always a strong distance runner, built more for comfort than speed many would say, and I've always enjoyed my training. How we train has changed massively over the years and the focus on strength and conditioning has, over the last twenty years, completely changed both the players physical conditioning and how the game is played. It was a tough trip but I really enjoyed it.

In December we headed first to Pakistan for a warm-up tour and then on to Dubai and Sharjah to play in the Akai-Singer Champions Trophy, also featuring West Indies, India and Pakistan. This was my first visit to Dubai and the place is now unrecognisable from back then. The city was tiny really, but still very clean and very safe. The Jumeirah Burj al Arab, the hotel that looks like a sail, was just being completed as was the Jumeirah Beach hotel. Around it at the time was nothing. A few years ago I went back and played the Emirates golf course, which we'd done as a team in 1997. I couldn't get my bearings at all. In 1997 the course was like an oasis in the desert, today it is surrounded on all sides by huge buildings and housing developments.

While I played one of the warm-up matches in Pakistan, I didn't play at all in Sharjah. However, we played well and won the tournament, beating West Indies in the final. This was a very different looking one-day team with a number of limited-overs specialists led by Adam Hollioake. Dougie Brown, Ali Brown, Matthew Fleming and Nick Knight were all selected having had a lot of success in the county game and all played important roles during the tournament. In a sense England were 20 years ahead of their time, given that specialists across different formats are now accepted as the norm, but back then there was quite a lot of criticism about these selections. Winning the tournament in Sharjah helped in the short term, but it wasn't long before the selectors moved away from one-day specialists. The term 'bits and pieces cricketer' was thrown around a lot in reference to some of these players, quite unfairly in my opinion.

It was another very enjoyable trip, with lots of social time as a team in the bar, on the golf course and by the pool. There were a few practical jokes played along the way as well. One day, while quietly reading his book on a sun lounger, Matthew Fleming, known as Jazzer, was wheeled straight into the deep end by his Kent teammate Mark Ealham. He didn't move and just sank with the bed and his book. Ealy really should have known that this wouldn't go without some form of retribution, and Jazzer had his revenge on the last day of our trip. He persuaded the hotel staff to let him into Ealy's room, removed his smart travel trousers, a pair of light-coloured chinos, and had them professionally tailored and shortened by at least three inches. We were only required to wear those trousers to travel to and from the country, so imagine the horror on Ealy's face when he put them on an hour before we were due to leave the hotel and they were halfway up his leg. It was the early hours of the morning and nothing could be done. He isn't the tallest man anyway and he looked ridiculous as we left the hotel. We headed home for Christmas with more memories and a trophy to boot.

I didn't get much rest at home. We got back from Dubai a couple of days before Christmas and between Christmas and New Year I was off again, this time headed to Kenya for the first leg of our A tour that would also include Sri Lanka. It rained for most of our time in Kenya, and we got very little cricket in at all.

By the middle of January we were in Sri Lanka. I've toured there a number of times during my career at both A-team and senior level. It is an amazing country with brilliant people. It is also one of the toughest places to play given the conditions, particularly the humidity. That first visit was very different to many of my others as the country was on high alert due to the civil war. In Colombo there were road blocks almost every hundred yards which made it very difficult to get around. In the papers there were photos of body parts and dead bodies, the result of suicide attacks in the capital. Our tour was almost cancelled very soon after our arrival due to a suicide bombing in Colombo. In the end, we decided as a team that we would continue, but we weren't able to get out and about very much and were advised to stay in our hotel.

On the field the tour was a great success for both me and the team. I was consistent with the ball across both formats and in the 'Test' matches in particular I began to show my worth as a spin bowler in these conditions. I also scored some useful runs down the order. We won the Test series against Sri Lanka A 2-0, which was a fantastic effort in such challenging conditions. I took 13 wickets in the series, all of which came in the last two Tests. The one-day matches were a different story, and Sri Lanka won the series comfortably.

I loved that tour. It was very different from my first A tour the previous winter in Australia, which was a very social trip alongside the cricket. In Sri Lanka, drinking alcohol was a rarity. Dehydration was such an issue, particularly bowling the number of overs that I was, that you just couldn't afford to. As soon as you leave your room you begin to sweat, and you don't stop until you get back to your hotel. It was brutal, but I loved it. I also loved being able to play such a big role and bowl a lot of overs. It was a trip that was crucial in my development and it would play an important role in how I performed on future tours of the subcontinent.

Unfortunately, I left Sri Lanka with a really sore left Achilles tendon. It had been grumbling for some time and I'd already had a couple of cortisone injections to settle it, but my workload and the conditions in Sri Lanka meant that it was now worse than ever. I was like an old man getting out of bed in the morning until it began to loosen up as I moved around. When I got home the decision was made for me to miss the one-day tour to the West Indies in March and April and rest my Achilles ahead of the domestic summer. I was gutted when the squad left, sat at home in my little house in Edgbaston feeling sorry for myself. As it turned out, it was a decision that would change the rest of my life.

The day the squad departed, March 17, a friend of mine, Shaun, the landlord at our local pub, was at the Cheltenham Festival. He knew I was pretty pissed off and on his way home he called me. He'd been on the booze all day and was trying to convince me to meet him for a drink when he got back to Birmingham. I kept saying no but he was persistent. In the end I gave in and in the clothes I was wearing, a pair of old jeans and a fleece, I headed into town to Walkabout, the Aussie bar. It was soon after we got our first drink that I spotted a tall blonde girl across the room. She was very attractive and I struggled not to keep looking across at her. She started to look back and we began to make regular eye contact – all this despite her being with her boyfriend, which I didn't realise at that point. This went on for some time until the guy she was with went off to the toilet and I gestured to her. We walked towards each other and it was quickly apparent that she was pissed. We introduced ourselves and I asked whether she would like to meet me for a drink. She agreed and I told her I'd meet her in the same spot the following night at 8pm. I had no idea whether she would turn up and asked Shaun if he and his wife Anne would meet me there as well just in case I was left standing on my own.

The next night I arrived before time, shortly followed by Shaun and Anne. She was a little late but to my surprise the woman I'd met the night before turned up. I hadn't got her name the night before, the bar had been loud and busy, and she introduced herself as Stine, a student from Norway. Shaun and Anne stayed for one drink and then left us alone. We got on like a house on fire, and she was even more attractive than I remembered. She looked a little unsure when she asked what I did for work and I told her I was a cricketer. She later told me she thought that was my hobby. Later we joined Shaun and Anne across the road at another pub that was a little quieter and we had a great night.

For Stine and I that was pretty much it. We began seeing each other regularly and within a few weeks she had moved into my house. She was in her last year at uni and had to either go home to Norway or move in with me. One day she turned up with all her stuff and never left. I didn't resist much, to be honest. It did take her some time to get used to my job and the long hours in the summer. One day she went mad when, having left for the ground around 8am, I didn't return until about 7.30pm. "You couldn't have been playing cricket all this time, where have you been?" she asked me angrily. It took some time to explain but she got it in the end.

That was 27 years ago, and we are still together. We've had some highs and lows, as all couples do, but I am very lucky to have her and she is the real strength behind me, as are our children Anders and Tilly. Without that injury, and without Shaun pestering me for that beer, we never would have met.

10

Does the cap fit?

The call came on a Sunday morning, June 28, 1998. I was at home, just getting up to get ready to head to Edgbaston where we were in the middle of a four-day game. I picked up the phone and the voice at the other end was a familiar one. I had toured Australia with David Graveney as part of the England A team in 1996 when he was our team manager, and then in 1997, in his role as chairman of selectors, he had informed me of my selection for England's one-day team for the first time. After a few pleasantries Grav told me the good news: I had been selected in the Test squad to play South Africa at Old Trafford.

My girlfriend Stine could tell this was an important call, but we'd only been together for a few months and being Norwegian she'd had very little idea of what cricket was when we first met. It was only when I said, "I can't believe it, I've been picked for England" that she seemed to realise that this was *really* good news and gave me a hug. I called Mum and Dad, who were absolutely over the moon.

When I got to Edgbaston the guys were quick to ask me if I'd heard any news. I told everyone. It was a weird feeling. I felt excited, nervous and almost scared at the same time. Was I ready for this? Was I good enough? I guess they are questions that everyone asks themselves after being selected. It's how you answer those questions that matters.

For the next two days I had a game to concentrate on at Edgbaston. We batted on the third day and Nick Knight, who had also been called into the squad, celebrated with a big hundred. With declarations and forfeits we contrived a game on the last day which Lancashire won by four wickets. I bowled OK, but only got myself one wicket for 60 runs in 30 overs.

At the end of that match I remember being incredibly nervous leaving Edgbaston. I was being taken out my comfort zone. It's a feeling I had felt before and would certainly feel again in my career.

My selection for Old Trafford was a surprise to me but not a total shock. The papers had begun to talk a lot about me over the last couple of years. I was aware of this and enjoyed it; it's great as a young player to be considered a future England prospect. Now I was in, and the pressures changed straight away. It's always easier being on the outside looking in, but once you've played at the highest level, that is what you are judged on. I came to learn quite early on that your stock with the media is generally a lot higher when you are out of the team, even if you've been dropped. But I looked forward to playing alongside the best cricketers in the country. Yes, I had been involved with the one-day team, but this was *Test cricket*.

My competition in the squad was Robert Croft, the Glamorgan off-spinner, who had played the first two matches of the series. He was also my main rival for the England one-day spot. Crofty had done well in one-day cricket but never really made his mark in Test matches. He was yet to take a wicket in the South Africa series. I was fairly convinced that he would still play ahead of me but there had been a lot of speculation about the Old Trafford wicket and whether or not it would turn. The general feeling was that it would.

For years Phil Tufnell had been England's first choice left-arm spinner. I was a great admirer of his bowling and at his best his flight was textbook. He had that fantastic ability to make the ball drop suddenly out of the air and completely stuff the batter on length. To me he seemed a natural-born spin bowler. It looked so simple. In the other areas of his game Tuffers was far from an international cricketer. I really don't think he enjoyed batting or fielding much. But bowling? Hell, the bloke could bowl.

Not for the first or last time, Tuffers was out of favour. Crofty offered a more rounded game; he could bat and had made good runs in county cricket.

Most of the other players were already in the dressing room when I arrived at Old Trafford. There were lockers along the back and side walls with long wooden benches underneath. To the front was the viewing area with large windows and cinema-style seating raised above the rest of the dressing room. I found a spot near the entrance. Most of the guys had unpacked and there was equipment everywhere. I had never seen so many bats: different sponsors, different colours but all beautifully cared for. Pristine. Some of the team were still manicuring their bats. I'd come to learn that this was a favourite pastime for Graham Thorpe and Nasser Hussain. Replacing or adjusting grips, putting on stickers or taping up minor blemishes. I only had two bats. I suddenly felt like that wouldn't be enough.

Everyone greeted me and wished me luck. Some lingered longer than others. I was amazed at the names I was now sharing a dressing room with: Alec Stewart was captain, Atherton, Hussain, Knight, Ramprakash, Thorpe, Cork, Croft, Ealham, Gough and Fraser. I hadn't been around an England dressing room since my debut in the one-day team in 1997, and I felt a little awkward. We were still two days away from the Test match but I remember the dressing room being surprisingly quiet. No one really seemed to say a lot. Gough and Cork, who were having a friendly go at each other, were the only voices you could hear. Everyone else seemed more concerned with their locker or their bags. I remember thinking at the time that these guys had played a lot together and I expected there to be a lot more banter. That dressing room was very different to the England dressing rooms I experienced later. But it was more a product of the system than of the people. No one really knew whether they were going to be in the team from one week to the next. There were no central contracts, and there was very little consistency in selection. The number of players picked in a series often exceeded 20 and was sometimes closer to 30. Players were unlikely to focus on the team first in these circumstances. Most were only concerned with getting picked for the next match, or being selected for the winter tours.

I was fortunate to play most of my Test cricket at a time of greater consistency in selection, a period that saw England enjoy its finest Test results for decades. England teams have become far more professionalised, and enjoyed huge increases in investment and support. The focus has certainly become 'England first', which I don't believe was always the case. Central contracts also enabled the ECB to manage the workloads of our best players, particularly the bowlers, so that they are available and in peak condition for the most important matches. England winning has to be the most important thing, and our county system should support this. Yes, many of us in the game are paid by counties to improve performance and win trophies. By creating the right environment for success and producing an oversupply of high-quality England-qualified players, we should be able to do both. The two things should work together, not against each other.

In 1998 the England team was treading water. I'm certainly not saying that the dressing room was full of bad people or led by a bad coach. I played with many of these same players under Duncan Fletcher after central contracts had been introduced. They were different players and people to the ones I played with in the 90s. They were more open, confident and willing to share. The likes of Stewart, Hussain and Thorpe were very different at the back end of their careers.

David Lloyd, the coach, was also being failed by the system. He was never sure what team he might be getting from week to week. At the end of a Test match his players would be off, back to their counties. He'd have no control about how much cricket they played or how many overs his bowlers would bowl. At the time I was surprised how little technical or skill development work Bumble did with the players. I was used to Bob Woolmer and, later in my career, Duncan Fletcher working tirelessly with players on improving their techniques and teaching them the finer points of the game. But I realise now that there was little point in Bumble trying to 'change the world'. He didn't know what his team would be from one week to the next, and his immediate focus had to be on winning; not next week, next month or next year, but now. The system led to short-term thinking, fear and a lack of consistency.

One player who was brilliant with me at Old Trafford was Darren Gough. I have always loved this man. He was a joy to play with. Every match he played as if it were his last, and what a great servant to English cricket he was. During my first one-day series he personally took a bat around the dressing room to get it signed by everyone and presented it to me. I'll never forget that. I still have that bat. Goughy gave me the lowdown on everything, from where to eat, where the nets were and what times to be places. He also took me to the club shop to get a print of the ground to get signed and keep as a memento.

I found out I was playing just before we started warm-ups. Alec Stewart reached out a hand and I was in. I don't remember much else before the start of play. I hadn't expected to make the final XI but I was about to become England's 590th Test cricketer. South Africa were a strong side. They had some quality performers in their ranks including Hansie Cronje, Jacques Kallis, Gary Kirsten, Lance Klusener, and my teammate from Warwickshire, legendary fast bowler Allan Donald.

Stewie lost the toss and on his way back from the middle he stopped and met me outside the front of the Old Trafford Pavilion to present me with my England cap. I was so nervous when we took the field, and everything seemed to be happening at high speed. All I could think about was when I was going to get my first bowl, and that call came just before lunch. One over. As nervous as I was, I negotiated it pretty well. I was in the game.

The third Test was a match we needed to win but certainly couldn't afford to lose. The first Test at Edgbaston was drawn and we'd lost the second match at Lord's by 10 wickets. At Old Trafford things weren't looking good for us. The wicket, as cracked and dry as it looked, was a road. It was a long first day and at the end of it South Africa were 237-1. They hadn't scored at a rapid rate and we'd stuck to our guns well but only had one wicket to show for it. I felt I'd acquitted myself quite well on my first day of Test cricket.

I felt more relaxed on day two but on the field things didn't get a lot better for the team. Kirsten was like a wall and the wicket resembled the M1. There was no sign of it breaking up yet and Kirsten and Kallis both got hundreds. They'd put on 238 for the second wicket when Goughy bowled Kallis for 132.

It was in the third session of day two that I opened my account in Test cricket. On 75 Daryll Cullinan gave himself room and tried to cut a ball that was too full. It clipped the top of off stump and I had my first wicket. It had been a long slog for all of us in the field and when I dismissed Cullinan the score was 457-4! None of us were doing cartwheels but I was chuffed. Whatever happened from here, no one could take this away from me. Mum and Dad were there to see it, as they had been for every step of the journey to get to this point. South Africa's first innings went on well into day three until they eventually declared on 552-5. Kirsten went on to get 210.

Our reply didn't go according to plan. It's always tough for a side that has just spent more than two days in the field, however flat the wicket is. Apart from Atherton and Stewart, who both got 40-odd, the batting was pretty dismal. By the end of day three, with the score on 162-8, I was having my first bat in Test cricket. Overnight I was 1 not out and my partner Goughy was unbeaten on nought. The next day we limped to 183 and were forced to follow on. I was 16 not out at the end and pleased with how I'd played on debut.

The follow-on didn't start well either when we lost Knight and Hussain cheaply. We were 11-2 with the best part of two days still to play, looking down the barrel in the match and series. However, thanks to a fantastic partnership between Atherton and Stewart, the rest of day four was a complete turnaround, and we didn't lose another wicket in the day. At close of play Atherton was 82 not out and Stewart had driven, hooked and pulled his way to an unbeaten 115. We suddenly had a hope of drawing the match. It would be a big ask but it was possible. We were 211-2.

Day five started OK but with the score on 237 Atherton was out to Kallis for 89. Ramprakash joined Stewart and they put on 57 but on 293 we lost two wickets: Stewart went for 164 after playing one hook too many to Donald, and then Thorpe rounded off a dreadful match with a third-ball duck to complete a pair. Cork didn't last long and went for 1. Suddenly we were 296-6 and in big trouble. Ramprakash and Croft got us to 323 before Ramps was out to Donald for 34 in a 149-ball stay.

The fall of the seventh wicket bought me to the crease. It was a real pressure cooker. Paul Adams, and his 'frog in a blender' action, was bowling from one end and Donald the other. On a relatively easy-paced wicket, Donald was still bowling with good speed. Even on a fifth-day wicket, Adams wasn' really spinning it. The wicket was still holding together.

I only stayed at the crease for 15 deliveries but in that short space of time I had my first taste of Test-match sledging. Adams was bowling with men around the bat and Brian McMillan was on the field as 12th man, fielding at silly-point. Reportedly he wasn't best pleased at being left out of the XI. Brian is a big man and had a reputation as someone not to mess with. He was immensely strong. Adams over-pitched and I drove it, out of the screws, straight into McMillan's shin. He wasn't wearing any pads but didn't rub his leg. He just looked at me and said, "Hey Ashley, those County bats, they aren't very good are they. How about you borrow one of mine?" It wasn't abusive. Quite gentle really. Just trying to get in my head. But for some reason, quick as a flash I responded: "Well, I might as well," I said, "you won't be needing them will you."

It was a pretty good reply, I thought. McMillan didn't. He was pissed off at being dropped for the match and I had just made the situation much worse. I wasn't out there much longer but for every second I was in the middle I was getting abused by McMillan. He called me everything under the sun. He was still going at me when I got out, caught at slip off Donald, by McMillan of all people, for just one run. It was a lesson learnt. We were now 329-8 with about 26 overs left in the day. The odds were stacked against us.

Crofty and Goughy battled hard and gradually we moved closer and closer to stumps. Then another drama. Goughy, who had batted for over an hour and faced 76 balls, got out to Donald. He was bowling like a man possessed with the third new ball in his hand. It was a nail-biting finish to my first Test match. Somehow we survived. Or rather Crofty and Gus Fraser did, with the former batting for over three hours and facing 125 balls to get us to safety. Fraser would never have made a more important 0 not out. Donald had bowled 40 overs and taken six wickets for 88 runs.

The match turned out to be the turning point in the series. After scraping the draw at Old Trafford, England went on to win at both Trent Bridge and Headingley to record a memorable victory.

However, I'd played my last part in the series. The following Sunday my phone rang again. It was Grav. I had been left out of the squad for the Trent Bridge Test, with Crofty also dropped. We had been replaced by Ian Salisbury, the leg-spinner from Surrey. I was disappointed and didn't rush to call Mum and Dad to give them the news. It didn't need explaining to Stine either. I wondered at the time whether I would play another Test match. As it turned out I was the only England spinner to take a wicket that summer, with Salisbury going wicketless at Trent Bridge and Headingley.

The week at Old Trafford had been a valuable learning experience for me. Was I ready? Probably not, yet. But at least I now had an idea of what to expect, and knew the level I'd need to perform at to earn a regular place in the team. This was a common theme throughout my career, at every level. Each step up was a new challenge, and I made it my goal to make sure I'd meet this one.

At Trent Bridge a certain Andrew Flintoff became England's 591st Test cricketer and was presented with his cap. It wouldn't be until the end of 2000, over two years later, that I'd get a chance to wear mine again.

11

Baby steps

Most people imagine that making your Test debut is just fun and exciting; that you are bursting with pride from pulling on the England cap and sweater that nothing else matters. You've made it. I think the reality for most people is very different from that. Yes, it is everything you've ever wanted to do: play for your country, make your family and friends proud, realise the dream and give a nod to those who have helped you on that journey. However, the pressure in that environment is intense. Once you are selected, no one talks about the journey you've made as the young lad on the village green, dreaming of playing for England, to the Test arena. You are judged on what you deliver, and that judgement can be harsh and difficult to take as a young player. There is no hiding place.

I'm not sure I had been on the team long enough for anyone to judge whether I was good enough for Test cricket. But I now knew what it was about. I knew I didn't want to be a member of the 'one Test wonder' group, and despite having just been dropped from the team, I don't think I ever felt I would be.

As I returned to Edgbaston and my Warwickshire teammates having made my Test debut, I remember feeling the weight lift from my shoulders. My first Championship match back was against Hampshire, and I had a great game. I hadn't carried the disappointment of being left out. I'd played Test cricket, I could say that at least, and perhaps I wasn't quite ready for it, but I hadn't felt out of my depth. Against Hampshire, I took nine wickets for 57 in the match and scored 75 in the first innings. It was my best performance of the season in the County Championship.

Overall, 1998 was a good and significant year for me. On the field, I played one-day cricket against South Africa, taking 2-37 in 10 overs at The Oval in May, and in July I'd made my Test debut, a massive milestone for a young player. In the County Championship, I took 35 wickets at an average of 26 and scored 472 runs at 31. It was a solid year. In the AXA one-day league, I'd had another strong year, taking 18 wickets at an average of just 14, and we'd finished runners-up. Off the field, I settled down and began to grow up a bit. Meeting Stine helped me massively, and I didn't go out or drink as much. I was probably difficult to live with in those early years with Stine. I'd had a couple of relationships previously, nothing longer than two years, and the most recent one was a long-distance relationship with a South African woman. I was used to looking after myself and doing what I wanted. I also found the pressures of professional sport, and the highs and lows that go with it, quite difficult to deal with and communicate to Stine when I was younger. I was moody and quiet at times. She'd probably say I still am. Luckily, she put up with me, and our relationship went from strength to strength.

Although I missed out on the Ashes that winter, I was selected in the squad for the Wills International Cup in Bangladesh, which was the very first Champions Trophy, as well as the one-day squad that would fly to Australia and play a triangular series against Australia and Sri Lanka at the end of the Ashes.

We arrived in Bangladesh soon after the end of the domestic summer, and after a couple of warm-up matches we took on South Africa. We scored 281, which had looked a decent score, but South Africa romped home with almost four overs to spare. I bowled well, at one point conceding just 14 runs in seven overs. Later, Hansie Cronje got after me, and I ended with 1-41 in my 10 overs. That match was Jack Russell's last in an England shirt, one of our best wicketkeepers with the most beautiful hands.

By the end of the summer of 1998, Stine and I had started talking about moving out of Birmingham to somewhere quieter, particularly given that I was hoping to continue travelling with England. I wanted

Stine to feel safe when I wasn't around. So, between the trip to Bangladesh and heading out to Australia at the end of December, we began researching different areas and looking at homes. I suggested we go to Droitwich in Worcestershire. I had been there a couple of times for appointments at the knee clinic and had enjoyed wandering around the town. We explored a new estate, College Green, built on an old school's grounds. We warmed to it immediately and found a plot and house type that we both liked and was within our budget. We didn't commit that day but left excited by what we'd seen. After Stine had gone to work the next day, I returned to Droitwich and reserved the house. Then, on my way home, I stopped at Rudells, a jeweller in Harborne, and bought a ring. I'm not sure what came over me, but it felt right, and I knew I'd met a good one in Stine. I rang her and told her I had reserved the house and suggested we head out for dinner that night to celebrate. I booked a table at the Garden House, a lovely pub we often visited on the Hagley Road. I was quiet throughout dinner, particularly given we were supposed to be celebrating, and Stine even remarked on it at one point. Once we finished eating, I prepared myself and asked the question. Thankfully, Stine said yes. We had a drink to celebrate and then went home to call our families. What a day.

We celebrated Christmas in Ripley with my parents and then I was off on tour again, headed for Australia with the one-day specialists. Soon after we arrived, I was told I would be flying to Sydney to join the Test squad as they were considering playing two spinners. I spent New Year with the Test squad on a boat near the Harbour Bridge, which was fun, but I couldn't help thinking that I might not be best prepared for Test cricket given that I'd just got off a plane and hadn't played any red-ball cricket for over three months. I trained with the team but, in the end, I didn't get picked and headed back to join the one-day boys. Australia won the Test and, with it, the series 3-1.

The one-day series was a triangular tournament, and we played Australia and Sri Lanka five times each. I only played two of those matches, one against each opposition. It was quite a spicy series with some major talking points, bordering on a full-on international incident in one case. At Adelaide in our match against Sri Lanka, Ross Emerson, one of the umpires, called Muttiah Muralitharan for throwing. The game was stopped, and it all kicked off. I was the 12th man and ran out with drinks for Knight and Hick, who were out in the middle batting, and watched as the incident developed. Arjuna Ranatunga, the Sri Lankan captain, was furious and ultimately took his team from the field. We weren't sure whether we'd even go back out again, but in the end everything settled down and the match resumed about 20 minutes later – with assurances, I think, that Murali would not be called for throwing again.

The two matches I played were both at the Sydney Cricket Ground. Having been given some rough treatment in my first couple of overs against Australia by Mark Waugh, going at 10 an over, I came back and bowled the last three overs from one end, bowling tidily, and we won the match. I'd managed to keep Michael Bevan quiet, who at the time was one of the best players in the world, and also picked up the wicket of Greg Blewett. It was great to play such a key role in such a big game, and at the SCG. At the end of the match, Shane Warne went out of his way to say well bowled to me, which meant a lot. A few days later, I played against Sri Lanka. We performed poorly and lost the match.

Despite that loss, we did enough to qualify for the best-of-three finals against Australia. The first game was again at the SCG. Chasing 232, we were cruising at 198-4 in the 43rd over. Nasser was playing particularly well but, inexplicably, he ran down the wicket and tried to hit Warne out of Sydney and was stumped. Warne had been in his ear, and it had worked. Next ball, Adam Hollioake was out lbw sweeping and, before you knew it, we were all out, 10 short. We'd thrown away the perfect opportunity to go one-up against the Aussies, and Bumble, our head coach, went ballistic. I'm not sure I've ever seen a coach so upset. After the match, he said little or nothing. At the time, I thought he might need some time to calm down, but he didn't.

He didn't speak to the team for the three days between matches and then, at the team meeting on the morning of the second game in Melbourne, he continued his silence and let Stewie run the meeting. It was bizarre. I'd never seen anything like it. I had my moments as a coach later in my career, but I don't think I could ever have stayed silent for so long. I'm not sure he helped the team much either, as we lost the second final comprehensively. Pressure does strange things to both players and coaches in these environments at times, even the best of men like Bumble.

On the way home, I was told I almost certainly wouldn't be in the 1999 World Cup squad, which was to be played in England. I wasn't that surprised given I'd hardly played in Australia but it was still disappointing to miss a home World Cup.

When I got home from Australia, I had quite a lot to think about and organise. At the end of February, we moved into our new home in Droitwich. It felt huge compared to my first house in Edgbaston, a two-up and two-down. We had four proper-sized bedrooms, a big kitchen diner and a separate dining room. We didn't have enough furniture to fill it. We also had a wedding to plan, as we'd set a date of October 9 the same year. It's said that getting married and moving house are two of the most stressful things you can do, and we took on both in the same year.

I didn't feature for England in the summer of 1999 and, in hindsight, it was probably helpful to be distanced from it. England didn't get past the group stage in the World Cup, which was a huge disappointment, and then got beaten in the Test series 2-1 by New Zealand, who were nowhere near as good as they are today.

I did OK with the ball again in the County Championship and the National League one-day competition, but I struggled with the bat in the Championship, averaging just 14 with a highest score of 30. My only meaningful score came against Oxford Uni, scoring 123 not out.

Our wedding was beautiful, surrounded by our families and friends. The Norwegians turned up in force, most of them in their distinctive national costume. Their arrival at St Andrew's Church in Droitwich caused quite a stir with the locals. Stine was very tired on the day, partly due to all the organisation she had put into it, but also because she was six weeks pregnant! We'd agreed that we wouldn't share the news with everyone at this point; only our close families knew. However, when it came to my speech, I couldn't help but let the cat out of the bag by saying, "The three of us will be going on honeymoon to Florida".

We celebrated way into the night and spent most of the next day with our families at the hotel. The day after we left for Disney World, which would have been great fun if Stine could have gone on any rides. We were so careful we avoided anything with even the slightest health warning. However, we still enjoyed our trip and in more recent years Florida and Disney have come to hold a very special place in our hearts as a family.

Following the summer's disappointing results, there was a double change in the England hierarchy. David Lloyd stood down as head coach, and Duncan Fletcher was appointed. Meanwhile, Nasser Hussain took over as captain from Alec Stewart. I missed out again on Test selection for the tour of South Africa but was picked for the triangular one-day tournament with South Africa and Zimbabwe which followed. It was great to go back to South Africa with England, having played so much cricket there when I was learning my trade. However, I didn't play a single match on the whole tour. It was incredibly frustrating, and challenging to remain focused and motivated when being dragged around as a spare part. Don't get me wrong, I did what I was supposed to do regarding my responsibilities as 12th man, working on my game and helping everyone else, but it was hard work. It was also becoming a trend. I'd been selected for numerous England tours but only played a few matches.

When I returned to Warwickshire at the start of the 2000 season, there had also been a change in leadership there. Bob Woolmer had returned to replace Phil Neale, who had taken on the manager role with the England team. I'd enjoyed being coached by Phil and would work with him much more in the future, but Bob returning brought a different challenge. He had been with South Africa for five years and knew what it took for players to succeed at the highest level. He was also a brilliant technical coach when it came to both batting and bowling. In 2000, everything ramped up for me. I'd recently bought a new house, I had just got married, and by the middle of the year, I would be a father. Don't get me wrong, I could still party with the best of them, but my focus had changed, and so did my responsibilities. I'd already had a taste of Test cricket and been involved with the one-day team, but made little impact. I wanted more.

The 2000 summer really couldn't have gone better for me, apart from international selection. From the pre-season tour in South Africa onwards, I felt like my game, and my bowling in particular, was in good order. In the County Championship, I took 52 wickets in 12 matches at an average of 23. With the bat, I averaged 40, scoring over 400 runs. One of my highlights was putting on 289 against Sussex with Dougie Brown for the seventh wicket. Doug got 200, and I finished 128 not out, my highest first-class score. I always enjoyed playing in Hove and generally did pretty well there. It's a lovely place, too, and being by the sea makes you feel good. I often said that if I were to play anywhere other than Edgbaston, it would be Hove. To share that stand with Doug was special. We were very close from the moment I joined Warwickshire and did just about everything together. In the NatWest Trophy, I got the opportunity to bat three in a couple of matches, and against Derbyshire at Edgbaston in the fourth round I scored my first List-A hundred, finishing 107 off 97 balls. My good form in the one-day league continued, taking 22 wickets at 19 and scoring 221 runs at 20.

But whatever highlights there were on the field, nothing could beat the arrival of Anders Fraser Giles on May 29. Nothing can prepare you for that moment, and I cried as I held him for the first time. I picked Stine and Anders up from the hospital the following day and brought them home. Now, that is a strange feeling – bringing a little person home you have total responsibility for and no real clue what you're doing. Fortunately, Stine was a natural. Two days later, I returned to cricket and celebrated becoming a dad by taking 3-32 against Notts in a win at Edgbaston.

Until the very end of the summer, I had no involvement with England. I was happy keeping my head down, getting on with my cricket and focusing on my job and family. As we reached the end of August, I knew the winter tour parties would be announced soon. I was at Lord's, just getting my pads on in the NatWest Trophy final, when I got a call from Grav. It wasn't a long call, but he told me I'd been picked in the one-day squad for the Champions Trophy and series in Pakistan, as well as the Test squad for Pakistan. It was my first overseas Test selection. I was delighted but had little time to think about it as I was soon batting. I scored 60 batting at three in very tricky conditions at Lord's, but we lost a rain-affected final to Gloucestershire. A couple of days later, I joined the Test squad for the last match of the series against West Indies at The Oval. I didn't play but being around the team again was fun, particularly knowing I would be touring with them for at least the first half of the winter.

On reflection, 1999 and 2000 were incredible years for me both on and off the field. It was two years since I played my first Test, and a lot had changed in that time. Now I had a second chance, and I was determined that this time I would take it.

12

Out of the dark and into the light

My return to international cricket was almost over before it even began. I got injured after just five balls in a warm-up match against Australia ahead of the Champions Trophy in Nairobi. I'd made the perfect start to my winter by dismissing Michael Bevan caught and bowled but in the process I pulled something in my lower left leg, and it was immediately apparent that it was pretty bad. I tried to carry on, attempting to finish the over, but there was a shooting pain up my calf and I was forced to leave the field. I had been struggling for years, on and off, with my left Achilles and had managed it with cortisone injections, anti-inflammatories and time out from the game when it became too sore. This time, it felt so bad that I immediately feared it would be the end of my winter tour. I was absolutely gutted as I headed back to the hotel.

Dean Conway, our team physio, arranged a scan for the next day and thankfully the results came back showing it was not as bad as we had first feared. The decision was made to keep me with the team and see how I was after a couple of weeks of rehab. I spent a lot of time on that trip on the bike in the gym. I was very grateful to Deano and Duncan Fletcher for keeping me out there and giving me the chance to prove my fitness. I had toured a lot with Dean before this trip and he is an excellent man. Far more than just our physio, he was a friend, confidant, and social secretary amongst other things. He was also very funny, and I trusted him. Thankfully, so did Duncan, largely due to the time that they'd worked together at Glamorgan before Fletch had taken on the England job, and he took Dean's advice to keep me with the group.

Paul Grayson, the Essex left-arm spin-bowling all-rounder, was flown out to Kenya as cover while I continued my rehab. In Kenya, we beat Bangladesh in the first match by eight wickets but then lost to South Africa by the same margin five days later and were knocked out of the competition. In all we spent almost three weeks in Kenya for just two competitive matches. In some ways it was a lot of time doing not much at all but for me it was just about enough time to get myself fit for Pakistan. Thankfully I was given the all-clear to continue my winter with England.

In Pakistan we were into our cricket quickly and I was back out in the middle. We started the tour with the one-day series, which we lost 2-1, but I bowled pretty well and consistently and it was a relief to get through three matches. Two other things stick with me from that series. Firstly, in the second ODI in Lahore, millions of midges engulfed the ground and found their way into every nook and cranny imaginable – ears, eyes and mouths, it was horrible. Then in Rawalpindi, for the third ODI, there was a riot outside the ground due to too many people turning up without tickets. The police used tear gas a couple of times to control the crowd and because of the direction the wind was blowing it blew across the field and stopped play. On one occasion this happened when I was out in the middle batting. It is a weird feeling, like the hardest hit of wasabi you've ever experienced.

Despite losing the series I felt pretty happy with my contribution and thought I'd demonstrated that I wasn't going to be overawed in this environment. The red-ball matches would be a different challenge altogether. There had been a lot of discussion about the quality of our spin department compared to Pakistan's. Ian Salisbury and I were the only two frontline spinners and both of us were relatively inexperienced. We were going up against Saqlain Mushtaq, Mushtaq Ahmed and a young Shahid Afridi. Most people gave us little chance of drawing, let alone winning, the Test series. That took the heat off us and it felt like we almost had a free run at it.

The first warm-up match in Rawalpindi was far less eventful than the ODI and, thankfully, no one got tear gassed. I put in a steady performance, picking up a few wickets, getting some overs under my belt and making a few runs. We won easily, by an innings.

For the second warm-up fixture we travelled to Peshawar in the north-west, close to the Afghanistan border. Peshawar is reportedly where Osama bin Laden entered Pakistan from Afghanistan, and one of his ex-wives is quoted as saying that this was the first place he visited in Pakistan post 9/11. In 2000 the city had an uneasy feel about it. As a team we were made to feel very welcome and were well looked after, but there was also a certain feeling of tension and anti-American sentiment. One day at breakfast one of the young men serving me pointed at a t-shirt I had on and said, "That is no good sir, you are a nice man, but that is no good". I remember looking down at my shirt to see what he was talking about. It read: 'GANT – USA'. I found it remarkable at the time and the strong anti-American feeling worried me. A month before our arrival in Peshawar the USS Cole had been bombed in the Yemen, and Al-Qaeda had claimed responsibility for it. There was talk in the media of retaliatory strikes in Afghanistan by the US, using Pakistan air space. If this happened, given that America was one of the UK's closest allies, we were worried that the anti-American and anti-West feeling may intensify in Pakistan and disrupt the tour.

Despite this, on one of our days off in Peshawar we were offered the opportunity to take a trip up the Khyber Pass to the border of Afghanistan, stopping on the way back at a tribal leader's residence for food and entertainment. Not everyone went on the trip, but it was a no-brainer for me. I have always enjoyed my history and this was an opportunity not to be missed. We had a huge amount of security with us, but it was a fantastic day out. At the border with Afghanistan we got out and had a look around at the guard post and Andrew Caddick and I had photos taken sitting on the big guns. The visit to the tribal leader's home was incredible and we were made to feel very welcome and safe. It was one of those trips I will never forget and I'm so glad I took that opportunity. I can't imagine an England team doing that now. Back in Peshawar we visited the markets in the city. We were looking for DVDs and PlayStation games. They were available of course, and so was just about everything else. From AK-47s, handguns, to pornographic material and pashminas, you could get anything. It was bizarre.

On the field, the warm-up match was uneventful and we won by eight wickets. We were as well prepared as we could be by the time we reached the first Test. We'd worked hard on the skills we'd need to win in Pakistan, in particular playing their spinners, in defence and attack. We worked a lot in pairs, throwing balls to each other on roughed-up parts of the practice wickets, which on more than one occasion upset our hosts. We focused on having a solid defence as much as our scoring options, as we knew the conditions would require patience and that the match would speed up at the back-end as the pitch started to break up. We also learnt from the local players. We watched them facing young ball boys on the outfield during the breaks after the match. We realised that, because of the soft and grippy nature of the outfields, it was a fantastic way to learn to play with softer hands, using your wrists and playing late. We all started doing it.

As we expected, the first Test in Lahore was a protracted affair. We won the toss and it was an easy decision to bat first. We batted for 196 overs in our first innings, and reached 480-8 before declaring, taking the slow and steady approach. Thorpey got a fantastic hundred supported by several others, and I managed to score 37 not out by the time we declared. In response Pakistan scored 401 in 163 overs. It was certainly a game of patience. I bowled better and better as the innings went on, and getting that volume of overs under my belt set me up well for the rest of the series. I took 4-113 in 59 overs. The match eventually petered out into a draw, which at the start of day one we certainly would've taken. A few of us had got ourselves into the series with important runs and wickets and we hadn't lost, as many were predicting we would.

Off the field it was a really enjoyable trip. A lot has been said about touring Pakistan, much of it derogatory, but some of my best memories of touring are from that trip in 2000. We would spend a lot of time together in each other's rooms, watching films, listening to music and talking. Between matches we'd find alcohol from somewhere, often the high commission if there was one locally, and sit around drinking and laughing. We spent many nights down in the shops connected to the hotels looking at rugs for hours on end, bartering over prices. Most of us bought some and had them shipped back to the UK. I bought three and we still have them today. We also enjoyed a couple of nights out at the high commission offices in Islamabad and Karachi. You could get very familiar food in the high commission, like egg and chips and steak, for next to nothing. You could also buy stuff to take away with you, like alcohol, sweets and chocolate. I must admit I was careful when it came to food in Pakistan. At the hotel I ate pretty normally, but at the cricket I survived on rice, baked beans and toast. The weight fell off me in Pakistan, even with the occasional beer or whisky thrown in. One of our best nights out was to a dinner for Imran Khan's cancer charity at a hospital he had helped fund. Special guests were Boney M and they played all their biggest hits. It was a great night and Boney M became the sound of the tour, with many bus trips having a singalong to 'Rivers of Babylon' and 'Daddy Cool'.

The second Test in Faisalabad was another long affair. We lost the toss this time and fielded first but we made good progress throughout the first day and at one point had Pakistan 151-5. By the end of the day they'd recovered to 243-5 through Yousuf Youhana and Moin Khan. On day two we roused ourselves again and bowled Pakistan out for 316. I had a really good couple of days, taking my first Test match five-wicket haul, 5-75 in 35 overs. We scored 342 in response with Thorpey again in the runs, making 79. Pakistan played much better in their second innings and the match once again ended in a draw. It was another good result for us. In footballing terms we were getting men behind the ball, defending really hard and waiting for an opportunity to counterattack. If we drew the series 0-0, we would have been delighted. We were exceeding people's expectations and personally I'd done far more in two Tests than most had thought I was capable of, taking 10 wickets.

The final Test, in Karachi, started much as the others in the series had. Pakistan won the toss and after electing to bat first finished day one on 292-3. It was a long day in the field for us but on day two we stayed disciplined and it paid off. I was perhaps fortunate to get Yousuf Youhana caught and bowled off a full toss, a sharp, low chance that I took one-handed to my right. It opened the door for us. It was the first of four wickets for me and Pakistan fell from 323-3 to 405 all out. I finished with 4-94. In reply, we set out to bat time and see where we'd get to. There was no point thinking about winning at that stage because we were so far behind. We had to earn that right and Atherton was the perfect man for the job, scoring 125 off 430 balls. We made 388 in 179 overs and were within touching distance of Pakistan. Again, we had no huge expectations as we went out to field in the second innings, but we knew that taking wickets and controlling the scoring rate would keep us in the match and make it interesting. Pakistan dug a hole for themselves in the end as we chipped away, bowling them out for 158 in around 70 overs, leaving us needing 176 to win. I took another three wickets in the second innings including a beauty that bowled Inzamam. That gave me 17 wickets in the series, the most by any England bowler in a Test series in Pakistan.

Having played the long game, we now had an opportunity to win the series, and we were going for it. It was a tough chase, and Pakistan used every tactic possible to try to slow the match down and wait for the light to get to an unacceptable level. Umpire Steve Bucknor knew exactly what Pakistan were trying to do and kept us out there. Just as it was getting dark we got over the line and won the Test, Thorpe 64 not out. It was an incredible finish to a memorable series and the 'win in the dark in Karachi' will go down as one of England's greatest ever Test wins, resulting in a first series win in Pakistan since 1961/62.

We left the ground pretty quickly after play as we were heading out of the country that night and had to get back and sort out our kit. We got changed and met for a beer before we headed to the airport. On the plane out of Karachi, as we roared down the runway, the whole squad began whistling the tune from 'The Great Escape'. It had been a tough series, and yet we had come away as victors

We arrived at Heathrow the next day and Stine and Anders, just eight months old, were there to meet me. I looked so skinny in the pictures that appeared in the paper the next day. I'd lost around 10kgs. I came back looking different, and I also came back feeling different from the bowler who'd left the UK three months earlier. It had been a long tour, but I'd loved every minute of it.

13

Sweating it out

As a result of my performances in Pakistan, I was getting a lot more attention from the media when I got home. It was completely new to me and I didn't have anyone at the time who really looked after this area for me. I was asked to go on *They Think It's All Over*, which I couldn't say no to as I'd always been a fan, and I was on Jonathan Ross' team. What a professional he is. The whole thing was scripted, and before the show was filmed we sat in a room for a couple of hours and went through some of the themes, questions and potential jokes. He wrote most of it on the spot, and it was brilliant to watch. A very clever and funny man. We were also on *Through The Keyhole* and were visited by Loyd Grossman at our house in Droitwich. Funnily enough the panel didn't guess whose house it was!

Pakistan had been rewarding for both me and the team, but my body needed a rest and my left Achilles in particular was really bothering me. I wasn't able to do a huge amount between tours and the priority was to rest it and let it settle. The cortisone injections I'd used to calm it down were having less of an impact, to the point where I was without soreness for as little as four weeks after the injection. My biggest fear was that at some point the tendon would just snap, which would be a disaster.

Soon after we arrived in Sri Lanka for the second leg of England's winter Test tours my Achilles started to flair up again and I battled through the warm-up matches. I'd also arrived with a new status in the side as our first-choice spinner following my 17 wickets in Pakistan. This brought a different level of pressure. Whereas Pakistan had almost been a free hit, with little expectation of us winning, people were now thinking we could win in Sri Lanka too.

I had a new spin partner in Sri Lanka in the form of Robert Croft. I had played with Crofty in my debut Test in 1998 and had been his understudy in one-day cricket. I knew him and got on very well with him. I felt for Ian Salisbury, who had played alongside me in Pakistan but had struggled to find any consistency and had been left out of the Sri Lanka trip.

The country, and Colombo in particular, was a completely different place to the one I'd visited in 1998 on an England A tour. We were able to move around freely, visiting other hotels, restaurants and coffee shops. Terrorism was less of a concern and the capital had a really relaxed feel about it – we were even able to have a tuk-tuk race one evening as a squad. The police closed the road for us while we raced along the sea front, round a roundabout and back to the hotel.

Sri Lanka as a team were a different prospect in 2001 from what they had been 10 or 15 years earlier, particularly in their own conditions. They had some world-class players in their team. Aravinda de Silva, Kumar Sangakkara and Mahela Jayawardene are three of the best batters I've played against and they also boasted players of the quality of Sanath Jayasuriya, Marvan Atapattu and Chaminda Vaas in their ranks, all very dangerous cricketers. However, we knew that the biggest threat would come from one player in particular, and that was Muttiah Muralitharan.

Murali was an incredible bowler. The ball fizzed when it came down at you, in his first few overs especially. There has been a lot said about Murali's bowling action, and whether it was legal or not. To be honest, I don't know. It was certainly very different from anything anyone had seen before. But he was great for cricket both in Sri Lanka and across the world and in many ways, alongside Warne, he changed the game. He was lethal in the right conditions and could rip through any batting order in the world. He would finish his career with an incredible 800 Test wickets, the most by any bowler.

Going up against Saqlain and Mushy in Pakistan had been hard, but I knew going toe-to-toe with Murali would be that much harder. We framed it as our whole bowling unit taking him on, but I undoubtedly felt the pressure as the senior spinner in our team and him in theirs, as I would when I came up against Warne later in my career. The other thing about Murali is that he is one of the nicest men in the world. Not only does he smile non-stop, which isn't that surprising given how many wickets he took, but he is also incredibly humble, kind and generous. A true gentleman.

The first Test was played in Galle, a beautiful coastal ground with the incredible fort as its backdrop. We stayed just up the road at the Lighthouse Hotel, one of my favourite hotels anywhere in the world. It has a colonial feel and the rooms are gorgeous, the food is magnificent, and staff lovely. During Covid we had the whole hotel to ourselves during our two-Test series in 2021. That was a weird experience, but there aren't many hotels you'd rather be confined to in those circumstances.

The Galle Test of 2001 also coincided with families visiting, and Stine and Anders flew out for about 10 days. We had a lovely time with him. I'd take him in the pool with me in his inflatable ring and he'd often fall asleep in the cool water. He also got a lot of attention from the other wives and girlfriends.

We lost the toss in Galle, Sri Lanka elected to bat, and we spent almost two days in the field – 170 overs in total. It was tough work. As part of our physical preparation and maintenance we weighed ourselves before play, at the end of each session and at the end of play. During that Test I was losing between two and three kilograms a session! That is vital fluid that needs replacing to avoid dehydration, so at each break we tried to get as much in as possible. It is hard to drink that much water in such a short period, a litre for each kg lost. It's also crucial to get some food in you, even if you didn't fancy it at all. At the end of each day my head would be pounding. It had never felt so good to get back to an air-conditioned bedroom.

Sweating also causes other issues, like struggling to keep the ball dry. We tried to give it to certain individuals on the team who either didn't sweat as much or weren't bowling. Whether you are trying to swing the ball conventionally or get reverse swing, keeping the ball dry is crucial. In Sri Lanka, and Galle especially, this was near impossible. Tres was the go-to ball-shiner in our team as he generally stood at slip, so didn't move much. I was almost constantly dripping wet and at every break would have to change top to bottom. Just taking those wet clothes off was such a relief.

Sri Lanka ended up declaring on 470-5, and two of those were run outs! Atapattu scored 200 not out, and Aravinda got a century. It was like bowling on a road. I bowled 48 overs in the innings and took just one wicket for 134. Matches can often get ugly in these circumstances, and this one certainly did. Apart from Tres, who scored a brilliant hundred in the first innings and half-century in the second, no one else really got going.

Tres was one of the very best players, across formats, that I played with or against. His ability to play the extremes of very fast bowling and high-quality spin was as good as anyone I've seen in an England shirt. I also used to enjoy practising against him. Bowling spin can be hard work at times in the nets as batters often see it as an opportunity to smack a few and free their arms up; playing in a way that they are never likely to in a match, at least back then. Tres was different. He'd talk to me about what he was looking to get out of the net, perhaps just looking to sweep for the whole session. I could try and combat this with my pace and line, getting valuable specific practice myself. On another day he might practise using his feet and coming down the pitch. Those sessions with Tres were some of my most enjoyable.

In Galle we followed on and ended up losing the match by an innings and 28 runs, Murali taking seven wickets. Going behind in a three-match series is difficult to come back from but we had to try to put it behind us and move on. Cricket in these conditions can look very one-sided at times. The pitch can be incredibly flat for two days, but once it begins to break up the match can move forward very quickly as it becomes increasingly difficult for batters. Galle was renowned for this and losing the toss had been crucial to the outcome. It's embarrassing to lose in this way, but it happens, even to the best teams. The umpiring at Galle had also been interesting at times and this would continue throughout the series, adding another level of spice.

We moved on to Kandy, stopping overnight in Colombo, partly to break up the trip and partly to drop off the families who would be returning to the UK. Kandy is in the middle of the country, slightly elevated and therefore cooler and less humid than Galle. We were very surprised, and pleasantly so, when we saw the pitch at the Asgiriya Stadium. It had quite a lot of green grass on it and was chalk and cheese to the pitch we'd played on in the first Test. Sri Lanka won the toss again and elected to bat. They scored 297 but our seamers, Gough and Caddick particularly, bowled beautifully.

When it was our time to bat Nasser was the star for us, scoring 109, and was well supported by his two most senior pros, Stewart and Thorpe. Nasser played some of his best innings for England in the most challenging circumstances. This was one of them. Whilst our seamers had dominated, Murali bowled 60 overs of high-quality spin. Nas may have had a little bit of luck along the way, but he played an incredibly dogged and skilful innings. Nas was also often at his best when he got into a bit of a scrap with the opposition, and in Kandy that was easy given the series was starting to become an ill-tempered one, with a lot of verbals going on around the bat from both sides. Nas loved that sort of conflict, he almost needed it. If I was playing against him I think I would have just ignored him and not wound him up. He even looked to do it with his own team at times before a match, just to get his intensity up and his mind right. We'd all fall foul of this at some point. It was quite funny really and you could often see it coming from a mile off a couple of days out from a Test match.

As a captain Nasser brought a different level of intensity to everything we did, and to the dressing-room environment particularly. There was a lot more stick than carrot in Nasser's management style and everyone was treated equally, whether you were a junior player like me or one of the seniors like Stewie or Ath. I liked that. There was no hierarchy or special privileges given to older members of the team. You pulled your weight, you worked hard, you played for the team first, or you got a bollocking off Nas. Sometimes a severe one. On reflection, we needed that as a team, and it was absolutely crucial to the progress we would make over the next few years. We had been a bit soft, but now we were becoming more hardened.

I'd felt that Nas hadn't really rated me before my performances in Pakistan. I knew he'd always been a Tuffers fan – which I was too, to be fair – and had been reluctant to pick me. However, once you proved your worth to him and demonstrated that you would do the hard yards, even in the most challenging conditions, he backed you to the hilt. Alongside Dermot Reeve and Michael Vaughan, Nas was one of the best captains I played for.

He got us to 387 and a crucial lead of 90. In the second innings we bowled Sri Lanka out for 250, Goughy taking his match haul to eight, and my spin twin, Crofty, taking three. I finished the Test wicketless, which was disappointing, and I didn't bowl with any decent rhythm or control.

We needed just 161 to level the series, but Sri Lanka made us work hard for every run. Thorpe played particularly well and while everyone else had struggled to score fluently, he managed 46 off just 58 balls and turned the match in our favour. Craig White also played well and it was great to be out there with him as we got over the line. It was an amazing feeling to level the series and it made the bus ride back to Colombo for the third Test very entertaining. We managed to find a few beers to celebrate but in that climate it didn't take much to make you feel light-headed.

We lost the toss again in Colombo and knew we'd need to make inroads. Despite Sri Lanka getting past 100 for the loss of just two wickets, we steadily chipped away and bowled with great discipline. Crofty took four wickets and I took two as we bowled them out for 241, a fantastic effort having lost the toss. I'd bowled better than I had on the rest of the tour. My pace was good, I bowled with real energy, and was much more accurate. I felt completely different and had a real bounce in my stride which I'd lacked for the rest of the series.

It was hard work with the bat, scoring 249 in our first innings. The difference for us, and the only reason we got a small lead, was Thorpe, who continued his form from the second innings in Kandy. He batted for about five and a half hours for his 113 not out, in the toughest of conditions. It was an innings of patience mixed with the very highest skill, against the spin of Murali and Vaas's left-arm reverse swing in particular. Thorpey's ability to manipulate high-quality spin was incredibly impressive. Murali bowled 41 overs in the innings and took just one wicket. When I was out we were 181-7 and looking at a significant first-innings deficit but Thorpey managed the tail brilliantly and we added 68 for the last three wickets.

From there, the match went into overdrive. We spent just 28.1 overs in the field in Sri Lanka's second innings and bowled them out for 81. We shared the wickets but I picked up 4-11 in 9.1 overs and felt like I had some reward for how well I'd bowled in the first innings. It was a great bowling and fielding performance from the whole team and suddenly, similar to the Karachi Test before Christmas, the series was within our grasp. We were left needing just 74 runs to win.

We lost some early wickets but never really looked like not getting there, largely thanks to Thorpey again who backed up his unbeaten hundred in the first innings with 32 not out. By this time he was practically on his knees with exhaustion having spent all but about 30 overs of the match on the field. I was with him at the end and had the pleasure of hitting the winning run. Thorpey was so tired he hardly had the energy to celebrate what was an amazing match for him. It was a performance that won us the series.

We had turned up to the ground on day three 175-4 in our first innings and would never have been able to predict how things would develop over the next few hours. We certainly weren't thinking we'd have won the series by the end of it. We went back to the hotel and celebrated hard and deep into the night in the bar in our hotel, the Taj. It was the culmination of an amazing winter for the team, a springboard for me personally, and an important step on our journey to 2005. However, another huge challenge was approaching fast. 2001 was a home Ashes series and a chance to see how we matched up against the best in the world.

14

Rough patch

When I got back from Sri Lanka I needed to take another break from cricket. My Achilles was worse than ever and the decision was made to take six weeks off and try to get myself ready for the Ashes series starting in July. I returned to cricket on May 29, Anders' first birthday, in a match against Notts second XI at Trent Bridge. After that I was able to play in four one-day county matches and two County Championship fixtures ahead of the first Test at Edgbaston. I didn't do anything spectacular in that time but managed to get some overs under my belt to test my Achilles. Despite the rest it was clear that it still wasn't settling and it was far from perfect as we reached the first Ashes Test.

After of our winter successes, we went into the summer with high hopes, or higher hopes than previous Ashes series anyway. However, in the one-day triangular series we had lost six out of six against Australia and Pakistan – not a great way for the team to start such an important summer.

The Australian team was full of super stars, players I'd watched for years in Test cricket and admired. I had played one-day cricket against them, but this was different. This was the *Ashes*. Slater, Hayden, Ponting, Mark Waugh and Steve Waugh, Martyn, Gilchrist, Warne, Lee, Gillespie and McGrath. That was the Aussie team for the first Test. A serious line-up.

We batted first and managed just 294 but it would have been much worse if not for a century partnership for the 10th wicket between Stewie and Caddy. The Aussies came hard at us from ball one and got off to a flier. I took the first wicket of the innings thanks to a stunning one-handed catch by Craig White on the leg-side to remove Hayden but at that point they were already on 98 after just 15 overs. At the end of the first day Australia had reached 133-2 off just 22 overs and it felt like they were well ahead in the game. The pain continued throughout the next day, although we were able to slow the rate a bit, and going into day three they were 332-4.

The next day was absolute carnage. It was my first experience of being on the receiving end of Adam Gilchrist. He hit the ball to all parts in an innings of 152 off 143 balls. All the bowlers got smashed apart from Mark Butcher, who came on relatively late in the innings to pick up 4-42 in nine overs. Australia finished on 576, with Steve Waugh, Damien Martyn and Gilchrist all scoring centuries. I'd taken just one wicket.

In our second innings, after a fairly positive start, we capitulated and were all out for 164 to lose by an innings and 118 runs. It wouldn't be the last time I'd come up against an Australian performance like this, but it was the first, and I felt a bit shellshocked at the end of the match. It already felt like a long way back, perhaps too far. I remember sitting in the shower area at Edgbaston at the end of the game wondering what had just happened and realising that beating this lot was a completely different challenge to the one we had faced over the winter.

At the end of the match my Achilles flared up again and I wasn't selected in the squad for the next Test. I played a couple of one-day matches for Warwickshire as we considered how to manage the injury but I had already had too many injections and I was now looking down the barrel at surgery. As it transpired, I played my last match of the 2001 summer on July 25 and soon after headed to Swindon for an operation to decompress my Achilles and remove the sheath around the tendon. It would mean a long recovery and a battle to be fit for the India Test tour later in the year.

The operation went well and I spent a couple of weeks on crutches. After I was able to put weight through my left leg, I started getting my head around rehab. Unfortunately, just before I started doing anything meaningful I picked up an infection in the wound and it felt like it was going to burst wide open. Fortunately, it settled with some antibiotics and I was back on track.

Despite the introduction of central contracts in 2000, which were so good for the players in so many ways, the science and medicine support was still lagging behind and it would take years yet to bridge the gap. If you were around the team you got excellent support from our physio, Dean Conway, and our trainer, Nigel Stockhill. But that was about the extent of the science and medicine department. So post-op, I was sent to the Lilleshall national rehabilitation centre. I had some occasional contact from the medical teams at both Edgbaston and England, but I was basically left with the guys at Lilleshall to crack on until I was ready to play cricket again. My experience there was a good one. The medical team clearly knew their stuff and gave me loads of support. There could be anywhere from five to 10 professional sports people, from a number of different sports, rehabbing at the centre on any given day. However, most of the people there were from football, and I was the only cricketer. It was a long summer and autumn, but I got my head down and did what I needed to do.

On September 11 I sat with Anders in our kitchen in Droitwich watching kids' programmes while Stine, now pregnant with Tilly, was at the hospital for a check-up. I was waiting to do my weekly column with a local newspaper when the journalist called and asked whether I'd rather do it another day given what was going on in New York. I had no idea what he was talking about until I changed the TV channel and almost immediately the second plane hit the Twin Towers in New York. I didn't move for the next couple of hours as I watched the whole thing unfold. The world had changed, including cricket.

My goal was always to be ready for the India Test tour at the end of November and thankfully I received the call-up. After 9/11 attention in the media turned to security and whether or not the tour would be affected. A number of us expressed our concerns about the situation. I don't think I was ever not going to go if the advice from the government was that it was fine to travel, but I really needed Stine to be comfortable with the decision given we had Anders, who was only 16 months old, and Tilly on the way.

In the end only Andrew Caddick and Robert Croft decided not to travel. However, due to our concerns, we were accompanied by two security experts on tour, something that has now become standard practice. Both men were ex-SAS and we loved trying to get stories out of them about their exploits. They humoured us, of course, and both men fitted into our group very well.

This was my first visit to India. I had heard a lot of stories but nothing prepares you for what it's actually like, particularly being part of an international cricket team. India is the one place in the world where, as a cricket player, you are treated like royalty. No matter how many matches you've played, everyone knows you, your stats, details on performances. It is extraordinary. Our hotel lobbies were always full of fans hoping to catch a glimpse of their heroes. We started in Mumbai and stayed at the Taj Mahal Palace Hotel, next to the Gateway to India, a beautiful and luxurious hotel on the sea front. All our rooms were gorgeous and the staff were first class.

While I had been passed fit to travel, on arrival I was still working my way to match intensity and getting my workloads up in the nets. As a result, I didn't take part in the warm-up matches in Mumbai or Hyderabad. I was picked in the match against India A in Jaipur, our last warm-up fixture, still with an outside chance that I could make the first Test in Mohali. I bowled 17 overs in the first innings, taking 1-48, which was fine for my first proper run out for four months. The issue was, as the innings developed and I spent more time on my feet, I started to develop a sore heel. By the evening it was incredibly sore, even to lightly touch. We won the match but I didn't bowl in the second innings and after the game had finished I was taken to get my foot scanned. The scan came back clear enough but that didn't change the fact that I could hardly put my foot down. This meant the first Test was out of the question for me.

I was gutted given the effort I'd put in over the last few months and wasn't sure I'd be able to play any further part in the tour. While the hotels were lovely, particularly in Mumbai and Jaipur, the evenings can be long in the subcontinent and, like the tour of Pakistan the previous winter, we tried our best to keep ourselves occupied. For some this was watching films or reading. For Michael Vaughan, Graham Thorpe and me, playing football on the PlayStation was how we spent most evenings. We'd spend hours playing round-robin matches, keeping a tally of the results. We even did a draft of all the best players around the world to pick our teams. Vaughany was Man United, Thorpey was Chelsea and I was Arsenal. I'm actually a QPR fan but I don't think they were on the game at the time.

As well as the football we did have another reason for spending so much time together. Thorpey had been having a difficult time with his marriage and had really been struggling on tour. Vaughany and I spent as much time as possible with him, trying to keep him occupied and being there when he wanted to talk. Nights alone in your room on tour can be long and lonely at the best of times. When there are things going on at home as well it can be almost impossible to keep everything in perspective. Thorpey hadn't been sleeping well and rather than him turning to drink we distracted him with football and some banter.

I spent a lot of time with Thorpey over the years. I first played against him when he was a colt at Farnham. Slightly older than me, he progressed quickly through the Surrey ranks and graduated to first-class and international cricket way ahead of me. I ended up playing quite a lot of cricket with him for England and always enjoyed his company. Later when I was head coach of England's white-ball teams he worked for me as batting coach and then, when I was managing director of England men's teams, he was one of Chris Silverwood's assistant coaches.

When I was white-ball head coach we had some of my most memorable nights on tour in each other's company. Thorpey, David Saker, Ben Langley (our physio) and I spent a lot of time together and shared many glasses of wine and laughs. In New Zealand, on more than one occasion I woke in the morning with sore ribs from laughing so hard the night before – another very good way of coping on long tours.

Thorpey was also one of the very best batting coaches I worked with. He knew from experience exactly what it took to have success at the highest level. But he also knew how to teach those important skills in a very effective and practical way, and he also had a great eye for spotting talent. Many of the players that won the World Cup in 2019 benefitted hugely from the work that Thorpey put in with them. He would spend hours throwing to them, working on very specific skills like playing the short ball, or manipulating spin with the sweep and reverse sweep. He will be missed forever. Covid was a dark and terrible time for so many. In my view, Thorpey was another of its victims.

Back in India, we lost the first Test in Mohali by 10 wickets. Thorpey left the tour after that match and returned home. During the match I had an injection into my heel to try to settle the pain and thankfully the soreness disappeared. I was able to return to full training and was picked for the second Test in Ahmedabad.

We won the toss and put a healthy 407 on the board. In response India scored 291, with Sachin Tendulkar making a hundred. This was my first taste of Sachin Mania. I had heard the stories about how grounds in India would fill just to see Sachin bat and in Ahmedabad that was certainly the case. In fact, in the second innings the crowd cheered when India lost their second wicket, bringing Sachin to the crease. His century was a knock of real class. The seamers bowled with a seven-two off-side field to him to try restrict him to scoring on one side of the wicket. Several times he just moved across and timed it beautifully through the leg-side. He was playing a different game to the rest of us.

For me personally, Ahmedabad was a happy comeback. We didn't manage to get over the line and win the match and I went wicketless in the second innings, but in the first I bowled 43 overs and took 5-67. This was my first Test in five months, against some of the very best players in the world, and for the most part the pitch was flat. But I'd bowled with control and consistency. For the team it had been a much stronger performance and we'd stuck at the task well.

We moved to Bangalore for the third Test, winning the toss and putting 336 on the board. Our seamers bowled beautifully in conditions that really suited them but despite Hoggard and Flintoff picking up four wickets each in India's total of 238, the biggest talking point of the innings, match and perhaps even the series was a spell I bowled to Sachin. In Ahmedabad I had bowled over the wicket for periods to try to keep the scoring rate down and limit Sachin's options to one side of the ground, much like the seamers had done with their seven-two off-side field. I had occasionally gone wide into the rough but generally looked to bowl a tight leg-stump line and keep them playing. In Bangalore the middle part of the pitch was pretty flat and Sachin was once again scoring freely, so I used the same tactic.

Unlike Ahmedabad, in Bangalore the bowlers' footmarks had really roughed-up the area outside leg stump, probably due to the amount of overs the seamers had bowled in the match, and I was able to bowl a little wider down the leg-side to Sachin. The ball jumped and spat out of the rough and Sachin began to get frustrated. Many people seemed to think this was a master plan drawn up by Nas, Fletch and I. It was nothing of the sort. It was simply a way of trying to keep one of the greatest players of all time quiet at one end while we were taking wickets at the other. It certainly wasn't meant to be disrespectful to Sachin, I have the utmost respect for him. In the end, he ran out of patience and ran down the wicket at me. He was nowhere near it, went through with the shot and was stumped by James Foster. He had still scored 90 but the dismissal opened up his end and enabled us to bowl India out for 238 and take a first-innings lead for the second successive Test.

I hadn't realised how controversial that tactic would be, and it ultimately led to changes to the leg-side wide rule. Many will argue it was a bad look for the game. For me, it was just playing the situation that was in front of us and trying to get into a position to win the match. Surely that is part of this great game. It's about finding a way, building pressure when you need to, sucking it up when you have to, and creating moments that change matches and alter the outcome of series. It won't always be popular, and it certainly wasn't in Bangalore. In the end the weather won and there was no play on the last day, but that controversy is something I will never forget.

15

Another delivery

By January 2002, we found ourselves back in India for the six-match one-day series. I left behind a very pregnant wife, who also had our 20-month-old son to care for. It had never crossed my mind that I would skip the tour, and Stine certainly hadn't pressured me to do so.

It was a quick turnaround once we arrived in India. We played just one warm-up match, which we won easily, and two days later we were lining up against India at the colossal Eden Gardens in Kolkata. Over 100,000 people were present that day, and the noise was incredible. Trying to communicate on the field was extremely challenging, particularly when Ganguly and Tendulkar were together at the start of their innings.

India batted first on what looked like a belter of a pitch and scored 281. In reply we were cruising, largely thanks to a brilliant hundred from Tres. However, we consistently lost wickets and were bowled out 22 runs short of our target. It was a big opportunity missed. I bowled poorly and was dropped from the team, with Jeremy Snape preferred ahead of me. We won the next match but lost the following two, going 3-1 down in the series with two to play.

I was recalled for the fifth match in Delhi. We batted first and posted 271, with Nick Knight scoring a century. I got off to a terrible start with the ball, conceding more than 30 runs in my first four overs. I remember feeling pretty bad when I was taken off, not only because I'd let myself down but mainly because I'd let the team down, too. Ganguly had been particularly brutal, hitting me down the ground and over deep mid-wicket. I hadn't expected to get another chance to bowl in the match after that treatment, especially as India were cruising towards victory. However, with 10 overs left and India needing only a run a ball to win with seven wickets in hand, Nas brought me back on from the opposite end. In that first spell, Ganguly had run down the wicket at me outside leg stump and freed his arms to hit in an arc from mid-off to mid-wicket, depending on the length of the ball. When I came back into the attack, he was still in on 74, and the Indians were walking it.

Given how he had played me in my first spell, I decided to come round the wicket and try tucking Ganguly up, giving him less opportunity to free his arms. I think a message had come onto the pitch from Fletch in the dressing room that prompted this plan. I should have thought of that option myself but in those moments, particularly when you haven't played much of a part in the series, your mind can just be in a spin. It was also just my 11th ODI since making my debut in 1997. I had been involved in somewhere between 50 to 60 ODIs but had spent most of my time carrying drinks. The majority of that is my fault. If I had performed better when I'd had the opportunity, I would have been more likely to keep getting picked. But each time I got a chance, it felt like making my debut again. When I had first played one-day cricket for Warwickshire, it took me a long time to settle and work out my role. With England, you don't have that luxury. You don't have that time. It's just the reality of international sport.

The first ball of my second spell, Ganguly ran down the pitch and tried to launch me back over my head and over the boundary. This time, because of the line of the ball, he scuffed it as he tried to hit it. At long-off, Owais Shah ran in and took the catch. The plan had worked. We were still a long way from winning the match, but I was so relieved to see the back of him, and we'd opened up an end. Three balls later, I had the other 'in' batter Mohammad Kaif caught at extra cover by Thorpey for 46, and suddenly, we were back in the match. We were able to continue to pressure the new batter, and India began to implode. By the end of the 49th over, I'd taken five for 57 in my 10 overs, including 5 for 9 in 19 balls and turning the match on its head.

We went on to win by just two runs. I fielded the last ball at deep point, stopping the boundary, and I remember Tres running out to me and I jumped into his arms. From behind, we were pelted with plastic water bottles filled with urine rather than water. The old Delhi ground was quite small and open, and the crowd felt close. During the match, on the other side of the ground, both Vaughany and Fred had been shot with a pellet gun from the crowd. Vaughany had been out there first and waved to Fred to swap positions because he 'had a better arm'. Or that was his story. He didn't mention the pellets. Fred, having been shot a couple of times, did what Vaughany should have done and told the umpires what was happening. They reported it to the match ref, who in turn reported it to the police. They went into the crowd with their batons and, unsurprisingly, the shooting stopped. Whilst serious, it was also quite funny, particularly how our future England captain had manoeuvred himself out of the firing line.

It was a tremendous relief to win that game and play such an important role. I received the Player of the Match award, a significant turnaround having thought I might never play ODI cricket again after my first four overs. The victory also brought us back into the series, which now stood at 3-2 with one match remaining in Mumbai.

Upon arriving in Mumbai, we managed to take a day trip to the Taj Mahal, which was a wonderful experience. It had such a calming and peaceful aura and felt a world away from the noise of the stadiums we had been playing in across India. At the Wankhede we batted first and, after looking like we might post a good total, Harbhajan Singh ran through us, finishing with 5-43 as we were bowled out for 255.

The atmosphere in Mumbai was incredible, especially when Sachin walked into bat. While Eden Gardens was a vast and sprawling ground, Wankhede resembled more of a gladiatorial bowl. It had been hard to hear anything in Kolkata, but in Mumbai, during the early stages of the Indian innings, it was nearly impossible to hear any verbal instructions from Nas. The noise in the ground was astounding, and it felt like the crowd was right over you. In the end, Tendulkar went fairly cheaply, but Ganguly began to fill his boots again, and when he was out for 80, the Indians were cruising at 191-4 with 13 overs left and, like they had in Delhi, looked hot favourites to win. Somehow, we dragged ourselves back into the match, and Fred bowled remarkably well at the death. We fielded like demons for those last 10 overs and ended up bowling India out for 250. Fred celebrated in his unique style, taking off his shirt and twirling it above his head as he ran around the ground, closely followed by the rest of us. It was an amazing win in one of the best atmospheres I've ever experienced. From nowhere, we had managed to level the series, no small feat in India.

From the ground, we went straight to the airport to catch a flight to New Zealand. We had been treated very well in India, except for the experience on the field in Delhi. However, there was real excitement in the group as we took off from Mumbai. Part of it was undoubtedly the adrenaline of winning the match and levelling the series, but it was also the anticipation of New Zealand after a long and hard-fought Test and ODI tour of India. I think we drank until exhaustion overcame us on that flight, and then we fell asleep.

We arrived in Auckland early in the morning and had our bags at the hotel by midday. Most of us changed and headed out. While we were well treated in India, being in New Zealand offered a different kind of freedom that we hadn't experienced over the previous few weeks. This was my first visit to New Zealand and no one really knew who we were, allowing us to go out and live normally – something we certainly couldn't do in India. Later, things changed in New Zealand as the popularity and commercialism of cricket grew. The 2005 Ashes was probably another turning point and during my subsequent visits, people were certainly more aware of who we were. On that first night I don't think I got back until around 2am. It was quite a stint, and many returned much later than I did.

We were heading to Hamilton the next morning for two warm-up matches, and at breakfast a few casualties emerged. To be fair, Fletch was relaxed about it but we lost our first warm-up match after a Simon Doull cameo at the top of the order, scoring 80 off just 47 balls. Sometimes, danger comes from the strangest of places! I remember Nas being miserable as sin after that match; he hated losing. Those of us who hadn't played kept a low profile afterwards and stayed well clear of him. In the second match we won with ease, and I took 2-22 in my 10 overs, ensuring I kept my place in the team.

I ended up playing all five ODIs in New Zealand, the first time in a series of that length that I had participated in every match. We lost the first two but leading up to the third I had much more on my mind than simply getting back into the series. Stine had been due for a few days when we arrived in Napier. On the evening of February 18, I received a call from her saying that she thought things were progressing and that she was going into the hospital soon. I managed to sleep well that night but was woken around 5.30 am with the news that I had a baby girl, Matilde Louise, and that both mother and daughter were healthy. Stine was amazing. Apparently, she was in the hospital for only a few hours, as she wanted to be home to put Anders to bed. She'd given birth to Tilly, tucked her under her arm, and gone home. Mum and Dad had watched Anders, and a friend of Stine's had been with her at the hospital. All she asked for when she got home was for Dad to pick up a pizza since she was starving. Incredible, really.

Fletch had asked me whether I wanted to go home for a week for the birth, but we preferred things to progress naturally and so there was no guarantee the timings would fall into place. It was also a long journey to go and come back in a week while preparing for a Test match. So I stayed in New Zealand. Things were just starting to change around that time when it came to parental responsibilities. Where it had once been unthinkable to miss an England match for the birth of your child, it was at least being discussed. A few years later, it rightly became completely normal to go home for births. In hindsight, I wish I had been at home for Tilly's birth. They are special moments, and I should have been there to support Stine. Tilly still reminds me to this day that I couldn't be bothered to show up for her birth! The other detail, which is easily forgotten now, is that there wasn't video calling or picture messaging at this time. I only knew what Tilly looked like because one of the players' wives visited and brought some photos with her that Stine had sent. That seems like the dark ages now.

That morning, going for breakfast halfway around the world from my family felt strange. Pat Murphy, known for his work with the BBC and a friend of mine, was at breakfast when I arrived, and he was the first person I told. Two days later, we celebrated a win in Napier, followed by another victory in Auckland, levelling the series.

In the deciding match in Dunedin, we were comfortably beaten and lost the series 3-2. I only took two wickets throughout the series, but I was our most economical bowler, and despite the loss, playing every match was a win for me personally.

From there, we headed to Queenstown for the Test preparation period. What an incredible place Queenstown is! In fact, I loved every bit of New Zealand, apart from being away from my family at such an important time. The people, the food, the wine, the climate, and the scenery were all fantastic. On the day we arrived in Queenstown, a few of us went up Bob's Peak on the Skyline Gondola. We sat at the top and shared several bottles of New Zealand Sauvignon Blanc. Fueled by the wine, we then raced each other on the luge at the top. I ended up coming off on one of the corners and scraped my leg. It was nothing serious, but it ruined my trousers. We watched Craig White take on the bungee, and he lost his phone on the mountain. We finished the night with dinner and a few more drinks in Queenstown. That was the last time I saw Ben Hollioake. He wasn't on the Test leg of the tour and was enjoying a few days in Queenstown before heading back to Perth. A couple of weeks later, we received the awful news that he had been killed in a car accident. Such a loss to the game and to us all.

The first Test was truly a game of two halves. The pitch at Christchurch was a 'drop-in', basically a pitch on a tray favoured at multi-sport venues like Christchurch and the Melbourne Cricket Ground. On day one, the pitch was emerald green and difficult to distinguish from the outfield. We lost the toss and, unsurprisingly, got put in. We scraped to 228 all out, largely thanks to Nasser, who played one of the innings of his life in the toughest of conditions. I don't think it was particularly pretty, but it was exactly what we needed and the dogged, determined Nas at his best. In response, New Zealand managed just 147 with Hoggy cleaning up, taking 7-63 with a ball that hooped everywhere. At this point it looked like a quick game was going to be a good game, and the start of our second innings did nothing to change this thought. At one point we were 106-5 with a lead of just under 200, but that looked plenty.

Then the game changed, or rather, the pitch did. Its complexion had completely transformed over two days; it was now straw-coloured and absolutely flat. That morning Fred had one of the worst nets I'd ever seen and finished his session by smashing down his stumps. But it looked like a completely different game in the middle as he and Thorpey took control, adding a remarkable 281 runs in just over 50 overs. Thorpey scored 200 from 231 balls, while Fred hit his first Test century, finishing 137 off 163. We declared, leaving New Zealand needing around 550 and feeling comfortable with our position. What followed was one of the most remarkable innings I have ever seen. Nathan Astle scored 222 in 168 balls, making Thorpey's double-hundred look pedestrian. He hit a couple of balls literally out of the ground, possibly out of Christchurch. At one point, balls were going so far that those of us who weren't bowling had a little smile to ourselves – out of view of Nas, of course. Chris Cairns, who picked up an injury during the match, came in at 11 and he and Astle put on a hundred in 55 balls for the 10th wicket. Despite the onslaught, I don't think we ever really thought they would win, and eventually Astle was out, caught behind off Hoggy with New Zealand 98 runs short. Caddy got plenty of stick from Astle but finished with 6-122, and we were up in the series.

The second Test in Wellington was overshadowed by the news from Australia that Ben Hollioake had died in a car accident. It was difficult for any of us to concentrate on cricket, but we continued with the match. We had the upper hand during the game, but it ultimately ended in a draw. I took four wickets in the first innings and bowled OK. We moved on to Auckland for the third and final Test, one up, and having played the best cricket in the series so far. However, we let ourselves down in the final Test, which was a low-scoring affair. We lost by 78 runs and I only bowled two overs in the match. It was a disappointing way to finish the winter, leaving us without a series win in either India or New Zealand despite having played some decent cricket along the way.

I couldn't wait to get home, and at the airport Stine was waiting for me with Anders and Tilly. Tilly was six weeks old by then, and this was the first time I held her. Stine told me that Tilly hadn't yet slept through the night and she was exhausted from looking after the two of them. That night Tilly slept right through, and she never looked back. I looked forward to a couple of weeks getting to know my family again before returning to work.

16

In Harmy's way

Long tours can be challenging for relationships. Strangely, coming home can be just as tough. It sounds weird, but being on tour for months on end is, in many ways, quite a selfish experience. Everything is taken care of for you: your food is prepared, your bed is made, your clothes are washed and ironed, and even your schedule is organised for you. All you have to focus on is your game and your physical and mental state. This is quite different from what is expected of you when you return home: to pitch in, take out the rubbish, cook, and look after the kids. These are all very reasonable expectations, of course. I certainly know it was difficult for both of us. We each had our routines and had got used to life apart from each other, and although we clearly missed each other, you have no option but to adapt. It could drive you mad otherwise. It probably took us a couple of weeks to get used to each other again whenever I returned home from tour, sometimes culminating in a clear-the-air argument.

At the end of the 2001/02 winter, we probably had enough to think about without worrying about how we were as a couple. We now had two children, a six-week-old and a 22-month-old, so both were a real handful. I was given a month off before I had to report back to Warwickshire, and it was an important time to spend with Stine and the kids, as well as relieving some of the pressure on her after she'd basically been a single parent for the last couple of months.

My season began with a handful of one-day matches and a couple of Championship fixtures for Warwickshire, leading up to our first international matches of the summer against Sri Lanka. Given how little I bowled in the longer format before that series, I was pleased with my performances against Sri Lanka, taking six wickets at an average of 31 in a 2-0 victory. I claimed wickets and scored a few runs in the win at Old Trafford, including a century partnership with Stewie in our first innings.

A few days after the Old Trafford Test, Nas and I found ourselves back at Lord's but on opposing sides, contesting the first final of the year, the Benson & Hedges Cup. We won the match easily and celebrated another Bears trophy. The next day, the ODI squad met down in Cardiff and Nas, Tres, Vaughany and I agreed to meet up and play golf. Vaughany and I always played together, and Tres partnered Nas. Vaughany and I loved playing mind games against those two and there would be a fair few verbals as we went round. As Tres stood over a drive we'd often remark about his grip, or how his technique had changed, or why he wasn't hitting it as far. Anything to put him off. Nas was a bit more straightforward with his 'feedback', which was often very blunt and full of expletives. We'd take most joy when we managed to get Nas having a go at his partner as well as us.

This round, I had a particularly special surprise for Nas on the first green. As we all approached the putting surface, I found myself closer to the hole than Nas and had to mark my ball. Normally, you would use a coin or a specially made marker similar in size to a two-pound coin. On this occasion I pulled my winner's medal from the day before out of my pocket, minus the ribbon, and placed it on the green where my ball had been resting. Nas didn't notice it at first, but once he saw the large marker on the green, he began swearing and walking toward it to see what it was. Once he realised what it was, a huge smile spread across his face, and we all started laughing. We had a fun round and Vaughany and I took the money.

Of the six matches we played in the one-day triangular series against India and Sri Lanka, I featured in three, but we did enough to reach the final at Lord's and I was picked in the XI. The match, against India, was an absolute classic. We posted 325 on a great pitch, with Tres and Nas both scoring centuries. Nas had faced some criticism in the media for batting three in our one-day team, some questioning whether he was worth his place, and after completing his century he pointed at the number on his back, which was also three, and gestured up to the press box – his passion for playing for England shining through once again. In response, India were 146-5 almost halfway through their innings. I'd taken the wickets of both Sehwag and Tendulkar in my 10-over spell, and we were firmly in the pound seats.

That day felt like playing in India. The crowd was predominantly India's light blue rather than England's darker blue. As India began to rebuild with Mohammad Kaif and Yuvraj Singh, the crowd grew louder and louder, and what had seemed an almost impossible chase started to appear increasingly achievable. We had a couple of opportunities to take the match away from India, but we missed them. Kaif finished 87 not out, leading India to victory with three balls to spare. The crowd went wild, and on the balcony Sourav Ganguly took off his shirt and twirled it above his head, mimicking Fred's celebration in Mumbai when we levelled the series just a few months earlier.

In the Test series that followed I played three of the four matches. We won the first comfortably by 170 runs, with Simon Jones making his debut. The young Jonah was raw and very fast. His control wasn't always great at that stage but he had genuine pace. In fact, everything he did was done at pace. Just three years later he would reinvent himself as one of the best reverse-swing bowlers in the world.

We drew at Trent Bridge, a match I didn't play, and then got hammered at Headingley by an innings and plenty. I picked up just one wicket for well over a hundred. I wasn't the only bowler to struggle as the Indian batting line-up put over 600 on the board. I had Dravid stumped, the only time he was ever stumped in Test cricket. Unlike my dismissal of Sachin at Bangalore the previous winter, this time it was from around the wicket. And unfortunately, Dravid had already scored 148!

The final Test at The Oval was a very high-scoring draw and the series finished 1-1. I picked up just five wickets at 70 in the series but I felt I'd bowled OK, apart from getting smashed at Headingley at the back-end of their innings.

Michael Vaughan came of age in the series, scoring over 600 runs and averaging more than 100. He had already established himself as a fixture in the team, but 2002 was the year he announced himself as a world-class player.

I think it was around this time that I started to feel the weight of pressure and criticism that was beginning to be pointed in my direction. Since the Sachin incident in Bangalore – where I'd bowled wide outside leg stump, frustrating him, until he ran down the pitch and got stumped – I felt more and more negative stuff coming my way. I was starting to both listen to it and read it, and this was the first time it had started to get to me.

Much has been said about me bowling over the wicket and the 'negative' role I played in the team. The reality is that it was extremely rare for me to bowl way out into the rough, as I did in Bangalore. Most of the time, I aimed to bowl close to the stumps, enabling all modes of dismissal by trying to bowl wicket to wicket or clipping the edge of the bowler's follow-through. It is strange how an off-spinner bowling over the wicket to a left-handed batter is hardly ever criticised, yet me coming over the wicket to a right-hander was discussed relentlessly. It's simply no different. I once did an exercise of going through my Test wickets, ignoring dismissals of left-handers, to see how many wickets I took bowling round and over the wicket bowling to right-handed batters. It was almost identical. I felt the events of Bangalore lingered for much longer than anyone would have expected, perhaps even to this day.

Reflecting now, later in my career, from a physical perspective it was much easier for me to bowl over the wicket than round. The more I've thought about it, the more I remember finding it difficult to get back around and over my front leg from the wide angle I bowled around the wicket as time progressed. I think there was every chance this marked the beginning of my struggles with my right hip, which eventually ended my career. Later, when my symptoms worsened significantly, I found it almost impossible to spend enough time on my right leg to generate the energy I needed to get through the crease and create the right amount of pace and spin on the ball. Bowling over the wicket allowed me to bowl over my front leg more, rather than around it, resulting in far less torsion and pressure on my hip.

Between the end of the season and the 2002/03 Ashes tour we travelled to Colombo for another Champions Trophy. We got beaten comfortably by India and, before we knew it, we were back on a plane and heading home. A month later, by mid-October, we were in Perth preparing for the Ashes. After some time on the west coast, we moved across to Queensland for a final warm-up match ahead of the first Test at the Gabba. I remember feeling pretty good in the lead-up. Although the warm-up match wasn't ideal for us, as it was played on a flat pitch and Queensland had no interest once they won the toss of doing anything but batting for as long as possible, it meant I got to bowl 40 overs and find some rhythm, picking up three wickets. It wasn't the best build-up for our batters, who spent almost 160 overs in the field before getting a chance themselves, but Vaughany banged out another hundred. I've always needed a certain workload to feel like I'm ready and confident. Perhaps that is why I had a lot of success in the sub-continent, as I was always going to bowl a lot of overs in those conditions.

The weather on the first day at the Gabba was gorgeous. We won the toss and Nas elected to field first, which surprised many of us. It's easy to say in hindsight, and I'm sure looking back Nas regrets it, but it felt like a defensive call to me. Very quickly, the first day went from bad to worse. Much, much worse.

It became clear that the pitch wasn't doing much at all. Simon Jones came on and got Langer out but soon after disaster struck when Jonah went to slide for a ball he chased to the boundary, his knee got stuck in the ground and you could tell immediately that he was in big trouble. He was stretchered off the ground and his series was over. Ponting and Hayden then piled on the pain, putting on 272 in just over 60 overs. We didn't help ourselves with some very average fielding. By the close of play, Australia were 364-2. It had been an awful day, the worst possible start. For a team that had played some really good cricket over the previous couple of years, we had let ourselves down.

Day two we dusted ourselves down and came again, putting in a much better performance in the field and with the ball. I bowled really well in the first innings, given the circumstances, and finished with 4-101. Australia finished on 492, and at the end of day two we had moved to 158-1, a really good fightback from us. Unfortunately, the rest of the match was all Australia. We ended up being bowled out for a disappointing 325, and in their second innings Australia declared on 296-5, leaving us around 460 to win. We didn't even get a quarter of that, bowled out for 79. We were behind in the series, a fast bowler down and pretty bruised as we moved on to Tasmania for a tour match between Tests. Personally, I'd bowled as well as I had for some time in Test cricket and took six wickets in the match.

I didn't play in Tasmania and we moved on to Adelaide to prepare for the second Test. On the first day of prep we went out to the middle for warm-ups and fielding practice before we were due to head to the nets. Leant against the coaches' bag was the whiteboard with the order for the batters and bowlers for the net session. As I approached, Nas and Stewie were already looking at it. As I scanned the list, I got to my name and realised that I was lined up against Steve Harmison. The ongoing joke, or not, on that trip was who got Harmy in the nets. He bowled the speed of light on that tour and didn't hold back in the nets. I said jokingly to the two senior players, "Well, that's me going home tomorrow".

I went into the spin net first, with Rob Key in the quick net, facing Harmy in the lane next to me. Just from the noises Keysey was making I could tell it was lively in there. After 10 minutes we swapped nets. At Adelaide the crowds used to be able to come and watch practice and they could sit right up behind the net. As I got into the net they were already egging Harmy on. He ran in and bowled one back of a length that was as quick as anything I'd faced on the tour. Nets always felt about five miles an hour quicker because of being closed in, but this was really quick. Harmy got bounce from a full length and while I'd prepared to play back and defend the ball, it beat me for pace and smashed into my wrist, between my arm guard and glove. If I wasn't fully awake before that, I certainly was now. I knew immediately that I could be in trouble because it had been a straight impact with no sign of deflection. I batted on for the next 10 minutes with Nas and Stewie stood at the back smiling at me. Behind me, the Barmy Army kept encouraging Harmy to bowl quicker and I reminded them that we were all on the same side. I was quite happy to be told I only had a couple of balls left. Once I was done, I walked out and stood with Nas for a while and had a chuckle about my experience. After a couple of minutes I tried to move my hand and an awful pain shot up my arm. I was in serious trouble. The adrenaline that had got me through the net had worn off, and I actually started to shiver. I called for the physio and we moved to the dressing room to escape the media's prying eyes. We got some ice on my wrist and our team doctor began organising an x-ray. I had no idea how bad it was but I was concerned that, given it was my bowling hand, I would struggle to be ready for the Test in two days' time.

Within an hour I was heading to the local private hospital and it didn't take long to confirm my worst fears: I'd broken my left wrist. My Ashes series, one I'd started pretty well, was over. I got back to the hotel and Harmy was waiting for me in the lobby. He was absolutely gutted. It wasn't his fault, injuries come with the territory, but the timing could have been better.

Two days later, while I packed my bags, I listened to the noise from the Adelaide Oval in my hotel room, a stone's throw from the ground, as the Test got underway. Later that day I made my way to the airport. As I'd predicted, I was heading home.

17

Out of Africa

I spent the best part of seven weeks stuck at home waiting for my wrist to heal. While it was nice to have extended time with the family, it was frustrating to be sat at home watching the series unfold, especially after I'd started so strongly with the ball. Ultimately, we lost the series 4-1, winning only the final Test in Sydney. It was a battering. One bright spot was Vaughany's performance, scoring 633 runs in the series and completing a remarkable year for him personally in Test cricket.

By mid-January I was heading back to Adelaide to join up with our academy boys who were on a training camp out there. I was also joined by Fred, who had also been at home with an injury. I didn't enjoy my experience there at all. Rod Marsh was the academy director at the time and when I arrived I couldn't have been made to feel more unwelcome. Given I was a centrally contracted player who, just a few weeks earlier, was playing in the Ashes, and was now preparing for a World Cup, I was made to feel like the spare part of the group. It was obvious there was some uneasy tension between Fletch and Rod; in fact, they couldn't stand each other.

Where it should have been one of the most important relationships in English cricket, there was little or no communication. As a result, I think Rod saw his opportunity to use me as a pawn in this game. Monty Panesar, who was just coming through as a promising left-arm spinner, was one of Rod's favourites and I was in Fletch's team. It was no secret that Fletch had backed me and the all-round role I played in the team. I think Rod saw Fletch's group as largely protected and untouchable. If Fletch wanted it, he got it. Which is really how it should be if your neck is on the line as the head coach.

Given that the ODI squad was in the middle of a triangular series and the academy was in Australia, it was decided that Fred and I should go to Adelaide before linking up with the one-day squad ahead of the World Cup. There wasn't much cricket for us to play in Adelaide, but it was felt that continuing our rehab with the academy would be better than being a potential distraction around the team. After all, that is part of the academy's role; to support players returning from injury and prepare them to return to the main team.

Rod didn't receive that memo. There was only longer format cricket available for us in Adelaide, but I showed up for a match against Australia Under 19s hoping at least to get some overs under my belt and some time in the middle. It was agreed by both sides that the match would be 12-a-side. Almost as soon as I arrived, Rod pulled me aside and told me that I would be number 12 in the batting line-up and would not bat in either innings. I believe his words were: "'It's important Monty gets a chance to have a bat", or something along those lines. I was shocked. There was no relevance to Monty getting time in the middle, let alone the two or three batters ahead of him that I should have batted before in order to get some time at the crease. It was ridiculous and an obvious display of strength from Rod. We batted first, and outwardly, I carried on with my role as the '12th man', delivering drinks and running on with gloves for almost the entire innings. Inwardly, I was seething.

I did bowl in the first innings, getting 27 steady overs under my belt, which was great, but once word got back that I had been put at 12 in the batting order, Fletch pulled me from the match and asked me to join up with the one-day team, which I was pleased about. A few days later, I was in Sydney for the first final against Australia. We got hammered by 10 wickets and moved on to Melbourne for the second match of the best-of-three finals. That was a closer match, but one we also ended up losing.

During that match, I had an important conversation with Fletch about my cricket and my batting in particular. To that point, given that I had scored a lot of first-class runs for Warwickshire, I had underperformed with the bat in Test cricket. At the time, I had played 19 Tests and averaged only a little over 14, which was poor for someone with my ability. I chatted with Fletch about my technique but also my approach to batting: where I was going to score, what shots may be effective in first-class cricket but not Test cricket, what my weaknesses were, and where people would look to bowl at me, all that sort of stuff. It was great to spend time talking to him about cricket, but I was also aware of an element to the conversation that I needed to score more runs at No.8 if I wanted to stay in the team, which was a message I probably needed to hear. Looking back now, it was an important moment for me, and it worked. For the next 35 Tests of my career, I averaged over 24, which, at the time, was more in line with where I was batting and a far better contribution for the team.

With the one-day series in Australia wrapped up, we headed to South Africa for the World Cup, opting for a few days at Sun City for golf before heading to Cape Town. While we managed to play a couple of rounds, a significant issue loomed over us that began to be more of a talking point as we got nearer to the tournament. In fact, it felt like a juggernaut hurtling down the road at us, one whose true scale we probably weren't aware of until it was far too late.

As part of the group phase of the World Cup, we were scheduled to play against Zimbabwe in Harare. Ongoing unrest in Zimbabwe had frequently made the news back home, and while I was in England during the Ashes, waiting for my broken arm to heal, I watched a documentary about the situation on Channel 4. It depicted various atrocities committed by Robert Mugabe's ruling government against anyone who opposed them, including accusations of torture and murder, as well as bodies being left in bunkers on golf courses. It was horrific. At home, Tony Blair's government expressed concern about an England team playing in the country under these circumstances and made it clear that they would prefer us not to travel there. However, they did not explicitly tell us we couldn't go. Nas asked me what the sentiment was like at home regarding Zimbabwe, and all I could say was that it was becoming a significant issue.

When we arrived in Cape Town at the Cullinan Hotel, everything ramped up again. We'd not even bowled a ball in anger and we were embroiled in a debate over whether it was right that we should travel to Harare. We spent hours on end in a conference room in our hotel discussing whether it was right for us to travel given the treatment of the Zimbabwean people by the government. We knew that if we went to Harare it would more than likely lead to protests, which in turn was likely to lead to violence of some sort or another against those protestors. Which, given the evidence I'd seen in the documentary, might be brutal.

At first, the debate centred around whether it was right or not, and the security of people who might protest about our visit. Soon, however, once a letter from a group who called themselves 'The sons and daughters of Zimbabwe' came to light, the debate switched to our own safety and security, and even that of our families at home. Richard Bevan, the head of the players' association, was the person, I believe, who brought this out into the open. Bev has been almost omnipresent during my nearly 30 years, on and off, of being involved with England cricket. He has always been a trusted adviser, cool head and confidant during that time, which he certainly was during this saga.

Apparently, the ECB had been aware for some time of a letter from this group but had not shared it with us until now. They basically threatened that if we went to play in Zimbabwe, we would return to the UK in wooden boxes and that even if they couldn't get to us, they knew where our families were. During our time in that room at the Cullinan, a number of people came to speak with us, from the head of the ECB and the head of the ICC to various local and international security advisers, including the police. There were mixed opinions about the letter, with some saying they had never heard of the group and weren't aware of the letter, while one of the senior security advisers indicated it was a credible threat. Once the main issue shifted to our safety and security, we were convinced that the ICC must now see the light and move the match to South Africa. It didn't happen.

To be honest, the longer we spent in that room, the less likely it seemed that any of us would be happy travelling to Zimbabwe. Firstly, this was due to what we were hearing and witnessing. The letter that had come to light, the absence of any reassurance from the ICC, on top of the attitude of some of the security experts, which was basically that if there was any trouble, they would deal with it! This was one of our main fears: someone getting seriously hurt in Zimbabwe for simply protesting about our presence in the country. Secondly, the longer we remained in that room, the more tired and emotional we became. Several players broke down in those meetings, and most of us shifted in our stances over those few days. Each evening, once the meetings wrapped up, we would go out drinking and continued our discussions within the group well into the night, contributing to our fatigue.

As it became clearer to all parties that most of us weren't keen on going to Zimbabwe, the pressure started to mount. We were threatened that the game in the UK could be decimated by the financial impact of us not fulfilling our commitments. We felt isolated as a group and Nas, particularly, was visibly worn down by the situation. During this period, we took part in the World Cup opening ceremony at Newlands, which was a fantastic event and a welcome distraction, but the meetings went on and on. Later, we had a visit from two Zimbabwean players, Andy Flower and Henry Olonga, who suggested that we play the match, but wear black armbands in a protest against the government, and the 'death of democracy' in Zimbabwe. While we hugely respected their actions and bravery, I think many of us felt that it wasn't for us to get involved in their dispute with their government. That wasn't our fight. It was incredibly brave of them, though.

In the end, when it came time to decide, there were more last-minute arguments from both sides – go or no go – from within our group. The weight of the decision was starting to hit home for many individuals, who were rightly concerned that they wouldn't get another crack at a World Cup. Ultimately, we decided not to travel to Zimbabwe. Officially, we forfeited the match due to safety concerns. I was one of a couple of players asked to give my account of the situation to the ECB legal team, so that the events of the previous few days were recorded correctly. Our focus moved back to cricket, all knowing that the decision could easily come back and haunt us.

When it came to the World Cup proper, I played in two of the warm-up matches but didn't play in the matches against the Netherlands or Namibia, our first two group games. Ian Blackwell was preferred to me. However, I was recalled to the team for the match against Pakistan at Newlands. We won the toss and batted. Those first few overs will be remembered for Shoaib Akhtar bowling the first recorded 100mph delivery to Nick Knight. That is the sort of thing that gets the attention of the batting order! Knighty later recalled that the 100mph ball didn't feel that different to any of the others. At that pace, whether it's 96mph or 100mph, it really doesn't make that much difference; it's just bloody quick and going to hurt if you wear one.

With the bat, we struggled to really get the innings going at any stage. Vaughany got 52 batting at three, but it was tough going. I went in at 194-7 with just under 10 overs left and us feeling like we were still quite a way off from where we needed to be. Colly and I edged our way past 200 and Shoaib came back into the attack. He was the fastest of the Pakistan bowlers by quite a distance at that point. Wasim Akram and Waqar Younis were also in that express bracket in the earlier part of their careers, but now Shoaib was top dog when it came to pure speed. Early on in his spell at the back end of the innings he bowled me a slower ball. Why? I have no idea. His change-up was pretty easy to pick as you could see the change in his grip on the ball as he began his take-off. The ball was full and in the slot. With mid-off up, I just hit through it and remember thinking, as I did so, that I'd hit it quite well. In fact, I hit it very well and it went all the way for six over long off and into the crowd. Who would have thought that on the day Shoaib bowled 100mph, I would be the one to hit him for six back over his head?. While the six runs were an important addition to our score, I do recall thinking, I wonder how quick this next one is going to be! Well, it was about 20 mph quicker and went past me at about chest height before I'd really got my bat down. He gave me a look that told me I wouldn't be getting another slower ball any time soon.

I was out for 17, but thanks to a late charge from Colly with 66 not out, we scraped together 246. Not a great score, but something we thought we could defend. In the end, it was plenty, largely thanks to Jimmy Anderson, who ripped the heart out of Pakistan's top order. Jimmy had debuted in Australia during the triangular series, and in those early days, as well as swinging the ball around corners, he was also really quick. All our bowlers bowled well, but Jimmy was the standout and finished with figures of 4-29 from his 10 overs. I wasn't required to bowl at all. It was a fantastic win and kept us well in the hunt for the later stages.

I missed out on the match in Durban that we lost to India by 82 runs, meaning that almost everything now rested on our match against Australia in Port Elizabeth. If we won it, we'd go through, despite not going to Zimbabwe, but if we lost we'd be reliant on other results in the group to go our way. I was picked to play in Port Elizabeth where we batted first, having won the toss. We got a fantastic start putting on 66 for the first wicket, but then lost a clump of wickets and were 87-5. Fred got a battling 45 to get us towards a respectable score and we eventually finished on 204-8. Andy Bichel bowled out of his skin and finished with 7-20.

In the field, we bowled and caught like demons. Gilchrist got them off to a decent start, but once he was out with the score at 33-2, we started to squeeze Australia, and they fell to 135-8. Caddick bowled beautifully up front, taking the first four wickets. I took two catches early on to dismiss Hayden and Ponting at mid-on and long leg, respectively, which were two of the best high catches I had ever taken, given both the situation and the swirling wind in Port Elizabeth.

At that point, it looked like we were going to make it through to the later rounds, and our decision not to go to Zimbabwe would be vindicated. Enter Bichel, Australia's hero with the ball earlier in the day and now the perfect foil for Michael Bevan at the other end. In fact, it was probably the other way around as Bichel came in and scored at close to a run a ball with relative ease compared to how everyone else had struggled on the pitch. Bevan played the anchor role.

We went from what seemed like an almost unassailable position to losing the match by two wickets with two balls left. Bichel had one of the best days of his life, and Bevan finished with 74 not out. We were distraught given the position we had been in, and our World Cup was all but over. This was confirmed when the match between Pakistan and Zimbabwe was rained off a couple of days later, and as a result, Zimbabwe went through. Our decision not to go to Zimbabwe had quite likely cost us a place in the later stages, and once our exit was confirmed, Nas announced that he would be stepping down as captain of the one-day team. It was the end of an era.

An early photo of us four kids with our mum on the Green at Ripley. Me on Mum's lap, Tracy, Carrie and Andrew.

Primary school photo with my sister Tracy, around 1980.

With Ian Ward, with whom I opened the bowling for so
many years in Surrey youth teams. A great man.

Single-wicket competition at Ripley CC in the early Eighties. Many of my fondest memories are of being at the club in Ripley as a young boy.

Ripley second XI photo in the early Eighties (me front left), surrounded by family members including Dad (back left), my brother (front right), my cousin, my godfather and my brother-in-law… a real family affair!

Mum with Tracy and me in Austria in the early Eighties,
the first time I'd been abroad for a holiday.

Early days at Edgbaston with (l to r) my cousin Hayley, my sister Tracy
and my wonderful nan. Suited and booted was very much the order of
the day for match days back then… not sure about the trousers!

Stine and I, both in skirts, at my old mate Dougie Brown's wedding.

My wedding day with my family, Carrie, Dad, Mum, me, Tracy and Andrew.

Just married. St Andrew's Church, Droitwich, Oct 9, 1999.

At one of our Giles Trust events. I couldn't be prouder of all of them.

On the bus the day after we won the Ashes, taken from my phone.
We were stunned by the crowds that greeted us that day.

My rocks through so many ups and downs in my
career: Tilly, Mum, Dad, Stine and Anders.

Thanks Mum and Dad, for everything.

18

The black dog

By the end of the Test series against South Africa in 2003, I felt like my self-belief and confidence was beginning to unravel. The final Test at The Oval should have been reason to celebrate, recording a famous win to level the series, but I'd taken seven wickets at an average of 71 across the four matches I played and media criticism of my performances was ramping up. I was reading and listening to too much of it. It started to get to me early in the series and by the end of the summer my confidence was in freefall.

At Trent Bridge, where I had hardly bowled, I was also getting it from some sections of the fans. It would've have been a minority of supporters but my mind was scrambled and that was all I was hearing. It was all stuff that had been thrown at me before but for some reason it had chipped away at my resilience and I wasn't coping.

At The Oval I didn't contribute much, and when we were doing a lap of honour I remember feeling embarrassed. I didn't feel I'd done anything to deserve the ovation we were all receiving. I couldn't wait for it to be over and to get back to the dressing room. Of course I loved us winning at the end of what had been a really tough series against a strong South African team. But I just wanted the ground to swallow me up.

I proved a number of times in my career that I am mentally tough, probably as resilient as almost anyone who has pulled an England shirt on. But at the time I didn't feel that at all. Things had started to get the better of me and I wasn't able to control it. At The Oval those feelings came to the surface.

Given this was the last international match of the summer we had a huge celebration after the match and all sat in the plunge bath at The Oval and drank beer and sang songs. I joined in but while on the outside I was smiling, on the inside I was hurting. We sang the songs that the Barmy Army had made up for each of us. When mine came round I cringed, imagining my teammates feeling sorry for me. On reflection I think I was suffering from depression, and it was going to get a lot worse before it got any better.

We only had a short break at the end of the summer before heading to Bangladesh for the first tour of the winter. The break did nothing to change how I was feeling and my low confidence lingered, bordering on self-loathing. It was set to be a long winter, moving on to Sri Lanka after Bangladesh and, after returning home for Christmas and a six-week break, we were to travel to the West Indies for a full Test and one-day tour.

As a member of both the Test and ODI squads, I knew the 12-week tour of Bangladesh and Sri Lanka was going to be tough. Three months on the road is never easy, but the subcontinent can be particularly hard. I wasn't particularly looking forward to Bangladesh. I had been there once before for the first ICC Champions Trophy back in 1998. That had been just a three-week trip and we were looked after incredibly well. The Bangladeshi people are fantastic and always go out of their way to make you feel welcome, but it is a tough place to tour. When your head's not right, it can be an absolute nightmare, as I was to find out.

We arrived in Dhaka in the first week of October and were aware that we could slip up on this tour if we didn't take our opposition very seriously. Bangladesh were considered the whipping boys of international cricket and there was no other option for us but to win, and win convincingly. But on subcontinent pitches, if we weren't fully prepared, it could cost us a Test match and perhaps even the series. We would also be using Bangladesh as preparation for what would be a much tougher assignment in Sri Lanka.

As a team we identified that we needed to be as fit as possible given the cricket we had coming up that winter and with little else to do in

Dhaka we put a huge focus on our fitness and conditioning. I threw myself into it and also took the opportunity to work on improving my bowling action, doing a lot of work with Mike Watkinson, our bowling coach for the tour. In hindsight it was a stupid thing to take on at that time. There were a lot of people looking for reasons why I wasn't bowling well and while there were areas in the action that I needed to work on, the biggest problem was in my head – with my confidence and mindset.

Before long I was making big gains with my fitness through the extra sessions. We'd come back after long training sessions and even during matches and hit the gym before dinner. However, my cricket was going nowhere. I was trying hard with the technical changes and putting the hours in, but I continued to struggle with my game. Away from the cricket and extra training sessions there was also very little else to do and I spent a lot of time alone in the four walls of my room.

I'd performed OK in the first warm-up game, but they were poor opposition. From then on I struggled. I was bowling poorly, I wasn't batting particularly well, and I wasn't enjoying it. The first Test wasn't a huge scare for us but they certainly put us under pressure. We chased down a modest target and won by seven wickets but it was closer than we would have liked. I didn't get any wickets in the first innings and took just one in the second, bowling without any real penetration. My spin partner Gareth Batty out-bowled me, as he had done in the warm-up game.

At the end of the first Test we went out to a private bar for a drink and to watch some football. I felt angry and frustrated about my performance. In the subcontinent your spinners should take the lead role and I'd got just one wicket. I felt like all eyes were on me, judging me. My already fragile mental state was worsening as a result. I drank gin and tonic as though it were water that night. I was pissed off, feeling down and later sick from drink. I also managed to have an argument with Fletch that night. It was over something I said to him in a fines meeting after the game that he took personally and saw as disrespectful. I hadn't meant that to be the case at all. It was something I said flippantly after a few beers, but I made the mistake of swearing when I said it. Later, at the bar and fuelled by alcohol, it all kicked off. It's the only time I've had a cross word with Fletch. That in itself should have been an alarm bell for me and those around me, but we cleared the air the next day and our relationship returned to normal.

After the first Test several members of the media were calling for me to be dropped for the next match at Chittagong. Some of the reports from Dhaka were quite scathing and I too thought that there was a good chance I wouldn't play the second Test. Batty had bowled pretty well and it was looking likely that we would only play one spinner.

Two days before the second Test, Michael Vaughan came to my room to see me. We were close mates and spent a lot of time together, but this was an official visit. He asked me how I was feeling and whether I was OK for the next match. He told me it looked like we would only play one spinner and that he and Fletch had spoken at length about it. He then basically gave me the option: if I felt I was OK and ready for the match then I was in. I was still his senior spin bowler and he emphasised the importance of getting me right for Sri Lanka. I told him I wanted to play and that I would be ready. I had never taken the easy option before and I wasn't going to start now. As it turned out, I didn't play much of a role in the second Test. I only bowled seven overs and our seamers steamrollered the Bangladeshis as we won with ease.

At home Stine had started to become more and more worried about me. She knew based on the reports in the media that I would be feeling low, but when she spoke to me on the phone she became increasingly concerned. My room was both a prison and a sanctuary. To Stine my state of mind was obvious, even from thousands of miles away.

I tried to act as normal as possible with the team and staff, but I genuinely hated that trip to Bangladesh. One night I was so bad that Stine threatened to get on a plane and come out and get me unless I sorted myself out. At the end of the call I wrote a letter to Stine and the kids about how I was really feeling, how I felt so low and like I was letting everyone down. I never posted it, but it helped to get some stuff off my chest. Much later, the difference that writing that letter made became clear.

This all happened at the end of the Test series, before the one-day matches started. The one-day series actually went OK. I played the first two matches and bowled well. We won the series comfortably 3-0, and we were off to Sri Lanka. It was great to get out of Bangladesh. It wasn't so much the place, it was all about where I was at the time mentally.

This was my fourth visit to Sri Lanka and I'd always enjoyed touring there. I hoped this trip would help turn my fortunes around. After losing the first one-day international the rest of the series was a washout. On our last visit in 2001 we had recorded a historic 2-1 victory in the Test series. It had been a tremendously hard series and we didn't expect anything different this time around. In fact, we expected it to be even harder given Murali had now developed a ball that spun away from the right-hander. He had been difficult enough to face when he was just spinning it one way, so we knew we were going to be tested.

Largely due to Murali, the Test series didn't go our way. After two hard-fought draws at Galle and Kandy we suffered a huge defeat at Colombo, but personally I'd enjoyed a really good series, taking 18 wickets at 29. I felt much more at home in this environment and had reaffirmed my position as our number one spin bowler. Mentally I was also in a much better place, or at least thought I was, and I enjoyed the trip.

However, no matter how well I performed, I still looked for the negative comments. I didn't bowl many bad deliveries in that series but when I did I was already writing the headlines before the ball had even reached the boundary. I clearly had an underlying issue that I wasn't dealing with, but I guess I hoped that by burying my head in the sand it would all go away.

The personal success I had in Sri Lanka did allow me some respite at home for the six weeks between tours before we flew off to the West Indies, but only a bit. In the second week of January I found myself in hospital and on the operating table. This time it was nothing to do with injury, but for a tonsillectomy. I'd struggled for a while and was having bad cases of tonsillitis four or five times a year. During the World Cup in 2003 I had been badly affected, ending up on a drip, and more recently in Sri Lanka I'd almost missed the second Test in Kandy after another bout. As a child I'd had problems but hadn't had my tonsils removed. The problem came back intermittently, usually when my resistance was low or

I was tired. Over the last year or so the cases had got much worse and we'd made a decision that I should have them removed when a suitable window became available. This was my opportunity.

I was supposed to go in on January 7 after getting home from a break in Norway with Stine's family but after an examination at the hospital it became clear that I had tonsillitis, and so couldn't go into theatre because of the inflammation and the risk of spreading the infection. I was sent home with antibiotics and told to come back a week later. This made my window for recovery a little smaller as we were due to leave for the West Indies during the third week of February. I had always been told that having your tonsils out as an adult was worse than having them out as a child, and that recovery could take a while. Immediately after the op I couldn't see a problem. I was eating sandwiches within an hour and out of hospital after two days. The problems started after about a week. Every time I ate it was like chewing razor blades. I felt dreadful and became gaunt and weak.

By the time we were preparing to leave for the West Indies I was feeling a lot better but I still wasn't 100 per cent when I got on the plane. I felt quite down and tired and didn't enjoy the beginning of the tour at all. The issues I was having with my confidence and self-belief resurfaced, and my physical state didn't help. This had a knock-on effect on my preparation and performance. As soon as I had a slightly bad day, I felt the weight of the world on my shoulders again. I should have been having the time of my life: I was touring the West Indies with England, I was backed by my coach and captain, and had a very supportive wife at home. I was trying to compete with the opposition, but the biggest battle I was having was with myself.

I got a few wickets in the warm-up games and started the tour pretty well. In the Test series I didn't really get a chance to do a lot wrong. I missed the fourth Test due to illness and in the three matches I played I only bowled 31 overs, taking two wickets at an average of 69. Looking back, I'm amazed how down on myself I was given how little I actually had to do. I didn't bowl that well, but 31 overs is no time to find any rhythm.

I spent some incredibly lonely nights in my room beating myself up. When Stine came out with the kids and my mum for the family visit, she was immediately concerned about me. With the best of intentions, I remember Mum telling me I had to pull myself out of it and cheer up. I only wish I could have. I didn't enjoy that trip at all even though it was one of our greatest successes as a team, beating the West Indies for the first time in a series in the Caribbean since the 1960s. As a team we had taken another step forward but as an individual I was continuing my downward spiral.

I wondered after that series how much longer I would survive in the side. I didn't play a part in another rain-affected one-day series, partly due to the weather and partly due to injury. As I returned to England I had done nothing to change how I was feeling. I was on my way to a breakdown.

19

Breaking point

I remember taking a very quiet walk along Marylebone Road on a Saturday evening in May. During the week the road was a mass of traffic but that night there wasn't the normal hubbub of car and lorry noise that accompanies weekday rush hours. But it was also quiet for another reason. I didn't speak a word to Stine on our trip from the Landmark Hotel, our base for the Lord's Test match, all the way to Pizza Express on the corner of Baker Street where we were heading for dinner. I was lost in my own thoughts, in my own little world. I was desperate, to be honest. At the restaurant we were shown to a table and we got the kids into their seats. It was good to get out of the hotel and pizza was an easy option, particularly with the children.

Stine sat across from me and I remember looking up from my menu, preparing to speak to her. She too had been quiet on the walk. She hadn't tried to push me into conversation. She knew I was struggling and that whatever she said would probably have gone in one ear and out the other.

I'd almost begged her earlier in the day to get in the car with the kids and come down from Worcestershire to London to see me. They had been at a kid's birthday party that afternoon but left early because Stine had realised that something was wrong. I wanted them with me that night. It was unusual for me. I'd never pleaded with Stine to see them before. It was always difficult living out of a hotel room with a young family and it generally meant a broken night's sleep which, during Test matches, wasn't ideal. Tilly was just two years old and Anders was about to turn four. Stine was waiting for me to say something, and when I did, it all came out.

"I'm not sure how much longer I can do this," I said to her. "I don't know how much more I can take." I started to cry as I spoke. I remember the restaurant being busy and I was probably attracting some unwanted attention, but I really didn't care. The kids hadn't noticed how upset I was, they were busy playing with the crayons and colouring the waiter had given them. When he came back to take our order, I remember making an effort to take a deep breath and act as if everything was fine, much as I'd been doing for months. I'm pretty sure Stine ordered her usual, half a lager shandy, the kids had coke, and I ordered a Peroni and a bottle of red wine for Stine and I to share. I didn't make a habit of ordering bottles of wine during Test matches but, given where my head was, what the hell.

Stine waited for me to speak again once the waiter had left our table. I explained how I'd had enough of the beatings I seemed to be taking in the press. Every time I picked up a paper there seemed to be something derogatory about me: how we didn't have a decent England spinner, how I would never bowl England to a victory. I was also starting to hear the flak I was getting from supporters. It was really getting to me.

The reality was that I knew I was underperforming. I wasn't doing myself justice and some of the criticism was probably justified, but I wasn't managing it at all well. For a start, I was reading *everything*! There were definitely moments during this period where I hoped I would be left out of the next match. Not because I wanted to turn my back on the team, but because I wanted a break from what felt like an onslaught on and off the pitch. It might have given me a chance to get back to Warwickshire and find the confident cricketer in me again. I was in a downward spiral, and my descent was getting quicker.

I know now that my mind was scrambled and I was believing everything that was said and written about me. I no longer felt like I was in control of my destiny, I just felt like a pawn in the game. Even when I had success in this period, I don't think I ever really came out of that sense of despair. In Sri Lanka, just months earlier, I'd taken 18 wickets in the series, but that feeling of peace and calm only lasted a short period of time. I was already bracing myself for the backlash that would follow my next disappointing performance before I'd even had a chance to pat myself on the back. It was a self-fulfilling prophecy. I had become a puppet for my critics.

I was getting to a point where I was prepared to lose what I had worked so hard to earn, of quitting the game I loved. Cricket to me wasn't just my job, and when I started playing it certainly hadn't been to make lots of money and have nice things. The game had been in my blood since the day I was first pushed around Ripley village green in a pram. From the time I could walk I'd been playing with a bat and ball. From the age of about eight I had dreams of being an England cricketer. I was certainly not the best player to have represented England by any means, but when I looked at where my journey started... well, I should have been proud and happy.

However, at that point, cricket was tearing me apart. It was ruining my family life and making all of us unhappy. Criticism comes with the territory of professional sport, and everyone gets it at some point. But it felt like I was fighting a losing battle. I was just about ready to throw in the towel.

It was the first time I'd really spoken honestly to Stine about how I was feeling. She knew I was struggling and had asked me if I was OK on many occasions but I'd just brushed it off and cracked on, not wanting to talk about it. All the while, the situation had been getting worse. It wasn't something that had just happened overnight. This had been going on for months. In fact it was probably closer to a year that I'd been feeling this negativity creep over me. I didn't like to talk about it with anyone though. It seemed a dirty, disgusting thing to talk about; that you are struggling, that you don't feel worthy. It felt a particularly hard thing to talk about with my teammates, even those who were really close friends. I thought that sharing how I felt with anyone would have given a very clear sign that I was weak. I was worried they wouldn't feel comfortable lining up alongside me if they knew where my mind was. Gradually it chipped away at my armour, and by this point I was feeling broken. I tried to keep up the front of 'being OK' but it was beginning to wear thin. I truly believe I was depressed.

"If this is what cricket is doing to you, then you should give it up," said Stine. "It's hurting all of us – you're not happy, just give it up!" I can remember her words clearly.

So there we were, around the corner from the greatest cricket ground in the world, and Stine, like me, had reached a tipping point. She could see I was becoming increasingly down and desperate; cricket was ruining me, and ruining our family.

I didn't love cricket at that point. I don't think I even liked it. That worried me. I had some decisions to make, but I didn't feel ready to make them. We finished our pizzas and I drained the bottle of red. We then headed back to the Landmark to put the kids to bed. The next day we were in the field for the fourth day of the first Test against New Zealand at Lord's. I hadn't reached rock bottom yet, but it wasn't far away.

20

Beam me up, Scotty

I slept soundly that Saturday night at the Landmark Hotel. It might have been the red wine that I'd demolished at Pizza Express, but more likely it was the outpouring to Stine that had cleared my head a little. I think she was relieved too. For months she could see this regression taking place but was helpless to do anything until I decided to share how I was feeling. But while this may have been a first tentative step, I still didn't have a plan of what I was going to do about it.

In the short term, getting stuff off my chest did seem to have a positive effect on my performance that Sunday against New Zealand. The Test so far had been a close affair. New Zealand had won the toss and made a decent first-innings total of 386. We replied with 441 to give ourselves a good lead. Andrew Strauss on debut scored a brilliant 112 on his home ground and Marcus Trescothick made 86 as stand-in captain for the injured Michael Vaughan.

My game to that point had been pretty dreadful. In the first innings I'd only bowled five overs and taken 0-32. With the bat I scored just 11. Overnight New Zealand were 134-1, so 79 runs ahead. I remember being a little more relaxed that morning. I'd accepted that I was in trouble, mentally and physically, and wasn't sure how much longer I actually wanted to carry on playing. But I knew that I had important job to do and decided that I would try as much as I could just to enjoy it. If I was going to go out, I was going out fighting and with my head held high.

Not long into the fourth day I was called into action. I chose to immediately come over the wicket and try to block up an end and restrict the Kiwis' scoring rate. We couldn't afford for them to get too much of a lead too quickly.

At the other end Simon Jones got our first wicket of the day, the dangerous Brendon McCullum caught behind for 96. His partner Mark Richardson continued in his very watchful manner and he was joined by Scott Styris, another strokeplayer.

Thank god Styris came in at three, because he was about to initiate a confrontation with me that got me back in the contest, and possibly the summer and beyond. I really don't know why he did it, he must have been looking to intimidate me. If he'd realised where my head was, he wouldn't have bothered. I was my own worst enemy at that point and didn't need any help in that regard. Whatever he was looking for, I don't think it was the reaction he got.

I was still nervous after the way I had bowled in the first innings but I was desperately trying to look confident and show positive body language, hiding the fragility I felt inside. Then, next thing I knew, Styris let rip at me. It completely took me aback. I had never been sledged by a batter while I was bowling before, and initially I was stunned and just stared back. Styris was having a dig about me bowling over the wicket. It was something that I'd been criticised for before on many occasions, particularly by the press, who saw it as a negative tactic. But it was something that I did well, and would actually do more and more over the next few years. At this point I had only bowled a few balls at Styris, and he'd played them all back down the pitch. At the end of the over he went at me as I walked past him. "Come on Gilesy, why don't you come round the wicket, be more attacking? You're very negative, back yourself Gilesy."

He was goading me into a response, either to get me to come round the wicket as he wanted, or to lose focus and start bowling bad balls. Well, it wound me up. For the next six balls Styris was stuck with me at the non-striker's end while I was at mid-on. I let him have both barrels. I was absolutely fuming. If he thought that I would go into my shell, he couldn't have read me more wrong. He didn't come back with anything, just looked at me occasionally and leant on his bat. At the end of the over I couldn't wait to get the ball in my hand and get at him. It was the first time since the tour of Sri Lanka, before Christmas, that I'd had such presence and determination at the beginning of an over. Almost instantly I had a different bounce in my stride, and I was bowling the ball really hard. At that moment nothing else mattered apart from trying to get this bloke out. The nerves, the worries, the fears of failure had all gone. I was in the zone.

The first three balls passed and I could sense that Styris was eager to get off strike. I bowled the fourth ball and my sense had been correct. To a ball that pitched on the stumps, Styris tried to work the ball away through mid-wicket, getting an inside edge. The ball cannoned into his front pad and straight into Nasser Hussain's hands at silly-point. I'd got him!

I was never a big sledger, but if someone looked for a confrontation then they got one. I didn't say a word as I ran down the wicket towards my teammates and past Styris. As he raised his head I simply put my index finger to my lips and mouthed 'Sshhh'. It was a wicket I will always remember. I had rediscovered the real me and I have Styris to thank for that. It got me into the match and influenced the result.

Next man in was Craig McMillan, another of the Kiwi batters that liked to play his shots and someone who was particularly aggressive against spin bowlers. He blocked his first ball. We had two men in front of him now, looking for a bat-pad chance. I knew it wouldn't be long before McMillan played the sweep shot, it's a shot he played well, but I didn't expect it second ball. It can be a risky shot to play early in an innings when you haven't got used to the pace of the bowler and pitch, and the bounce in the wicket. The ball rushed McMillan and he too got an inside edge onto his front pad. The ball hit the pad hard and looped over Nasser at silly-point. Nas turned quickly and, as the ball came over his head, took a great catch at full stretch. I had my second wicket. I was overjoyed but more importantly New Zealand had slipped from 187-2 to 187-4, with a lead of 132.

Jacob Oram was then run out with the score on 203 and Richardson was joined by Nathan Astle, the pair putting on 84 for the sixth wicket. As well as taking wickets we had done a great job of controlling the run rate. I'd bowled at the Nursery End unchanged and we rotated our seam bowlers at the other. With the score on 287 Richardson went for 101 to Harmison. Three runs later Astle was out for 49. We realised we had a window of opportunity. The lead was 235 and we were just three wickets away from batting again.

On 304 Vettori also got out to Harmison, who had bowled beautifully. At the other end the very dangerous Chris Cairns was still there. We'd kept him quiet so far. I'd kept a couple of fielders out on the leg-side boundary, waiting for the big shot, but so far he had resisted. We all knew it would come at some point, he was just that sort of player. He'd hit me out of Edgbaston a couple of times before. Eventually, he took on the challenge. In this situation there is a moment where you consider the possibilities, almost in slow motion. The ball comes up and out of your hand and heads down the pitch. At the other end comes Cairns, bat raised, feet advancing down the wicket. He isn't coming down to block this one. I like to think it was a decent bit of bowling, but maybe I was just lucky. Either way, Cairns had run out of patience and tried to hit this one out of St John's Wood. He mishit it, and Mark Butcher ran forwards and took a good low catch at deep mid-wicket. We wrapped up the New Zealand innings for 336 and left ourselves needing 282 to win.

I was really chuffed with how the day had gone. We had stuck to our task brilliantly and kept the Kiwis under control. As a team we left the field happy and confident that we could chase down these runs on a wicket that was still playing well. I felt I'd played an important role and done my job well, bowling 39 overs in the innings and taking three wickets for 87 runs. My confidence had taken a huge boost.

I wish I hadn't picked up the papers the next morning. I thought I might read that we had taken control of the game with good discipline, controlled aggression and proper planning; that we were in a great position to win the Test and take a lead in the series. Instead, we were described as negative. It was said that we had given up on trying win the match. Apparently, I had bowled particularly negatively and for far too long. We also read that it was a run-chase we were very unlikely to make. I felt that I'd just had one of my best days for the team for a long time only to be shot down in flames. I felt terrible.

That Sunday we proved everyone wrong. We knew we could chase down 282. Whatever history said, this was a different England side.

It was to be Nasser Hussain's last Test match. He finished 103 not out and steered us to victory. We only lost three wickets and the innings was paced to perfection. I felt happy with our victory, but despite my efforts things still seemed to be getting worse before they got better. While we celebrated as a team that night, and all patted ourselves on the back, I wondered what I would have to do to change people's opinions of me.

In 10 days' time we would begin the second Test at Headingley. Before then, I played in a C&G Trophy victory against Kent at Edgbaston. It wasn't great preparation for the upcoming Test but I took a couple of wickets. I travelled to Headingley not sure whether or not I would be picked for the Test match. The Headingley wicket had been notoriously seamer-friendly for decades and the forecast told us that we might expect some damp weather in Leeds, another huge factor in picking a Test team at the venue. But playing a spinner always gives you balance. Often teams pay the price for leaving out a spinner in favour or an extra seamer or batter. There was talk of Paul Collingwood playing instead of me as an extra batter who could bowl a bit, but gut feeling was that after the role I played at Lord's in the second innings, I would keep my place. As it turned out I was picked in the side. It felt like a vote in confidence after my efforts at Lord's.

The first day at Headingley was a dull affair. We chose to stick the opposition in to make the most of conditions but managed only 19 overs in total, New Zealand reaching 41-1.

Day two gave us a full day's play. Michael Papps and Stephen Fleming played really well and got the Kiwis to 200 for the loss of just one wicket. I hadn't helped matters, dropping Papps at gully when he had 36.

After 143 overs in the field we bowled the Kiwis out for 409 on day three – a good total considering the conditions. I bowled 19 overs in the innings and took 0-67. I bowled OK, nothing special, but the wicket didn't offer me a lot. I got the usual jibes from the Headingley crowd about being in the side for my batting and heard the usual "Go on Giles, turn one" shout.

We realised that 400 was a good score on this wicket but Tres and Straussy were quick to put us at ease. Marcus was absolutely incredible and led the charge with his trademark thumps straight down the ground mixed in with cuts and pulls. In this form, there were few better or more destructive players in the world. At the other end Strauss was taking to Test cricket like a duck to water. We lost our first wicket, Strauss for 62, with the score on 153 in the 38th over. Our openers had given us a great foundation and dented New Zealand's hopes. Tres got to a very well-deserved hundred off 161 balls but the key partnership of our innings was still to come. Graham Thorpe was dismissed for 34 and we were five wickets down and still 70 runs behind. At this point they would have felt they could easily finish off our tail and take a first-innings lead, but Fred and keeper Geraint Jones turned the match on its head.

Geraint had made his debut in the winter against the West Indies and had immediately impressed everyone with his attitude and attacking batting style. I always felt happy batting behind Jonah in the batting line-up. I don't think he scored as many runs as he should have done, but I always had the confidence that he could. On this day he certainly didn't disappoint.

New Zealand's hopes of a first-innings lead were dashed by Flintoff and Jones' partnership of 118. It was the most controlled and patient innings that I'd seen Freddie play. He played some great shots but also reined himself in at the right time and kept Geraint going at the other end. The only mistake he made was his last shot. On 94 he tried to hit Styris over mid-off, completely mishit it, and was caught. He deserved a hundred but it wasn't to be. I joined Jonah with the score 457 and we put on a quickfire 34 before I was dismissed for 21. With the help of our tail Jonah scored his first Test hundred. We were all thrilled for him. We ended up with 526, and a lead of 117. We flew onto the field to get at the Kiwis, who were obviously rocked after letting such a strong position slip. Hoggard was brilliant on his home ground, on a wicket that was now starting to show signs of variability in bounce. At the end of day four the Kiwis were in trouble at 102-5.

I hadn't bowled in the second innings up to that point and was already feeling pretty down on myself again. We were in such a strong position to win the game and the series, but I felt terrible. I was hearing the idiots in the crowd again, poking fun and ridiculing me. Lord's had been tough, but the final day had given me some respite. Here I was back at square one again. I was fighting a losing battle with the demons in my head.

On the last morning we wrapped up the New Zealand innings quickly and set ourselves a target of 45. We lost just one wicket and chased it down in eight overs. We had won the match convincingly, and with it the series. We had identified at the start of the summer that the New Zealanders would offer us tough competition. They certainly had at times, but we had reacted positively and overcome everything they had thrown at us. We had grown again as a team. But personally I'd taken another step back. I felt as low as I ever had. I'm aware now that I was asking a lot of myself, but I felt as useless as many people were telling me I was. It wasn't everyone of course. My teammates, friends and family were all behind me and backed me 100 per cent. But the state I was in meant I wasn't listening to them and my confidence was shot. It was a great victory at Headingley but, yet again, I didn't feel worthy of the applause.

Jim Souter, who managed activations with our lead sponsor Vodafone, asked us if we would go outside and do a photo for the press and sponsors for winning the series. Series victories don't come around every day so you should celebrate them. You have plenty of bad days in cricket and many moments at the end of games where you can't get your head out of your hands. That's exactly how I felt now. I was quiet in the dressing room and I'd started to slowly pack my kit as everyone else moved upstairs to have lunch and do the photos. I finished packing and had a quick shower. I put on my England uniform, pulled my bags out of the dressing room and took them to my car at the back of the stand. I got in and drove out of Headingley. I hadn't said goodbye to anyone.

I went home feeling absolutely exhausted. It hadn't been a particularly tough game physically, and it certainly wasn't hot. But I was shattered. My body ached and my legs felt like lead. I didn't say much when I got home. I spent my day off just sitting in front of the TV still feeling terribly tired. I wasn't interested in playing with my kids and gave them no time at all. That's an awful feeling. I didn't leave the house all day and wanted to stay hidden away from the world. The next morning I had to be at practice in Nottingham. The day after that we would begin the third Test. I didn't know how I was ever going to be ready for that match. I wanted time to stand still. I'd reached rock-bottom, and I needed help.

21

Can't beat a bit of Bully

Practice that Wednesday morning was much the same as any other session that I'd had in the previous six months. I got on with it, did everything I had to, and put a brave face on. I was often one of the last to leave the nets and that day was no different. I finished my session by bowling a few balls on the square at Trent Bridge to Geraint Jones with bowling coach Troy Cooley watching my action. After a couple of dozen balls Troy pulled me to one side. "Looks pretty good," he said. "Yeah, it's alright," I replied, not very enthusiastically. "Physically it looks good, your action is strong, pace is good, and your areas are fine," Troy continued. "So what's wrong?" "My bowling feels OK, I'm just not here though. I feel totally fucked and my head is buzzing." "You need to get that sorted," said Troy. "You need to sort your head out."

With that we called an end to the practice and left the field. Most of the other guys had gone back to the hotel. Normally I would do the same between back-to-back Test matches but I guess I felt that the longer I spent out in the middle practising, the more chance I had of feeling 'normal' again. It was a ridiculous thing to expect. I'd spent the last few months retreating mentally into a bad place and a few extra balls out in the middle weren't going to make any real difference.

I was the last player in the dressing room, had a shower and got dressed. I picked up my wash bag and car keys and was about to leave when the door to the coach's office opened and out walked Steve Bull. I'd been aware that Bully was in Nottingham. He wasn't involved with the Test match preparation but, as our team psychologist, he had come up to speak to Duncan Fletcher about the upcoming one-day series before he sat with the team to discuss our goals.

"Hi Gilo, how's it going?" he said. "Hello Bully, yeah OK, how are you?" I replied.

I'd always got on with Bully. He's a nice man to be around and I'd always enjoyed our team sessions. In fact, I had always had an interest in sports psychology and its performance advantages. I just hadn't looked at it hard enough.

"You around today Bully?" I continued, "I could do with a chat." "Yeah, sure Gilo. Let's go for a coffee and a chat."

I don't know what made me ask the question. I was a split second from walking out of the dressing room. If Bully had opened the door a few moments later, I would have been on my way down the stairs to my car. But I'd passed the point of being able to sort myself out. I didn't really know it at the time, but by asking Bully for a chat I'd decided to do something about how I was feeling.

I had been in a downward spiral for about two years. I had doubts about myself, my worth, my job and my family life. I had doubts about everything and I didn't share those doubts with anyone. They were mine. For the previous six months I had been plummeting. It was a freefall that I had no control over. Stine had become aware that more than anything it was my job that was getting me down. I'd wanted to play cricket for a living for as long as I could remember, but I felt I was letting myself and my family down. When you have children all you want is for them to be proud of you. My performances were mediocre.

I've been asked how the people I spent most time with couldn't see what was happening to me. Why didn't they help? Well, in some respects they were trying to. I still felt I had their support, but it wasn't easy to talk about. By arranging to meet Bully for that coffee, I had taken a step. I needed to talk openly and frankly to him about my feelings, and I was ready to do that now.

I met Bully in the reception at Hart's Hotel and we agreed to take a wander into town and find somewhere to have a coffee and a quiet chat. I remember it being a cool place. The interior was very modern and sleek. One of the staff came over and took our order and we found a seat and waited for our drinks. We sat at a long, high table on stools in the middle of the room.

"So what's going on Gilo?" he asked. That was all I needed. I told Bully everything. As I delved deeper into how I felt I became more and more emotional. I didn't cry, but I was certainly welling up.

Bully probably wondered what he had got himself into. He thought he was going for a nice coffee and a general chat. He was now stuck with this nutcase of a left-arm spinner who was falling apart in front of him. I was glad to get this stuff off my chest and immediately felt as if I'd had a great weight removed from me. Bully dug deeper into my feelings about my worth in the team. He asked who I admired and looked up to from England's spin department of the past. I immediately said Phil Tufnell. I knew that he had got 120-odd Test wickets in his career, and I had always admired the way in which he bowled when I was younger. He had beautiful control of flight.

At that time, I would have laughed if someone had told me that I'd take more Test wickets than Phil. He was the benchmark for English spin bowling over the previous decade. I didn't even feel I had the right to compare myself to him. Bully pressed me on this and we talked about Tuffers' broader role in the England team. Cat is a lovely bloke, but never offered a great deal other than when he had the ball in his hand. He couldn't bat or field to any great level and didn't appear to be that bothered about fitness. Bully then got me talking about my roles in the team; not just as a bowler but also with the bat, as a catcher at gully, and a popular member of the dressing room. It was a difficult thing to do. It was even more difficult to talk about the good performances I'd had with the ball for England. But Bully pushed me on it. I'm sure he knew my best moments from his closeness to the team, but he wanted me to talk about them. Slowly I opened up and talked about my successes in Sri Lanka, India, Pakistan and during various Tests in England. It was as though I'd almost forgotten some of these moments myself. They had become hidden in all the other negative shit that was going on in my head.

Bully asked me if there was any other area that I thought I could attack. He already knew that fitness and diet was an important area of preparation for me, and I'm sure that was the answer he was looking for. I told him that it was probably an area that I had neglected as I had become more and more down. I was feeling a lot less emotional now, and more like doing something about the situation. But what?

Bully pulled out a small notepad from his pocket with the Hart's Hotel insignia on it and placed it on the table in front of him. "OK let's make a plan," he said. And so we did. The plan had three points to it, areas that we had already discussed. I still have that piece of paper, right here in front of me as I write. These were our three points:

- FITNESS & DIET
- ROBUST CONFIDENCE – back to significant successes – AFFIRMATION
- MY ROLE – broad-key contributor across at least three areas

A simple plan you might think, but one that at last had me talking and thinking about me. With this plan I would control the things that I could control. I couldn't control what anyone else thought of me. I couldn't control what people shouted at me or wrote about me. However, I could control these things that we'd spoken about and written down. I could get fitter and be careful about what I put in my body. I could choose to recall the good and positive times in my career rather than the more disappointing experiences. I could also certainly work and develop on my broad role in the side. Hard work and proper practice would support that. All these things worked together, hand in hand. The most immediate thing for me to tackle was the second item. I had to clear my head of all the negative stuff and start thinking and talking positively about myself.

I explored with Bully the best way to implement item two, the self-affirmation section. I had talked to him about how in Bangladesh during a particularly bad time I had written a letter to Stine and the kids talking about my feelings and how I thought I was letting them down. I hadn't written it as a form of therapy but I was going to send it to them because my conversation on the phone with Stine had been so dreadful.

As we discussed it, I remembered that writing that letter had had a positive effect on me at the time. Soon after writing it I went to Sri

Lanka with the team and enjoyed a successful tour. So Bully and I decided that if I enjoyed writing, it would be a good way to get my feelings out and reaffirm my strengths. We talked about performance and lifestyle diaries that other sportspeople and businessmen used and decided it would be a good thing for me to pursue.

We finished our chat, left the café and while Bully headed straight back to the hotel, I made my way into town and to WHSmith. I was in the mood now. I had decided to take action and I wanted it to all happen right now. I didn't expect it to have an immediate effect, but I wanted to get on the road to recovery, to get my life back in order. I bought myself a notebook and a couple of pens. I didn't waste any time and pulled out a pen and opened the first page of the notebook as soon as I got back to the hotel. I still have that book now.

This is exactly what I wrote. (I apologise for some of the language – and to my friends in the press – but I had a lot to get off my chest.)

Wednesday June 9, 2004

It's time to draw a line under all of this now.

I'm getting myself down. I feel tired. I feel low and emotional. I just don't feel very good about myself. When I get home I feel too tired to do anything. I can't enjoy my family. Stine, Anders and Matilde are also suffering with this. That's not fair.

I'm listening to the crowd too much, and I'm reading the papers too much. They shout things at me and it's started to get to me. They tell me I'm 'shit' and 'useless', 'you're a wanker Giles, get off'. It's got under my skin and I'm starting to believe some of the things myself. That's why it's got to stop.

I do have value in this team. I have always given my all. I've always stood up in tight situations – we always say we like a scrap as a team and I have never run away from one of them. I don't deserve this treatment and I certainly don't deserve to make myself feel like this.

I will one day get dropped from this team. That's just the nature of the game. But I can't go out like this. I will fight back. I have to get back in the gym. Get my energy back. I've got to start enjoying my cricket again.

Let's start tomorrow against New Zealand – let's enjoy it.

What the hell do these newspaper boys know anyway. Most of them have never played cricket. They spend most of the day not watching the cricket – they are wankers – most of them – not all of them but most.

AND THE CROWD – the ones who tell me I'm useless. Sad bastards. School bullies probably most of them. Very insecure all of them. Get a life lads… let's grow up!!!

BE CONFIDENT
HAVE ENERGY
COMPETE AND WIN
IGNORE THE WANKERS

I felt relieved when I closed my book. I felt different already, more positive almost as soon as I had finished writing. I had a few moments on my own watching TV and feeling quite relaxed before we met downstairs for our pre-match meetings. Afterwards I headed out for some food in Nottingham with a few of the boys. I had no problem going back to my room that evening. I was a lot less anxious than I had been of late. I picked up my diary and read what I had written. When I'd finished I picked up my pen and started a new page.

Wednesday evening

I feel relaxed and confident about tomorrow. I'm trying not to worry but look forward to the day.

I was still extremely nervous getting up on the first day of the match at Nottingham. I was anxious during warm-ups and as the coin went up at the toss. I know now that every one of us in that dressing room would have been feeling what I was feeling or similar. It is completely normal given the circumstances.

It's OK to acknowledge those fears are there, but not healthy to focus your attention on those doubts. None of us can control what has already happened but you can have a lot of control on what is happening now, in the moment. My last six months, at least, had been full of 'what ifs' and 'maybes', worrying about what had already happened and what people thought about me. Sometimes it's just how you frame things. The sweaty palms, the dry lips, and all the other signs of nerves – again, all very normal, and just your body's way of preparing you for something important, something that you really care about. It's just a mix of natural chemicals that prepare your mind and body for action. That's how I see it now anyway.

My meeting with Bully didn't suddenly change everything, of course. I wasn't suddenly a cross between Shane Warne and Brian Lara, and it certainly wouldn't be the last time that I battled my self-doubt. I was still getting up that morning clinging on to my Test place by my fingertips. I was hardly going to walk into the dressing room and say, 'OK, don't worry lads, I had a great coffee with Bully yesterday and everything is absolutely fine now. I am going to have a great game this week. So just chill out, take it easy, put your feet up.' But when I look back, I had changed. At least something in me had.

We lost the toss that morning and at the end of the day New Zealand were in a commanding position at 295-4. Not a lot to cheer about you might think, but I had really enjoyed it. I felt like I bowled well. I had good control and bowled well to any field that I set. I was trying to get into the batter's head and second guess what move he might make next. I varied my pace well and played an important role in controlling New Zealand's scoring rate. I got myself a wicket as well, that of Mark Richardson for 73. Today I had done my job. I was happy and it didn't matter what anyone said or wrote. I had also really enjoyed the crowd. I don't remember hearing any negative stuff, and I played along with them and had a laugh. My perspective and thought patterns had changed. I was, in Bully speak, controlling the controllables.

At the end of the day I was relaxed and went back to the hotel happy that I had done my job. In terms of figures, it wasn't the best day of my career, but it was a stepping stone – in fact, a huge leap in the right direction. That coffee with Bully was the precursor to the most remarkable comeback for me, and my involvement in a historic cricketing summer. I could never have imagined at that moment how 2004 and 2005 would turn out. Without that coffee, I'm absolutely sure I never would have made it to the 2005 Ashes. That night I sat on my bed in the hotel and wrote another entry in my diary. It read:

Thursday June 10

I've enjoyed today. It's been a very hard day. But I really have enjoyed it.

I bowled well today. I only took one wicket, but I carried out my role and did what was asked of me.

Think positively about bowling, not negatively. Don't think about failures in my action, or bowling a bad ball. Think about being strong at the crease, and bowling good areas with good energy and pace.

Good body language. Tomorrow I'll start again and do what is asked of me. You are not always going to do things that you would like. But give yourself a chance. Stay in your bubble and stick to the plan. I'm tired tonight but tomorrow I'll be fresh and ready. Plenty of energy and enthusiasm.

Good with the crowd today. Not so many wankers about. Still the odd one. Get your own lives and don't try to get involved in mine!!

* *Good energy*
* *Stick to the Plan*
* *Be Confident*
* *Be Positive*
* *WIN*

What's the point of Ashley Giles?

It was during the Trent Bridge Test of 2004 that the headline 'What's the point of Ashley Giles?' appeared on the back page of one of the broadsheets. This was taken from a question sent in to Sky during the second Test and was picked up by the written press. I spotted it as I sat at breakfast. I don't remember exactly what my reaction was, but I do know that I let it go quite quickly. A few days earlier, my reaction would have been entirely different. It would have been another nail in the coffin of my cricket career, and it would have stayed with me for days if not weeks.

However, at Trent Bridge my mindset had changed. So had my results, and my match got better and better. In the first innings, I finished with figures of 2-70 in 27 overs, which was a decent return, and more importantly, I felt as though I'd bowled with control and consistency. New Zealand, having been 272-2, were eventually bowled out for 384. In reply, a number of our batters got in but didn't capitalise and we were bowled out for 319. I made a good contribution with the bat and was not out at the end for 45.

In their second innings, New Zealand again started strongly and we were well behind in the match. I took the first wicket, trapping Richardson lbw, and this brought Brendon McCullum to the crease.

On just 4 he ran at me and had a proper hack at a ball that wasn't really the right length to take on. He nicked it, and Fred took the catch at slip. Then, as we did so often during that period as a bowling attack, we began chipping away at their line-up. I took two more wickets in the innings, the first of those an absolute beauty to Chris Cairns that pitched on leg and hit the top of off. New Zealand had again collapsed from a position of strength, leaving us needing 284 to sweep the series.

We started terribly, losing our first three wickets for just 46, but Mark Butcher and Thorpey steadied the ship. However, when Geraint Jones was out and I walked to the crease to join Thorpey, we were still 70 short of our target. It wasn't quite the drama that I would experience at this same ground a year later, but it was a tense run-chase. The Kiwis came hard at us, and me in particular, bowling a lot of short stuff. But in many ways their approach helped us and we were able to score pretty quickly. Gradually, we took the sting out of their attack and moved towards our target. Thorpey reached his century, another outstanding innings, and we got over the line, winning the Test by four wickets and the series 3-0. I finished 36 not out to wrap up an incredible comeback match for me. The difference in me from just a few days earlier was remarkable. I had hated cricket, and what it was doing to me and my family, but that night at Trent Bridge I felt a few inches taller again and the sick feeling in my stomach had gone. Most importantly it was great to play such a big role in a match in England, something I'd not done for some time, and help us win a Test.

At the end of the New Zealand series, I just wanted to keep playing Test cricket. I didn't want or need the one-day triangular series between us, New Zealand and West Indies. I played just two games in the series, one against each opposition. We were terrible as a team and won just one match from the six we played and missed out on the final. During this period I continued the work on my mindset, writing in my journal at least once and often twice a day. I also played a bit of cricket for the Bears, including in the T20 competition. I only played two T20s in my career but I really enjoyed the experience and would have loved to have played more of the format. It was just a year old at that point, and in those first couple of years it was seen just as a bit of fun and a bit of a slog.

Towards the end of July we met up at Lord's to prepare for our four-match Test series against West Indies. I was nervous, as normal, but also excited to get back into Test cricket on the back of my last performance. As a team we were also on course for our goal of a clean sweep summer, winning every Test match. Before the Test started we had the honour of being presented to the Queen on the outfield at the world's greatest cricket ground. It was a a great privilege to meet the Queen on more than one occasion. She was an incredible individual with such a warm glow.

West Indies offered a different challenge to New Zealand. They had a different style and I knew that Gayle, Sarwan, Chanderpaul and particularly Brian Lara would be a good test for where my game was. At Lord's we piled on the runs in the first innings with Rob Key scoring a double hundred, backed up by centuries from Strauss and Vaughan. We put 568 on the board in just 121 overs. In response, West Indies started very well but we then got four quick wickets and I got myself into the match with three of them, including both Gayle and Lara. This was the first time I'd bowled to Lara in a match, having played a fair bit with him at the Bears. On reflection, Brian was probably a little unlucky as replays seemed to show that the ball clipped his pad on the way through to Geraint rather than his outside edge. I wasn't complaining.

The pitch held together well and was pretty good for batting throughout the first three days. West Indies finished on 416, giving us a lead of over 150. I took four wickets and although it was hard work, I'd carried on pretty much where I'd left off at Trent Bridge. In our second innings, we looked to put pressure on the opposition and get ourselves to a point where we could declare and leave us plenty of time to bowl them out. Vaughan completed the incredible feat of scoring two hundreds in a Test, and we declared at 325-5, setting a target of 477.

We quickly had the West Indies two down, with one each for Hoggy and me. Gayle came at us hard and reached 81 at almost a run a ball before Harmy bowled him. Towards the back end of the day, I had Chanderpaul caught off his glove at short-leg and ran down the pitch to celebrate what would have been my 100th Test wicket, only for the umpire to shake his head. The next morning, I learnt from Fletch that someone at the ICC had wanted me charged for my appeal, as I hadn't looked at the umpire when I ran towards my teammates to celebrate. I perhaps wouldn't have minded so much if it hadn't been so blatantly out, and the fact it should have been my 100th Test wicket. I ultimately had no problem with the decision; you get some good ones and some bad ones. But it was crazy, given the circumstances, that I could have faced a fine for celebrating a clear wicket and milestone. In the end, common sense prevailed, and we got on with the last day.

Lara and Chanderpaul dug in for a while, and I recall beginning to feel the pressure of not making a breakthrough during that first session. However, I managed to control these thoughts and focused on my job, as well as where I wanted to bowl to these two great left-handers. Then, in the 46th over, with West Indies on 172, Lara came down the track to me, as he had a couple of times before in that innings. The ball dropped and spun, the length was perfect, and as Lara pushed forward the ball passed between his bat and pad. My first reaction was that I hoped Geraint would collect the ball cleanly in time to stump Lara, but I needn't have worried as the ball crashed into middle stump, almost knocking it out of the ground. It was an absolute beauty. Brian has since described it as one of the best balls he ever faced, which is high praise from one of the greatest of all time. I ran off towards deep cover, followed by my teammates. In that moment I couldn't have cared less about the Chanderpaul decision that had gone against me the previous evening. Lara had just become my 100th Test wicket. I had come a long way from that meeting with Steve Bull in Nottingham, talking about how down I was about my game and how far away 100 Test wickets felt. Within two Tests, I'd got there.

The wicket of Lara gave me and the team a huge boost. We opened up an end and removed their last opportunity to take the match from us. Soon after I had Bravo caught and bowled and then Hoggy and Harmy picked up one each either side of lunch to leave the West Indies 200-7. Enter Tino Best. Tino is an interesting character, full of it on the field and combative. With the bat he fancied himself as a right-handed Lara. After a couple of failed attempts to smash me out of Lord's, Fred stepped forward from slip and said, "Mind the windows, Tino". Everyone around the bat chuckled. The very next ball Tino came down the pitch and tried to hit the ball out of

London and was stumped by some distance. It was one of those fun moments in Test cricket that is easily remembered and continues to be replayed regularly on social media. A while later I had Pedro Collins stumped to claim my fifth wicket, and my ninth in the match. As we closed in on victory I desperately wanted to pick up the last and make it 10, but it was Fred who took the final wicket. We won by 210 runs and I was awarded my first and only Player of the Match award in Test cricket. I also had my name on the honours board in the home dressing room, something players strive for when they come to Lord's.

After a couple of nights in my own bed, I headed to Edgbaston for the second Test. We batted first again and made another huge score of 566, largely thanks to hundreds from Fred and Tres. In their first innings I took another four wickets, including a beauty to Bravo, similar to the ball that dismissed Cairns at Trent Bridge. During this innings I received one of the biggest compliments of my career from Lara during a spell I was bowling to him. I was bowling well and the pitch was gripping a little. Brian was trying to use his feet and sweep me. On one occasion, after getting a sweep shot away to deep backward square-leg for a single, he ran up to my end and said, "Giles, you have me confused". It made me feel a million dollars. Just a few weeks before I had felt little or no worth in the team and now I had one of the best players in the world telling me I had him 'confused'.. Lara scored 95, and the West Indies finished with 336.

After Tres repeated Vaughany's feat from Lord's by making two centuries in the match, we set West Indies 479 to win. The pitch had started to spin quite a lot and they never really looked like getting there despite 82 from Gayle. I took five of the first six wickets, including Lara, Chanderpaul, Sarwan and Gayle, and finished with 5-57 in 21 overs, completing another nine-wicket haul in the match. I never had such a purple patch in my career. There were certainly times when I bowled as well, mostly abroad, but I had never felt so confident bowling in Test cricket in England as I did at that time. This continued through the summer and while the third Test at Old Trafford was a bit closer, we ended up winning there and at The Oval, completing our goal of winning all seven Test matches. In the West Indies series I finished with 22 wickets at an average of 23, and also averaged 20 with the bat.

At the end of the Test summer we turned our attention to one-day cricket, with the Champions Trophy being played in England and Wales through September. Ahead of that we took on India in a three-match series as preparation, winning 2-1. I played in all three matches and bowled well again. In the Champions Trophy, a relatively short competition, we faced Australia in the semi-finals at Edgbaston following wins against Zimbabwe and Sri Lanka. Australia scored 259 and we cruised home by six wickets. It was at the end of this match that I think we first really felt that we could challenge Australia for the Ashes the following year. Yes, it was a different format, but we could see the Aussies were human after all.

We moved on to The Oval to take on West Indies in the final. In challenging conditions we scored just 217, largely thanks to a century from Tres. We added 63 between us for the seventh wicket, and I ended up with 31. Our total looked plenty with West Indies 147-8 in reply and all their frontline batters back in the pavilion, and we looked set to win our first global 50-over trophy. But Ian Bradshaw and Courtney Browne started chipping away at the target and slowly they got themselves into a position where somehow they were within striking distance. I remember us having a couple of very close lbw appeals turned down. With the conditions suiting seam bowling, I didn't bowl. I wish I'd run up to Vaughany and asked him to give me a spell. It was probably the right call to rely on our pace bowlers but the change in pace may have worked. In the end, West Indies got over the line and we missed our chance to win the trophy. It was a disappointing way to finish such an amazing summer.

Despite that loss, I have such fond memories of the 2004 summer. It had started at such a low point for me but became my best Test summer by some distance. I'd gone from a state of near despair and on the verge of retiring from the game to playing a big role in one of our most successful Test summers in history. As a team, it was another huge step in the right direction, towards our goal of winning back the Ashes. I can still recall how different I felt doing a lap of honour around The Oval at the conclusion of the Test summer, celebrating what had been an incredible achievement by the team. This time, there was no doubt that I had played my part.

With Ben Hollioake, a beautiful soul, and Nasser in Mumbai meeting
sick children from a local hospital in February 2002.

Cheers Harmy. A broken arm in Adelaide, November
2002 meant an early return from the Ashes.

Wheeling away against Sri Lanka at Edgbaston, June 2002.

364-2 after day one, Brisbane, November 2002. The Trafalgar
Square celebrations could not have been further away!

Proud Bear. I always loved playing for Warwickshire. Here against Sussex in May 2003.

A young Jimmy, still playing 22 years later! Here with me and Fred on his
way to 4-38 off 10 in the one-day series against South Africa, July 2003.

Harmy drenches Fred after our win over South Africa on the last
day of the fifth Test at The Oval in September 2003.

Dismissing Chris Gayle lbw at Lord's in July 2004, the second of my nine wickets. Along
with Duncan Fletcher, Michael Vaughan was the true architect of that amazing two years.

Man of the match against the West Indies at Lord's in July 2004. Getting Lara (twice!) was a real high.

An England training session at Centurion Park in January 2005 with one of the great men, Graham Thorpe.

Edgbaston August 2005, what a Test match.

With Hoggy after we had steered us to victory at Trent Bridge in August 2005.

What a moment – Ponting's dejection and my delight say it all, Trent Bridge August 2005.

Catching Brett Lee during the fourth day of the final Test at The Oval in September 2005.

With Kev at Trafalgar Square, the day after his astonishing innings, September 2005.

Who'd have thought it? Ashley Giles MBE, Buckingham Palace, February 2006.

23

Getting to the start line

Towards the end of the 2004 international summer, a familiar and concerning issue resurfaced. Following the Oval Test, we were called in for a team meeting with representatives from the ECB and our players' association. On the agenda was the planned tour to Zimbabwe, scheduled for November. Given what had transpired at the World Cup in 2003, the tour had been a topic of discussion for months. Despite some debate, we were informed that the advice from the government, security agencies, and our own association was that it was safe to tour and that we should honour our commitments. The meeting was relatively short, and everyone appeared satisfied to proceed. It was a relief that we didn't get caught up in the same distressing debate we'd experienced 18 months earlier in Cape Town.

Ahead of that series, we travelled to Windhoek in Namibia for a training camp and two matches against their national team. The plan was to use both Namibia and Zimbabwe as preparation to ensure we were in top physical shape before the Test and ODI tour of South Africa. Without getting too far ahead of ourselves, we knew that success in South Africa would be another important step on our journey towards the 2005 Ashes.

The significant addition to our squad for the ODIs was Kevin Pietersen. Even before Kev debuted in international cricket, he was at the centre of much debate and seemed, even then, to polarise opinions. Throughout the county circuit, there were varied views about his character and how he would fit into the England team and our dressing room. We had some strong personalities, and many believed his inclusion had the potential to go very badly, very quickly.

One could probably say we were prepared for him. As it turned out, in my opinion, we had no reason for concern. During that trip, Kev and I partnered for training, working together in the gym. I couldn't speak more highly of him during that tour, which we used as a training and physical camp to prepare for the rest of the winter. He was 100 per cent committed to everything we did and worked as hard, if not harder, than anyone else. It was also clear from early on that he was incredibly fit, and his running, in particular, was as strong as anyone in the squad. One thing that there was little debate about was his ability, and he practised as well and as hard as anyone else. We won the two competitive matches against Namibia comfortably, and Kev didn't really get to showcase what he was capable of.

We hoped our transition to Zimbabwe would proceed smoothly; however, just as we were scheduled to fly there, another drama began to unfold. Several British journalists, including those from the BBC, had been denied entry into the country, prompting us to delay our flight from South Africa to Zimbabwe. ECB chair David Morgan came out to speak with us, and we collectively agreed that we wanted this decision reversed before we were prepared to fly.

At one point, it seemed as though the tour might be called off, and we spent a night in a hotel near the airport while negotiations continued. The following day, the Zimbabwe government reversed their decision, and the tour was back on. However, due to the delay, the series was reduced to four matches, all of which we won comfortably. We swiftly moved to South Africa for what would be a two-month Test and ODI tour.

South Africa were a strong team. We knew that winning there would be a serious challenge and an important marker ahead of what was to come. Graeme Smith, Jacques Kallis, Shaun Pollock, Herschelle Gibbs, Makhaya Ntini, Dale Steyn, a young AB De Villiers – they were a serious cricket team.

To add to the difficulty, our preparation period wasn't particularly long, and only a week after playing the last ODI in Zimbabwe, we faced the South Africa 'A' team in Potchefstroom. We were caught cold and were comfortably beaten. The most electrifying part of that match was when one of the floodlight towers was struck by lightning while we were fielding. We could see the storm approaching, and when they hit that part of the world, they are intense. There were enough warning signs for us to leave the field, but we didn't, and I can still recall the noise and the flash before my eyes as the tower was hit. We ran from the field without waiting for a nod from the umpires. I immediately got a headache from the flash that shot across the ground. Only once had I come closer to lightning than that, which was on our return flight from a tour of New Zealand, just as we were approaching Heathrow, when the plane was struck. There was silence for a few seconds, until everyone realised we weren't falling out of the sky.

From Potch, we moved to Port Elizabeth for the first Test. Before the match started, we sat down as a team to review our goals and discuss how we wanted to play. We felt good and strong going into it, and the game couldn't have gone better. Despite South Africa posting a competitive 337, we went past them, bowled them out much cheaper the second time around, and set up a relatively simple chase of 145 to win the match by seven wickets. Strauss, the star with the bat, finished just six runs short in the second innings of two centuries in the game.

Ahead of the second Test in Durban the families arrived and we celebrated our first Christmas on tour as a family. It's a weird thing trying to enjoy Christmas with your family and prepare for a Test match at the same time. Christmas definitely isn't the same, as much as you try to make it so. The Boxing Day Test will largely be remembered for the tragic scenes that unfolded across Asia due to the devastating tsunami in the Indian Ocean. I can still recall seeing the images on TV coming from Galle, where we had played just over a year earlier, and not quite being able to comprehend at first the depth of the waters as they surged in and flooded the stadium, claiming thousands of lives.

I spent most of my time lying down during that Test after straining my back while batting in the first innings. I continued to bat but couldn't move and certainly couldn't get under the short ball. I was a sitting duck and was hit almost everywhere during my 36-ball innings, particularly by Steyn. It was dreadful. We were bowled out cheaply, and I couldn't bowl in South Africa's first innings. We faced an almost 200-run deficit after the first innings, and the game seemed almost lost at that point. Remarkably, we managed to bridge that deficit and more during the first-wicket partnership of 273 between Tres and Straussy, both of whom scored centuries.

From that start, we moved from a position of almost certain defeat to putting 570 on the board and setting South Africa 378 to win the match. My back loosened up enough to return to the pitch in the second innings, and at one point we had them 183-7. Pollock and De Villiers then put on over 80, and even though we managed to see the back of Pollock with about an hour left in the Test match, bad light played its part and the Test was drawn.

I experienced a bit of a confidence wobble after Durban. I believe it was a combination of the back issue, being out of the match for an extended period, and the subsequent impact on my bowling in the second innings, which wasn't as good as I had hoped. I felt that if I'd bowled better, we might have won the Test. I hadn't felt that way since the dark days of early 2004, and when we arrived in Cape Town, I set aside some time on my own to go through my routine of writing in my journal, ensuring I was giving it the proper attention, so that I was fully prepared for the match.

On day one, before the start, the two teams lined up, and Newlands fell silent for a minute in memory of all those who lost their lives on Boxing Day. Despite such a poignant and sad moment, my daughter, Tilly, only two at the time, managed to break the silence from the top tier of the stand where the families were seated, shouting, 'I'm up here, Daddy, I'm up here'. It was typical of our little girl whom Fletch would later nickname 'The Terrorist'.

We lost in Cape Town, primarily due to a poor first innings performance with the bat and the brilliance of Kallis, who scored almost as many runs as we did on his own, then followed up with 66 in the second dig. After a couple of nervy overs, I bowled quite well in the first innings, taking three wickets, and when I reached 29 in the first innings, I achieved the 'double' of 100 Test wickets and 1,000 runs. Just a year prior, at my lowest point, I never would have imagined getting there. At the time, I was just the ninth England player to accomplish this, and when I did, I slightly raised my bat to Mum, Dad, and my brother, who had travelled over from England.

It was also fitting that I should achieve this in the city and country where I'd learnt so much of my trade as a young player.

With the series level at one apiece, and leaving the families behind in Cape Town, we headed for Johannesburg for the fourth Test. After the first innings, the two sides were as good as level thanks to high-quality hundreds on either side from Strauss and Gibbs. It suddenly became a very important one-innings game. In our second innings, Tres played unbelievably, one of the best and most important Test innings of his career. He scored 180 out of our 332 and we declared nine wickets down with a lead of 324. This was smart and positive play from Vaughany. He knew that if they played out of their skin, they could still win the match with the amount of time left in the game, but he also knew that we needed to leave ourselves enough time to bowl them out. Sometimes, you have to be prepared to lose to win.

With the ball Hoggy was exceptional. Having taken five wickets in the first innings, in the second he got the ball to swing around corners and took the first six wickets of the innings, including the crucial one of Kallis, first ball. Hoggy was often the unsung of our exceptional seam bowling attack of that time, but, in the right conditions, he was lethal. South Africa fell to 118-6. Gibbs again stood out for them, rounding off his best match of the series, but when I had him leg-before for 98, they were in serious trouble. Smith came in later in the innings due to an injury and battled hard for 67 not out but at the other end we managed to chip away, and with less than 10 overs remaining of the match it was fitting that our man of the match, Matthew Hoggard, nicked Steyn off.

It was one hell of a game of cricket, and possibly one of our hardest fought wins to that point as a team. It had been a really even contest that could have swung either way for so much of the match, and to win it and go 2-1 up in the series was incredibly important after our heavy defeat in Cape Town.

Ahead of the final Test at Centurion, I received the news from home that my nan had passed away. I thought long and hard about whether I should go home or not, but ultimately decided that Nan, who was small and slight in stature yet an absolute powerhouse, would want me to stay on to do what I'd worked so hard to achieve.

After what had gone before, the match felt dull by comparison. Although there were still some outstanding individual performances, the game ultimately ended in a draw. With it, we had secured what we knew would be a tough series, 2-1. It had been our last significant challenge ahead of the Ashes. Straussy won the man of the series award for his outstanding three centuries and unbeaten 94.

In the seven-match ODI series that followed the Test matches, we were comfortably beaten, but the major talking point was Kevin Pietersen, who scored three centuries in the seven matches and announced very loudly to the world that he was ready for international cricket. His range of stroke-play, the force with which he hit the ball, and his ability to dismantle an attack was unlike anything I had seen in our one-day team up to that point. His performance sent shockwaves around the world and certainly through our dressing room. If he could do this in the one-day stuff, against a strong opposition, what could he do in Test cricket?

By the time the series concluded, it was mid-February, and we were ready for a break. I took the chance to reacquaint myself with my little family and work on my conditioning before the summer. Two months in my own bed was a rarity at that time. Our domestic season got underway on April 13 at home against Glamorgan, and it couldn't have started any better. I took nine wickets in that first match, followed by eight and seven in the next two against Kent and Middlesex. I scored a few runs as well.

Unfortunately, during the match at Kent, something occurred that, at the time, seemed rather innocuous, but which would become the first step towards my retirement just two years later. I was fielding at gully when I attempted to move to my right to cut off a ball. As I began to twist my shoulders and hips, preparing to take off, I felt something in my right hip catch, and an instant sharp pain shot through that area. I tried to shake it off for a few balls, but it remained sore, so I left the field to speak to our physio, Mossie. He examined it, stretched the area, and it seemed to settle, so I returned to the field.

Over the next couple of games, despite my success with the ball, my right hip felt heavier to move than my left. By the time we arrived in Sussex for our fourth match, I was beginning to struggle. We were soundly beaten at Hove, and I managed to bowl only 11 overs in the game, ending up wicketless. I had no inkling at the time, but that game in Sussex would turn out to be the last County Championship match of my career. I had experienced a lot of success at Hove, but this time I didn't take any wickets, and scored a duck in my last innings.

It was decided that I would take a break from cricket to rest my hip and prepare for the internationals. That break ended up lasting a month, and my first match back was on June 14 in Neath for Warwickshire's second XI. The day before, I had watched my England teammates face Australia for the first time in international T20 cricket at the Rose Bowl. It was such a difficult experience, as I just wanted to be out there with them. The atmosphere was so electric that you could feel it through the TV, and we won comfortably.

I played one more match for the Bears before rejoining England for the triangular series against Australia and Bangladesh, followed by the three-match rubber against Australia. The triangular was an enjoyable series, and there were already signs that the summer would be a good one, evidenced by the closeness of the matches and the spirit in which they were played.

It was so close, in fact, that we tied the final at Lord's, with Harmy and me scampering two off the last ball. During that series, we also demonstrated that we wouldn't take a backwards step against this Australian machine. At Edgbaston, things heated up for a while after Simon Jones hit Matt Hayden with a ball thrown at the stumps. When Hayden responded aggressively, several of our ring fielders surrounded him in a show of strength and solidarity. Kev continued his progress in our team, averaging over 45 across the two series, and made a compelling case to make his Test debut in the Ashes. In my opinion, the way he'd taken the attack to Australia was exactly what we needed in our team when we got to the Ashes start line. He was just different, perhaps always has been, and bloody good.

Thankfully, I came through the one-day matches well. I still felt some awkwardness in my hip and knew I would have to manage it, but it was fine, and I had no intention of missing what was to come. We had waited a long time for this opportunity, and over the previous three years in particular, had built a team that we felt was ready to take on one of the greatest teams in the history of the game. Still, I don't think any of us could have imagined what was to unfold over the next seven weeks.

24

Lord's

We arrived at Lord's on the Monday. Already it seemed everyone in the country had an opinion on the outcome of the most anticipated Ashes series for some time. Those views ranged from Australia annihilating us (Glenn McGrath, of course) to England winning our first Ashes in close to 20 years.

When we started our preparation on that Monday, I remember there being a lot of excitement and nervousness in our group and a general impatience to get on with it. In hindsight, the Monday start for our prep was too far out from the game and was a break from our normal preparation schedule. The reasoning was sound; first Test of the summer, get us together, make sure we aren't going in cold, and so on. But it was too long. We'd normally only ever start our prep for a Test on the Tuesday afternoon before a Thursday start. Those three days seemed to go on forever.

After my hip issues earlier in the summer, physically I was fine. Mentally, I may have felt a little undercooked in terms of game time, but it was about being as well prepared as we possibly could ahead of the start line. The atmosphere in London was one of great excitement, with people wishing you well for the series or wanting an opinion on its outcome, but there was also an edginess across the capital, following the awful terror attacks across the city on July 7.

After our team meeting on the eve of the game, a few of us headed out for fish and chips. We were broadly unbothered by the public, which would not be the case by the end of the summer. It was the calm before the storm.

On that first morning, July 21, 2005, most of us strolled the 15 minutes from the Landmark Hotel by Marylebone station, walking with the fans and MCC members on their way to the ground. Unlike us, they would have to wait outside the ground until the gates officially opened, but when that time came, the stampede of egg and bacon ties through the Grace Gates was a sight to be seen. On more than one occasion, we've hung out the windows at the back of the dressing rooms in the toilets and shower areas to watch this race for the best seats in the house.

The atmosphere was electric as we were warming up, and the crowd started to roll in. During warm-ups, there was one standoff when the Aussies came across to a pitch where a couple of us were bowling on the edge of the square. A few of them started lying down next to and, in some cases, on the edge of the practice pitch we were using. It felt like a bit of posturing, and after a brief pause, I decided I would keep on bowling. My next ball came very close to a couple of them, but after a bit of arm waving and a few verbals, they moved away from the pitch.

Ricky Ponting got the call right at the toss, and it was no surprise he elected to bat first. I think there were some overheads – a few clouds perhaps, but nothing major. The big addition for us was Kevin Pietersen. The rest of the line-up had been largely unchanged over the last year, barring a bit of rest and rotation during that period, or forced changes due to injury. There was great anticipation about how Kev would go against the Australians, but despite it being his debut, it was great to have him in our side given his form in the other formats. Unfortunately, Kev's selection meant that Graham Thorpe missed out, and as a result, announced his retirement that day from all cricket. Thorpey was one of the very best players I played with during my time with England, particularly in how he played spin. At that stage, it was a brave and bold call from Fletch and Vaughany.

I will never forget the atmosphere in the Long Room that day as we walked through to take the field just before 11am. It's normally a calm and very formal area, a few polite claps and good wishes as you pass through, but that day was totally different. The noise was on a different level to anything I'd heard there before. Once play got underway, from ball one Harmy set the tone and bowled with great pace and aggression. We set out that series to go toe to toe with the Australians and not to take a backward step. We had played that way for the past 18 months with great success and there was no need to change that now. We knew Australia would have plenty of good days in the series, and they were traditionally at their best when they had wrested control and then almost bullied sides into submission. They'd done it to us in previous Ashes series. We were very aware that when they had a good session or day in the series, we'd have to pick ourselves up and come again.

The early running at Lord's was ours. Second ball, Harmy hit Justin Langer, just above the elbow. It hurt him. In the eighth over, Hoggy took our first wicket, bowling Matthew Hayden, which brought the great Ponting to the crease. Soon after, Ponting got hit just under his eye by a short ball from Harmy that was too quick even for him. It drew blood from his cheek, and the match was paused while he got treatment.

No one from our team approached Ponting or asked how he was. Everyone will have been concerned, of course, you always are when anyone gets hit like that. But I think the whole atmosphere, the build-up, the Long Room, the crowd and the way the boys bowled got everyone so tightly wound up, on both sides, as though something could kick off at any minute, that we were all just frozen in the moment. Once play had resumed, I remember walking past Justin Langer and Ponting as they met in the middle of the pitch between overs. Langer was speaking quite loudly, certainly loud enough to make sure we could hear. "So this is how it's going to be, is it? OK, right."

Later, after the series, Langer recalled how this approach from our team was something he'd not seen before and was a bit of a shock. After that incident, and the aggression and quality with which we had bowled, Langer knew we were more than up for it this time round.

At lunch, the Aussies were 97-5, and the atmosphere in the Lord's dining room, which is relatively small, was pretty quiet. Most of our bowlers won't go up to the dining room if we are in the field, it's a bit of a trek, and they tend to want to have their food brought to them in the dressing room. I always prefer to go up, probably to get a better look at the pudding options, and the atmosphere in that famous room was always an indication of how the match was going. On this occasion, there was an unease on both sides, despite the score, and both sides were probably slightly shocked by the atmosphere and intensity across the first two hours of play.

After lunch the atmosphere in the ground changed for a while. An element of this would have been down to some regrouping by the Australian batting order led by Simon Katich and Adam Gilchrist and then, once Freddie had seen off Gilchrist, continued by Shane Warne. But the main reason for the change in mood was the news breaking that there had been more attempted terror attacks in London that day. Thankfully, the impact was nothing like that of the previous forntnight, and once this started to drip through, the buzz in the ground started to lift again.

Still, it was unsettling. Later that day, there would be some talk of the Australians being uncomfortable with the ongoing situation, particularly with their families being with them in London, and that some of them may have wanted to go home. Ultimately, those concerns were allayed, but it added to the air of tension, which had gripped the game itself.

Katich and Warne got the Aussies to 178 before Harmy blasted through the tail, finishing with 5-43. All our seamers had bowled really well and got themselves into the series. I hadn't needed to bowl in what had been close to a flawless performance, barring a couple of dropped catches. Bowling the Aussies out before tea on the first day having lost the toss was an incredible start to the series. We knew, of course, they would push back hard – and push back they did.

Glenn McGrath was brilliant in the opening spell that afternoon, and in no time at all, we were in the mire. By the 17th over we were 21-5, all taken by McGrath, with five of our top six going for single figures. Kev and Geraint put on over 50, but when Jonesey was caught behind off Lee for 30, we were 79-6, and I was in. Brett Lee bowled the speed of light from the Pavilion End, and came hard at me. I had always found it difficult at Lord's to pick up the short ball, and Lee had me pinned back against my stumps. My method against short fast bowling was normally to get under it, and get out the way. For some reason at Lord's, that just wasn't happening and I was a sitting duck against the short ball.

Early on, I got caught short leg off Lee, but it was called a no ball. Katich, at short leg, gave me both barrels. I remember thinking how was Brett Lee bowling a no-ball my fault? On 11, and in the last over of the day, I got out. In fact, I got out twice. Lee bowled another short ball, which I nicked down the leg-side and was taken way back behind the stumps by Gilchrist. At the same time, I'd slipped back slightly and stepped onto my stumps, so was out hit wicket. It was embarrassing to walk off in those circumstances at the end of what was an incredibly high intensity first day of the series, with us 92-7.

The next morning, Kev, Harmy and Simon Jones managed to get us to within 35 of Australia, and we were 155 all out. Kev gave us a glimpse of the quality player we'd come to see play match-defining innings over the coming years, and finished with 57.

We knew we'd have to get into their line-up quickly if we were to get back in the game. We missed a couple of chances during the day that could have definitely given us a sniff to get back in it, particularly when Ponting was out with Australia 100-3 and we then dropped Michael Clarke early on. Four down then, and we would have had a chance. But after that missed opportunity, Clarke and Damien Martyn began to take the match away from us.

They both played me pretty well. I couldn't control the scoring, and was going at five an over. That second day was chastening for me personally and for us as the team. By the end of it, Australia were 314 ahead, with the match firmly in their favour. Day three didn't start well either, and we missed more opportunities in the field. We had prided ourselves on our skills and maintaining our discipline over the previous couple of years, and we had already started to let ourselves down. We finally bowled Australia out after lunch, and left ourselves needing what we knew would be a very challenging 420 target.

Despite Tres and Strauss starting better in the second innings, by the end of the day we were 156-5 and as good as out of it. On the Sunday, bad weather delayed the start of play, and we were stuck in the dressing room for a long period. When we did get out in the middle, the match was finished within 10 overs, in which time we managed just another 24 runs. Hoggy, Harmy, Simon Jones and I were all out without scoring, and my second ball duck wrapped up a miserable game for me. I felt like I'd not even started the series yet. Apart from a catch and running Brett Lee out in the second innings I'd contributed next to nothing.

Warne and McGrath finished with four wickets each in the second innings, and McGrath nine in the match, including his 500th Test wicket. Day one seemed a lifetime ago. We'd been beaten by 239 runs, and we were well and truly behind in the series. We all knew we hadn't become a bad side overnight, something which was rammed home in the dressing room afterwards. We also knew the backlash in the media and from the public would be strong. But I probably wasn't prepared for how strong that backlash would be, or that I'd be dragged into the middle of it. To that point in my career, I'd had some difficult moments, but the next 10 days would prove to be some of the most challenging I'd ever dealt with.

25

Edgbaston

Most of us were physically and mentally exhausted by the time the last wicket fell at Lord's. Soon after it, the post mortems could begin. We knew we'd underperformed for the majority of the game, and parts of the media, and some of the public, were angry. Ian Bell, Geraint Jones and I bore the brunt of the criticism, with many calling for us to be replaced ahead of the second Test.

Given our performances we probably shouldn't have expected anything else, and I was particularly disappointed with my contribution, or lack of one. I struggled to shake this off and in the days after Lord's I definitely read and listened to far too much. This, added to my own frustrations, made me both angry and dark. I was beginning to doubt myself and my worth to the team, which I hadn't done since the bad days of a year before.

We had 10 days between the end of Lord's and Edgbaston, which should have been the perfect amount of time to get my head straight and work on a few things. Instead, I just couldn't let go of the defeat, and the criticism we were receiving from all quarters. Additionally, I'd agreed with Fletch to play for Warwickshire in a limited-overs game on July 27, only three days after the Lord's Test. By the time I arrived at Canterbury to face Kent I was in a really bad place.

It was at this point, just as I was dragging my kit from the car to the dressing rooms, that I was approached by a member of the written media, Chris Foye, who asked me for an interview. At that point, of course, I should have just declined the request, kept my head down and got on with the game. Instead, with only the gentlest of nudges, I took him up on it.

The floodgates opened. All of my frustrations poured out. I was laying into everyone, but particularly the media and certain past players who had been so strong in their criticisms post Lord's.

I don't think everything I said was unfounded or without some truth but there was no need for me to say it at that point. We'd lost the Test match in pretty poor style, and what that performance unleashed shouldn't have been any great surprise. There had been a huge amount of hype before the series and we needed to take it on the chin and come back stronger in the second Test.

Still, some of what was said, I thought, was unfair. One comment from Dave Houghton, the former Zimbabwe captain, and someone I knew well, I thought was particularly unkind. When asked for a comment he said, "Playing Giles is akin to playing 10 men" and this was the headline in the papers the next day. Given my state of mind following the Test, that comment in particular hurt me and I contacted Dave about it.

In the piece with Chris Foye I said something along the lines that some members of the media and past players didn't really want us to win the Ashes. That's probably unfair and unreasonable on my part. Anyone who works in the media has a job to do and a story to write. At that point, the Ashes was *the* sports story, and there was going to be comment. There was one headline in one of the papers which read 'Traitors' linked to some of my comments. I don't think I ever used that word, but that's the word that was used to describe my sentiments around the past players.

From the moment that article was released the rest of my week was a nightmare. I came under even more criticism because of my comments and a number of journalists wanted a follow-up comment from me. England players weren't protected from the media back then like they are now. In this modern era all enquiries will go through ECB and the team's media manager. Those 10 days should have been a period of rest, reflection and preparation. They'd turned into a nightmare.

By the time I arrived at Edgbaston, I was anxious and very tired. One of the first people I ran into on my arrival was Michael Vaughan, and he asked how I was doing and how my week was. "Not great mate to be honest, it's been pretty tough," I said. Vaughany said, "Why, what's happened?" I still don't know to this day how much Vaughany knew or didn't know about the week I'd had. What he told me was that he hadn't seen any of the media that week and had chosen not to read or listen to anything about our performance at Lord's, which in hindsight is exactly what I should have done. It was a valuable lesson for me for the rest of the series.

I still had work to do on my mindset to ensure I was prepared for the match. Weirdly, two comments from members of the Australian team helped me. One was as a result of a chance meeting with Matthew Hayden outside the Edgbaston dressing rooms. I was sitting outside looking onto the pitch when Haydos walked past me, having just finished his practice. Rather than keep walking, he stopped and sat down. "Looks like it's been a tough week, mate?" he said. Now, Haydos is a huge man and, as well as being one of the best players of his era, a fierce competitor on the field. But in this moment there was nothing but empathy and kindness in his voice. It immediately helped my state of mind, and rather than feeling sorry for myself and a bit 'poor me', it made me consider that no matter who you are, at some point all players go through a week similar to the one I'd just had. Whether you are me, Hayden or Warne, at some point you are going to get it, even if, in this instance, I could have helped myself by keeping my mouth shut. I really appreciated him stopping and speaking to me in that moment.

The second comment, from John Buchanan the head coach of Australia, was even more impactful and came following a session he'd done with the international media. He was quoted as saying something along the lines of, "We know that if we can get to Ashley Giles, we can get to the rest of them", the rest of them being our quick bowlers. John was basically saying that if they can get me out of the attack they can exert greater pressure on our quick bowlers, forcing them to carry more of the workload, tiring them and increasing the risk of injury. Rather than any negative effect, those comments had a hugely positive impact on me. After all, if they had a strategy for me, they must see that I have a value to the team, something I and many others had struggled to see that week.

I also spent some time talking to Steve Bull, our team psychologist, whose help and guidance had taken me from a position of near despair to enjoying the best summer of my international career. Steve helped me focus again on the good things I had done for the team over the last few years and on my role in the upcoming match. Essentially, the message was not to let the things I couldn't control get into my head. It's unrealistic to think that you never have those negative thoughts, but it's the ability to switch back to being in the moment, being present and controlling the controllables which is important. After Lord's I'd let too much of the outside in.

Ahead of each Test match we always held a team meeting to go through our tactics and approach, and before it the team management group, consisting of a few senior players, the captain and senior coaches, would meet ourselves. As the oldest member of the team, and one of the senior players, I was part of this group. At the start of it I remember Fletch turning to Vaughany and saying, "So, how do you want to play it?". He simply said "We went hard at Lord's, we go even harder here."

This was just one example of Michael Vaughan's excellent leadership in sometimes the most difficult and challenging times. It was also a move away from previous approaches when we'd found ourselves in similar positions. In the past, to use football parlance, having gone 1-0 down in the series England sides have probably tried to play it safe, get men behind the ball and get a draw. Not this time. There were many times that Vaughany will have been paddling like hell under the water while giving the appearance of being calm and in control above it, and this meeting was one of them. Both Fletch and Vaughan went on to remind everyone again how we'd played over the last couple of years, and that this was the time to reconnect with that.

Before a ball was bowled in anger two things happened that would go on to have a huge bearing on the series. Just as we got together as a team on the outfield to warm up, some of our team were distracted by a commotion on the other side of the ground, where the Australians were warming up. We all stopped to look and could see Glenn McGrath lying on the floor clutching his leg, surrounded by members of Australia's medical team and players. He'd stepped on a ball, twisting his ankle and was out of the Test match. No one wishes injury on any fellow player. But given his impact at Lord's and who he was, him not playing could only be a benefit to us.

The second moment came about an hour later. The two captains arrived together at the middle of the pitch with Mark Nicholas from Channel 4, the lead broadcaster, for the toss. The pitch did have a tinge of green in it and was fractionally damp because of bad weather the previous week. It was nothing significant though, and having played my entire first-class career at Edgbaston, we often said in these circumstances, you may think about bowling if you win the toss, you may even think about bowling again, but you still bat. While it might be tricky to bat for the first hour or so, the wicket would get better as the day went on. Most of us were back in the dressing room when the coin went up, and seeing Nicholas turn to Ponting, I was convinced that we'd be in the field first, so much so that I reached for my whites to start getting ready.

None of could believe it when it was announced that Ricky had elected to bowl first. To this day, I still can't understand why Australia made that choice. The only reason could be that given our poor performance with the bat at Lord's they thought we were vulnerable and there for the taking. But given McGrath's absence and, therefore, the increased importance of Warne's role, it only made sense that Australia would bat first.

So, we got first use of the pitch and Trescothick and Strauss made the absolute most of it. We survived one scare when Tres was caught off a no-ball for 32, but otherwise it was a blistering start from our openers who made the most of some loose bowling from the Australian seamers and, from ball one, took a proactive approach against Warne. We were 112 by the time we lost our first wicket, Strauss for 48, and in the over before lunch Tres took Brett Lee for 18.

After lunch the tempo continued. We had a bit of a wobble, going from 164-1 to 187-4, but this brought Flintoff in to join Kev and that's when the fireworks really started. We scored 157 runs in the afternoon session in 27 overs and when Flintoff was out for 68 off 62 balls the two had added 103 runs in quick time and taken us to 290-5. Fred, in just his second Test against Australia, was now very much in the series. Geraint Jones was out soon after but Kev and

I added 49 for the seventh wicket and although I only made 23, it was nice to contribute. Although Kev was out soon after me, Hoggy, Simon and Harmy did a great job to get us past 400 and we were eventually bowled out for 407 in the last over of the day. That many runs in a day 20 years ago was pretty much unheard of and, given our performance at Lord's, put a few ghosts to bed. Vaughany had asked for us to go even harder and that is what we did.

Day two started with a bang. Harmy hit Langer on the head and with his first ball Hoggy had Hayden caught on the drive for a duck, a well-executed and smart plan. This brought Ponting out to join Langer, and they steadied things to inch up to a comfortable position. By this time, I was into the attack.

I was still incredibly nervous. Playing at my home ground was helpful but I was desperate to get in the game. With the Australians on 88 I bowled a ball to Ricky from over the wicket that he tried to sweep down towards deep square. The ball bounced a little more, took the top edge of the bat and Vaughany completed the catch at short fine leg. I ran off to celebrate towards mid-wicket, pointing towards where the families were sitting as I knew my parents were there and had lived the last week as much as I had.

The sense of relief was huge. My teammates surrounded me, rubbed my head, slapped me on the back, and high-fived me. I knew I had their support but it was clear they knew how important this wicket was to me after the attention I'd had the previous few days. From that point we did what we'd done so well as a bowling unit in recent times and started chipping away at them. Every time they looked like putting a meaningful partnership together we would break it. Gilchrist finished 49 not out but ran out of partners. All out for 308, giving us a lead of 99 runs.

Personally I'd had a much better day, contributing three wickets, adding Clarke and Warne to Ponting, and I'd also added a certain amount of control for the team. Before the day was out, Warne reminded us of his class and that the game was far from won when he bowled Strauss with a beauty from around the wicket that pitched wide into the rough, turned viciously and bowled him behind his legs.

Day three didn't start well for us. Brett Lee was on fire and we soon found ourselves at 75-6, and under pressure. Enter Fred. If his performance in the first innings had been important, his runs in the second were match-defining. His 73 in 86 balls was a mix of calm control and brutal stroke-play. Geraint and I added partnerships of 26 and 30 runs respectively with Fred but it was the 51-run stand in 49 balls with Simon Jones that got us into a position where we had a lead of 281, and a decent total to defend.

Langer and Hayden came hard at us. In what seemed like no time they had reached 47 for no wicket, taking a big chunk out of the target, when Fred came on to bowl at the Pavilion End. This was his moment, and the crowd sensed it too. His first ball was fast and on the money. His second, again from round the wicket, bounced a bit more and clattered into Langer's elbow and then on to the stumps. This brought Ponting in, and the next five balls (including a no-ball!) were some of the most challenging he would have faced in his career. I'm not sure how he felt, but it was scary enough standing at a wide slip position 20 yards further back.

Every ball was a brute, moving through the air in both directions, and the last delivery of the over that moved away from Ponting, bounced a little more, and took his outside edge. Geraint took the catch above his head and Ponting was gone. Australia were suddenly 48-2 and Fred had turned the innings on its head. Hayden followed with the score on 82 and when Martyn chipped one to mid-wicket off Hoggard, the Australians were tottering on 107-4. Soon after that I dragged Katich forward to one that he nicked to slip, Tres juggling at first but then safely pouching it, which brought the great Adam Gilchrist to the crease.

As he was making his way in, Vaughany and I discussed the field we would have for him and, in particular, whether we would stick a man out on the long-on boundary, a favoured area of his to get things moving. In the event we decided to leave him up, hovering slightly deeper than a normal mid-on position.

It didn't take long for Gilchrist to take the bait. But as he came down the pitch, the ball gripped slightly from the rough, caught the inner half of his bat and having tried to drop-kick it over mid-on, he only managed to scuff it to the very safe hands of Andrew Flintoff. In that scenario, when the ball is in the air and you have time to watch it all the way, there are very few other people that you would want that ball to go to. He completed the catch and booted the ball about 40 yards as I ran to give him a kiss. It felt like a huge moment in the match and, personally, to remove such a dangerous player, and at that point, was a great feeling. That brought Warne in to join Clarke, and of course he came hard at me again, as he had tried to do in the first innings. This time round he hit me for a few boundaries and just when it looked like we would end the day with Australia seven wickets down, Harmison, in the day's final over, outfoxed Clarke with a beautiful slower ball yorker.

It left Australia with 107 still to win, and just two wickets left. It had been another extraordinary day of epic highs and desperate lows. At one point we looked like we might not even get a 200-run lead. Suddenly, we were on the brink of levelling the series.

I'm often asked how we felt on that Sunday at Edgbaston. I can tell you that not one of us thought that the job was done. You can't think like that against Australian cricket teams. The atmosphere in the ground was incredible and it was a packed house, which in normal circumstances would have been a surprise given the match situation. The expectation, however, was clear: we had to win.

It was wild. Whatever we threw at them, Shane Warne and Brett Lee resisted. It wasn't until the runs required was down to 65 that we finally got Warne out, slipping as he moved back to a short ball, treading on his stumps to be out hit wicket. If we felt at that point that we were almost home and dry, Lee and Kasprowicz thought otherwise and slowly the two men started chipping away at the target. Before we knew it, the runs needed was below 30, and then 20. With 15 needed we had our opportunity. Kasper threw his hands at a wider short ball and top edged it down to third man where Simon Jones was fielding. It certainly wasn't a simple chance, and Jonah had to come forward to take the ball that was dying as it reached him, but as he hit the ground the ball popped out of his palms. At that point, a few of us feared the worst.

In no time they needed four to win. Steve Harmison to bowl. I was down at fine leg and the atmosphere was pretty sullen. Harmy ran in and bowled an attempted yorker that had too much width on it. From where I was I couldn't see exactly where the ball was heading, but I knew Lee had smoked it and for a moment I thought the match was over. The ball went straight to Simon Jones on the cover boundary; five yards either side and it would have gone for four.

Harmy came in again and, with everything he had left, bowled a short one into the pitch in the direction of Kasper's ribs, who fended at it and only managed to glove it down the leg-side. As this played out I remember starting to move to my right to prepare to cut the ball off if it beat the keeper, but Geraint moved down the leg-side and rolled as he took the catch.

Everyone in the ground was celebrating way before Billy Bowden raised his finger. The Test was over and we had won by just by two runs. As everyone started to celebrate I ran towards the middle. The crowd was going mad, but as I was running in Geraint started running the other way, heading towards a group of Aussie supporters who had been giving him a fearful amount of abuse the whole match. Tres and I set off after him and pulled him back towards the rest of our team. There was a huge sense of relief in the dressing room after the match, accompanied by feelings of euphoria and extreme tiredness.

We shared a beer with the Australians and then went back to the hotel where we sat for some time and had a few drinks together. Later we wandered along Broad Street to carry things on. The previous 10 days had been some of the toughest for my career. In the end the win had never really been about proving anyone wrong. It was about playing to our potential and getting ourselves back in the series. Personally, it was just nice to contribute. Edgbaston was one of the greatest Test matches of all time, a Test full of drama and excitement, where every session felt as long as a day and the match as long as a series. It was exhausting. Andrew Flintoff was awarded man of the match for his coming-of-age performance and, as a team, we were right back in the series.

26

Old Trafford

When I look back, it was around Old Trafford that things really started to change. Not just the momentum of the series, or the form of the two teams. It felt to me that the whole profile of cricket in the country started to shift and, arguably, it's never looked back.

We'd had little time to reflect or recharge following the drama of Edgbaston. Back-to-back Tests can be challenging physically, but in this case, still riding the high, it felt good to know we were moving on quickly and, in no time, preparing for the next match. We had few concerns over player fitness, unlike the Aussies who continued to have issues with their bowling attack, McGrath and Lee in particular, and we were buzzing during the practice days.

The mood had flipped in just a few days and suddenly everyone wanted to talk about those last few overs at Edgbaston. Personally, following my experiences after Lord's, I had decided to avoid all the media – written, radio and TV – and just focus on my role in the rest of the series. It was something I maintained until we'd finished at The Oval. Instead, I almost exclusively listened to just one album on CD for the rest of that summer. It was James Blunt's *Back to Bedlam* debut album, and it became a huge hit. For me it was a distraction, but I still love that album and each time I listen to songs from it, memories flood back from that summer. Between Tests, given our family home in Droitwich being just 20 miles from Birmingham, I managed to nip home and see the family, do some washing, and get some fresh kit before heading north.

The day before the match started we held our normal pre-match team meeting at the team hotel and our analyst, Tim Boon, had put together a nice little highlights package from Edgbaston. It was my job to provide the music during these moments. I never prepared anything specifically and never really worried about the timing of any highlights package that Boony had put together. On this occasion, weirdly, having chosen *Mack the Knife* to play along to the video, the final beat of the music played just as Geraint Jones rolled to take the catch that won us the match, which brought cheers and laughter around the team room. It was a nice moment.

On day one there were no dramas around the toss this time. We won it and on a firm and decent looking pitch Vaughany had no hesitation in choosing to bat first. In the end, both McGrath and Lee were passed fit to play. Given McGrath's injury on the first day at Edgbaston it was a remarkable effort to get him ready for a Test match just a few days later. Our team was unchanged again.

Straussy was out early, bowled by Lee, but otherwise we carried on where we left off at Edgbaston. Vaughany, who had struggled so far in the series, started to look like his old self and with Tres they began to put together a really good partnership. Vaughany had a little bit of luck being both dropped by Gilchrist and bowled by McGrath off a no ball when he had 41, but who didn't need something to go their way, particularly in that series?

There are few players who, when they got in, sniff out the big score more than Vaughany. He regularly said to me that he couldn't understand how batters gave it away once they'd got to fifty. He always said that if he gets to fifty, he should be getting a hundred. There is no excuse, he used to say. His conversion rate was remarkable, as was the elegance of his stroke-play and the control he had over himself. In the early 2000s, before he had properly broken into the team, I remember saying at a management meeting: "I don't know how exactly, but we have to get him in the team, I can't bowl at him in the nets." It was true, of all the players I bowled to at that time he was the most challenging. Thorpe and Trescothick were both great players of spin but Vaughan seemed to be able to play me the full 360 degrees with ease. It wasn't long after that that he did break into the line-up.

Vaughany and Tres added 137 for the second wicket before Tres became Warne's 600th Test victim with the score on 163. Warnie was simply the best cricketer I played against during my career. To have achieved what he did as a leg spinner alone was incredible; but then to consider his impact on the world game through drawing new people in to watch it, and getting young cricketers interested in playing it – well, the legacy is off the charts. Just the theatre he created out in the middle of a cricket field was worth the entrance fee. He was also a very kind man.

At the other end Vaughan had continued to play his game and after reaching his century, he picked up the pace even further and moved from 100 to 150 in just 39 balls. In the end, what had been a beautiful piece of batting was undone by a full toss from Katich that Vaughany hit down long on's throat. He had scored 166 out of 290-3 when he was out.

Bell had joined Vaughany, dug in, and also got himself into the series. He battled hard that day and we were all delighted when the baby of our team got himself a half century. However, having lost Kev, Hoggy, who had been nightwatchman, and Belly for 59, we slipped to 346-6 on day two. The innings could have gone either way at this point but Fred and Geraint steadied the ship, adding 87 for the seventh wicket. This would prove particularly important as once we lost Fred with the score on 433 we lost our last wickets, including me for nought, for just 11 runs, finishing on 444 all out.

Australia started well with the bat and had got to 58 without loss when I had Langer caught at short leg by Belly. It was a blinding catch, one handed to his right with real pace on it. One of those that either sticks or not. Ponting was out soon after to Jonah and on 86 I had Hayden trapped in front, stuck on the crease to one that had spun and kept a little low. Katich was out to Fred with the score on 119 and suddenly the Aussies were four down.

Then, with the score on 133 I bowled a beauty to Martyn that pitched just on the line of leg stump and, with the batter just prodding forward, beat his outside edge and hit the top of off stump. It was a beauty. Richie Benaud was commentating at the time and said, "Any time you see a spin bowler persuade a batsman to cover his stumps with what seems the perfect defensive shot, and there is a crash of ash, you know you've seen something special".

I rarely watch my performances back, but I must admit to watching that ball, as much for Richie's commentary as anything else. Even Geoffrey Boycott, often one of my harshest critics, said, "What a good ball". In truth, I had bowled similar balls in the previous year to dismiss Chris Cairns at Trent Bridge and Dwayne Bravo at Edgbaston, but given the situation neither of them compared to this one. Australia finished day two on 214-7 and way behind the game.

Much of the third day was interrupted by rain. Once we did get out, and with the score on 231, Australia still short of the follow-on, Warne came down the track to me. The ball spun, beat the outside edge and I thought I had him, but the ball slipped through Geraint's gloves and the chance was gone.

Across the whole series I look back on this moment with the most frustration. Not at Geraint, of course, God knows we have all dropped catches or got things wrong. It was just the situation, for me and the team. A wicket at that point would have given me four in the innings with a chance to have a go at the last two and us an opportunity to bowl Australia out within the follow-on. It would have given me a huge surge of confidence heading into the rest of the match and series, as well as putting us in a very strong position. Geraint had a really tough day. Along with the missed stumping he also missed a catch off Fred. He was in bits at the end of the day's play and the daggers were out for him again in the media. I remember him sitting quietly in his corner at the end of the day deep in his own thoughts and self-doubt. It's a position I'd often found myself in and an extremely lonely place. Of course, everyone rallies round you in those situations but it doesn't stop the demons.

In the end Australia got themselves to 302 all out, largely due to Warne's 90. Simon Jones was incredible for us, finishing with 6-53 in the innings. The pitch had proved quite abrasive and we had quickly got the ball reversing. Both Jonah and Fred were brilliant in these conditions and throughout the series our ability to get the ball reversing and then make the most of the situation was a huge factor in the series. We had a lead of 142.

When we batted again it was Strauss this time who showed his class. He had taken a heavy knock from Brett Lee on his left ear, for which he wore this giant white bandage, but the way he played made him look anything but silly. The pace at which we scored showed our clear intent to get to a position to declare and during the middle session of the day we scored 102 in 27 overs. I remember us not wanting to go too hard. If you press that button too early there is a chance you lose a clump of wickets, finishing up shy of the lead you are looking for, keeping the opposition in the hunt. We really didn't want to be doing this with Australia. Belly and Straussy put on a telling stand, with the former registering his second fifty in the match. In the end, it was a little cameo from Geraint that got us into a position to declare scoring 27 off 15 balls. I was out in the middle with him at the time and was still on nought off just four balls when the declaration came. I was delighted that we had got ourselves to a lead of 423, and that I hadn't bagged a pair! At the end of day four the Aussies were 24-0.

The final day of the Old Trafford Test of 2005 has a special aura all of its own. The ground was already full by about 9am. Tickets had been offered at the bargain price of £10 per adult and £5 for kids, as they often were on the last day of a Test match. Apparently, the authorities had expected around 13,000 people to turn up, and had never imagined the scenes that greeted everyone on that last day. There were queues snaking around the ground, thousands of people stuck outside with no hope of getting in. Many had been waiting to buy tickets since the early hours of the morning. I was always one of the first to the ground on game day, and I couldn't believe what I saw when I arrived. Many of our players had huge trouble getting to the ground that morning and a couple were late for warm-ups. We had never witnessed anything like this in England before and was a clear indicator that the country was now gripped by this series. The atmosphere was again electric, and the task was also clear. We needed 10 wickets to take a 2-1 lead in the series, and Australia a further, and most unlikely, 399 runs.

We couldn't have started any better when Hoggy had Langer caught behind with only a single added to the score. Ponting joined Hayden and immediately looked in good touch. The two of them got the score to 96 when Hayden was out, bowled by Fred behind his legs. For the most part, at one end we managed to chip away at the line-up. But at the other Ponting was phenomenal. Martyn was out with the score on 129 and Katich fell to Fred, slashing one to me at around fourth slip that went high and fast, and was probably the best catch I've ever taken, with the score on 165. When we got Gilchrist cheaply to leave them five down, we were way ahead of the game, and firmly in charge.

Ponting and Clarke then frustrated us for the best part of 20 overs. I didn't bowl very well on that last day. The harder I tried to force it, the more loose balls I bowled. Warne had also gone wicketless in the second innings and the pitch appeared to die a bit for spin as the game went on. Fortunately, the abrasive nature of the pitch meant the ball was reversing again and while I couldn't say they were bowler-friendly conditions, we had the right attack to take advantage of the situation. In the 76th over Simon Jones obliged. He bowled a huge inducking reverse-swinging ball to Clarke that he could certainly be forgiven for leaving. It knocked his off stump out.

When the normally very dogged Gillespie went for nought, Australia were 264-7, and we were just three good balls away from winning the match. Unsurprisingly, Warne had other ideas and forged a strong partnership with Ponting, who by this time had scored his 23rd and, given the match situation, one of his best centuries in Test cricket.

When Warne had arrived at the crease there had been 31 overs left and he and Ponting had slowly chipped away, bringing that number down bit by bit. Just after the last 15 overs of the day had been called by the umpires, with Australia 314-7, our chance came. Warne clipped a full toss from Jonah to mid-wicket to Kev's right hand. He dropped it. It wasn't an easy chance but you'd back Kev to take it.

Finally we got Warne, caught behind off Flintoff via Straussy's thigh at second slip. It was an extraordinary catch in the end from Geraint, who reacted sharply to dive low and one-handed in front of Tres at first slip, to complete the wicket. With 9.4 overs left they were eight wickets down.

Ponting hadn't looked like getting out all day but with just 24 balls left he nicked one down the leg-side off Harmy for 156 off 275 balls. It's one of the tougher ways to get out, particularly when you've played that well, but we'd take anything we could get at that point and it gave us a sniff. Australia were nine down.

We threw everything we had left at them for those last 24 balls. During the last over Harmy was almost on his knees. The last ball in the end was clipped for four and the Test was drawn. The immediate feeling was of disappointment and missed opportunity. It had been an incredible Test match and gone right to the wire. Before we left the field Vaughany pulled us together in the middle of the ground, he thanked everyone for their efforts, told us to walk off with our heads held high and to take a minute to look at the Aussie viewing area, where they were celebrating a draw as though they'd just won the Ashes. It was another example of Vaughany's astuteness as a captain.

One thing we knew for sure: going into Trent Bridge the Ashes was alive, and for the first time in a long time we had the momentum.

22

Trent Bridge

I couldn't help but think that we'd missed our chance. That was an opportunity you don't get very often against this Australian team. We could have won in Manchester. We should have won. We could have been 2-1 up in the Ashes series heading to Trent Bridge – just one game away from regaining the urn. Instead the series was level in what was developing into the closest and most exciting Ashes in many decades. Some would say we should be happy, given what happened at Lord's, that we were still in this series. But we'd played some brilliant cricket over the last two Tests. We had outplayed the best cricket side in the world. But when we had our foot on their throat, we'd failed to kill them off. I just hoped we wouldn't live to regret it.

I spent the time between games trying to clear my mind of that last day at Old Trafford. I needed to start my preparations for Trent Bridge, but I was putting much of the responsibility for us not winning at Old Trafford on my shoulders and I couldn't shake it off. I hadn't taken a wicket on that final day and wasn't happy with how I had bowled. I couldn't help but blame myself. It was in a sombre mood that I travelled back to Droitwich on the evening of that fifth day. I re-lived every minute of what had happened. What could I have done differently? Why didn't I get a wicket? Have I cost us the Ashes?

I had returned home to an empty house; Stine and the kids had gone to Norway to visit her family and wouldn't be back until Trent Bridge was well under way. In most circumstances this wouldn't necessarily be a bad thing. After such a tough couple of weeks I needed to relax, have time to reflect and clear my mind. But right then, that was the last thing I needed. Old Trafford was doing my head in. I finished off a couple of beers in quick time that first evening and got to bed. I didn't sleep well, but that was becoming the norm, and the next couple of days were spent doing not much at all. Fortunately I had been asked to play golf for one of our sponsors at the Grange near London on the Friday of that week. Immediately after the match had finished at Old Trafford I had regretted the decision but after a couple of days at home on my own I looked forward to the opportunity to get out of the house and be around people.

With an early start for golf on Friday morning we were put up at the Grange on Thursday night. I found out that Paul Collingwood and Kevin Pietersen were also playing and we arranged to meet up in the bar for a quiet drink. Needless to say I went to bed pretty hammered. The next morning I began to regret my decision again to play golf when I woke up with a blinding hangover. To make matters worse, when I opened my curtains, it was wet outside. In fact it was absolutely tipping it down. I'm a fair-weather golfer, so I wasn't looking forward to coming off the course with a score way over a hundred and pneumonia. As it turned out, I didn't play too badly (with the aid of a couple of Ibuprofen and a case of Red Bull) and the three guys I played with were good fun.

The next morning, following a few more drinks that evening, I headed back up the M1 to Edgbaston where Warwickshire were playing Lancashire in the semis of the One-Day Cup.

The Bears won and that evening I joined them for a drink to celebrate getting to another Lord's final. It was good to be back with the boys away from the international spotlight, just having a laugh and a few beers. I stayed in Birmingham that night at Dougie Brown's place. On the Sunday an old school friend came up to see me at home and we played golf, had a good laugh and ate dinner.

I didn't make a habit of getting pissed during a Test series but those three nights were a great release for me. I'd started thinking less about Manchester; I still had that niggling feeling that we had missed an opportunity and I missed the family, but that week did me the world of good. I hadn't let my situation deteriorate by hiding myself away and stewing on my thoughts. I had got out and spent time with different people and felt happy talking about the previous week. In a few days the fourth Test would begin and the pressure would be back on.

I made sure I was super sharp during the practice days. Vaughany and Fletch both knew how disappointed I was at Old Trafford and I was sure they would be keeping an eye on me over the next couple of days. I bowled OK in the nets and looked forward to the week. The weight had been lifted from my shoulders from that previous week and I enjoyed our preparation. I also tried to be overly upbeat and have some fun in the build-up. We couldn't let the Old Trafford result affect our preparation. We needed to ensure that we maintained the momentum we'd gained over the last two Tests, and not hand that advantage back to Australia. The Aussies had also come out on the offensive in the press, reminding us that it was us that needed to win one of the next two matches, not them.

When we arrived at Trent Bridge on Thursday morning the groundstaff had done a brilliant job to get the ground fit for play after heavy rain the previous evening. Even with wet weather around there was little doubt what we would do if we won the toss. The coin came down in our favour and Vaughany announced an unchanged team and a desire to bat. It was becoming realistic to think that an England cricket team could remain unchanged for a whole Ashes series.

Glenn McGrath failed a fitness test just prior to the toss due to an elbow injury. This was a great shock to us, and a boost, with Shaun Tait playing instead. We knew he had an unusual slingy action and raw pace, and could be a handful, but he was inexperienced and would probably offer us a chance to score. In that morning session Tres jumped on anything slightly loose and thumped it around Trent Bridge in a way only he could. The openers put on a century stand inside 22 overs before Strauss was dismissed. Vaughany then came in and played beautifully, as he had done in Manchester, only for rain to interrupt our flow during the afternoon session, giving the Aussies a chance to regroup.

Tait took two wickets after the delays and after playing so well again for 58, Vaughany nicked one behind off Ponting. He didn't show it – outwardly he kept his cool all summer – but I knew Vaughany would have been really pissed off. We finished on 229-4 with Kev and Freddie at the crease.

When we lost Kev early on day two, we were five down with Geraint Jones joining Fred.

For weeks now, Jonah had been under a huge amount of pressure from both media and spectators. At Old Trafford he had made a couple of big mistakes and I could sense that things were really starting to get to him. As a team we were right behind him. He was an extremely valuable member of the team, but if ever we needed him, it was now. At 241-5 our innings really could have gone either way.

His timing couldn't have been any better. The two played beautifully for a partnership of 177, with Fred's 102 the best innings I had seen him play. There had been a change in Fred. About eighteen months out before the Ashes, he'd gone from this unpredictable, loose individual, to someone who was much more focused, much more precise, much more on it. He started using sports psychologists around then, and he seemed to develop a clearer sense of what he was and what he wanted to be. Whether that was with the Ashes in mind specifically, I don't know. But you could see it. The change was obvious.

At Edgbaston he had thrown caution to the wind and been destructive. At Trent Bridge he played a calm, calculated innings of true class, while at the other end Geraint had played the most important innings of his life. He continued to have his critics throughout the rest of the series and beyond, but without that partnership we simply wouldn't have won the Ashes. Yes, there were many reasons why we beat the Australians in 2005. But that partnership would be one of the biggest ones. Jones made 85. We finished on 477.

In reply we couldn't have started better. Hoggy bowled beautifully and at the close Australia were 99-5.

We knew day three was key. This time we got it right. Apart from a quickfire 47 from Brett Lee at the back of the innings, Australia had no answer for some brilliant seam bowling, particularly from Simon Jones. Simon had taken six wickets in the first innings at Manchester and was superb again here, taking 5-44 in 14.1 overs.

Hoggy got three and Freddie and Harmy one each. I didn't have to bowl. Australia 218 all out. It was on.

On our way off, Vaughany had an important decision to make. Do we enforce the follow-on? We certainly had the Aussies on the ropes. He called us round to address us all, but the bowlers in particular. He wanted to know whether we were truly up for this, and still fresh enough. The adrenaline was flowing and we were all pumped. We were in agreement; we should make them bat again.

Towards the end of his spell Simon had started to get some discomfort in his ankle. This discomfort had become a little worse as he had gone on, but he'd kept bowling and was sure he could go again in the second innings. It was only when he got back to the dressing room that things took a turn for the worse. Simon's ankle started to seize up and he was in trouble. Quite possibly, so were we.

He did manage to come out and bowl four overs at the start of the second innings, but after that he limped off. Before long he couldn't walk and his match, with the ball at least, was over. We were down to four bowlers and had lost, on current form, our most dangerous one.

The Aussies started well, reaching 50 for the first wicket and 129 for the second when I had Langer caught at short leg. At last I was in the game with the ball. The next wicket will go down in Ashes legend.

Damien Martyn pushed one into the off-side and called Ponting, who was on 48 and cruising, through for a run. It was always going to be tight. The man it went to was Gary Pratt, Durham lad and exceptional fielder, who was on for Simon Jones. Pratty picked up and threw down the stumps. Ponting was short of his ground and absolutely fuming. But, quite bizarrely, he was more upset with us than his partner. He let rip at us on the pitch and then had another go at Fletch on his way up the steps of the pavilion. Apparently Ricky's problem was that he thought we had overused our 12th man during the series to allow our bowlers to go off and rest. His other problem seemed to be that the lad himself was such a bloody good fielder. It honestly hadn't been a plan for our bowlers to go off regularly and I can say hand on heart that our boys only ever went off for a quick shirt change or to go to the toilet. But why wouldn't we pick the best fielder as substitute? It's just foolish to do anything else.

More than anything it was a sign that the pressure was really beginning to tell on the Australians and their captain. I have a massive amount of respect for Ricky Ponting, but he got it wrong here. If anything, the Pratt incident was an example of the fantastic attention to detail we showed in our planning for the Ashes, and how small things can make big differences.

Martyn fell soon afterwards but then Clarke and Katich put on a hundred to take the Aussies into the lead. Losing Simon early on had made it that much harder for us, but we couldn't let them get too far ahead. Not with Warne around.

On the fourth morning we bowled really well as a unit and with great discipline. We didn't get a wicket straight away but the Aussies didn't get away from us either, and our patience eventually paid off with the wicket of Clarke. We had opened an end up – and Gilchrist duly followed shortly afterwards. Warne came in and smacked us for a quick 45, but we kept chipping away and eventually bowled them out for 387. It had been a fantastic effort. We had just spent 170 overs in the field. For the last 120 we were one bowler down. Our efforts had left us needing 129 to win the match, and us four bowlers led the team from the field. We had shared the workload and the wickets.

The atmosphere in the ground was electric as Tres and Straussy started our second innings. In the dressing room it was one of tension, excitement and nervousness. I remember hoping that this would be a breeze. A couple of wickets down, a few beers, a huge celebration and off to The Oval.

We started well enough, with Tres thumping it again. He'd scored 27 runs off 22 balls when he was out to Warne's first ball, with the score on 32. Vaughany went soon afterwards, also to Warne and then, with the score on 57, we lost both Strauss and Bell. Warne was bowling beautifully at one end and Brett Lee, with a reversing ball, was fired up at the other.

I had my thigh pad on, and I'd already sat everywhere in the dressing room looking for a safe or lucky spot that would see us home. I passed many of my teammates on my travels, often without saying a word. Cricketers are a superstitious bunch.

When Kev got out, I was in the coach's room, sat next to Fletch. That position hadn't worked either. I moved again and found a seat in the main dressing room. I was next in.

"Come on you two," I was saying to myself. "Just like the first innings. Get us home." I was praying that Freddie and Jonah would get the job done.

My match wasn't done yet. With the score on 111, Freddie got bowled by a reversing ball from Lee. I was shaking with adrenaline as I stood to put on my gloves and helmet. It was hard work negotiating the steps down from the dressing room to the pitch.

"Come on, relax, don't lose this now." As I got towards the boundary rope, mentally I started to switch on. While sitting waiting to bat so much goes through your head. Much of it fear, anxiety and what ifs. You have no control and that is dangerous for the mind. Once you cross the boundary line there is no place for negative thoughts. I had to stay focused on the here and now, how I was going to play and where I was going to score my runs.

I joined Geraint in the middle, but with the score on 116 he ran down to Warne to hit him over mid-off, mis-hit it and got caught. I knew before he played the shot that he would probably take that option on. It was one of his strong areas, it just didn't come off.

I was joined by Hoggy who was smiling nervously under his helmet, his blond locks pushing from under its sides. "What's happening?" he said. "Well, Brett Lee is bowling 90mph inswingers and Warnie is turning it square… so good luck." That was all I said as I turned and walked away.

I had every faith in Hoggy. He worked hard at his batting with Phil Neale, as I did, and he hated getting out. He's a gutsy bugger and a good friend. After nicking ourselves a couple of singles we needed eight to win. Hoggy then played a shot off Lee that will stay with me forever. He generally scored his runs with nudges and nurdles and the odd sweep from the spinners. Lee had bowled well and fast, but he over-pitched this particular delivery, attempting another rocketing, in-swinging yorker. It also hung out wide of off stump. Hoggy smashed it through extra cover. For a moment we didn't move, both in awe of his cover drive. Eventually we started running but it went for four and we were now just four runs away from victory. At the non-striker's end I prayed that Hoggy would play the same shot again – and it would be over. He couldn't manage that, but he got half a bat on the next ball that went down to long leg and we ran two. The last ball of the over Hoggy survived a massive leg-before appeal from the Aussies, but it was never hitting.

We met in the middle of the pitch and agreed that I wouldn't try and force the issue against Warne. Playing out a maiden wouldn't make any difference, we only needed two to win which might be easier to get against the pace of Lee. The first three balls passed without incident. I was sure that Warne was trying to set me up for a straight ball and the LBW. I kept my front leg out the way and played everything with the bat. The fourth ball was a full toss and I timed it as well as I'd timed anything all summer. It thudded into Katich's leg guards at short leg and went nowhere. I shared a nervous smile with the Aussies fielding around the bat.

I must have lost my focus a little as I threw my hands at the next ball. I thought it was offering me width as it came out of the hand but it ended up passing between bat and off stump. How it missed my off stump I still don't know. I had to check the replay on the big screen to reassure myself that I hadn't been bowled. I met Hoggy in the middle of the pitch and decided that I would block the next ball and get out of this over. We would then take our chances against Lee.

The sixth ball came down. It started straight. Drifted straighter and was full. I didn't really try to hit it, but leant on it and timed it beautifully. It beat the leg of Katich this time and the man at mid-wicket, and made its way almost effortlessly across the outfield. I was sure it was going for four but we made sure we completed the two runs we needed for victory.

In that moment I suddenly noticed everyone in the ground going wild. Before then I hadn't even been aware they were there. I was so focused on the game that as far as I was concerned only Hoggy, myself, Brett Lee and Shane Warne were out there playing our own private game on this wonderful Test ground. Now the noise flooded into my ears. On the balcony my teammates were celebrating madly. I wanted to be with them. As we walked off to a standing ovation I turned to Hoggy and said, "Tonight Hog, we are Kings!" He laughed back at me.

I remember the euphoria in the dressing room and being wrestled to the ground by Steve Harmison as I got through the door.

Downstairs, Mum was crying her eyes out. She had been like that for 20 minutes apparently. I went down and gave her a huge hug. They were tears of relief as much as happiness.

It was an amazing feeling to be there at the end. Almost eight-and-a-half million people watched me hit those winning runs. Just a year earlier, at this same ground, my fortunes had transformed after a chance meeting with Steve Bull. I'd been close to giving up in 2004, I'd reached rock bottom and my career was going nowhere. Now we were 2-1 up in an Ashes series and at the gates of dreamland. The nation was going cricket mad.

22

The Oval

"I've had a really strange dream." Stine's words barely registered as I continued to pack in preparation for our final road trip of the summer. "Did you?" I responded vaguely.

The truth was, 99 per cent of my mind was miles away from this conversation, from my bedroom, from Droitwich Spa. As an individual and as a team we were heading into the most important week of cricket in our lives. Part of me just wanted to get in the car and get down to London to get on with it. Get it over with. The other part of me wanted to hide under the bed until it was all over, to escape the pressure, the anxiety.

"We were all on a bus," Stine continued. At this stage, even with the very little attention I was paying her, it didn't seem a very exciting dream. "Me, you, Anders and Tilly." No stopping her now. "We were all on an open top bus in London."

With her final statement she had got my attention and I stopped packing for a minute. Stine could see I was interested now. "Everybody was waving at us. There were thousands of people shouting and waving at us." "Are you serious?" I said. "Absolutely, why?"

I had heard a rumour that the ECB were discussing the possibility of an open top bus parade through London if we managed to win it. It was a rumour that had stayed in the dressing room and I hadn't shared it with anyone, particularly Stine.

I asked her how she had found out about the ECB's plan, but of course she knew nothing about it. She had just had this dream.

On the way down to London I popped into the Lane 4 headquarters to see Steve Bull, and one of Lane 4's founders Adrian Moorhouse, the former Olympic swimmer. Lane 4 work with mental skills in both sports and business and Bully had spoken to me earlier in the year about doing a couple of workshops alongside him with some corporates. Me relaying my experiences in cricket and Bully putting them into a business context. I really enjoy the mental side of our game and its benefits to me and the teams I have played in. Part of me wished I had rescheduled this appointment though. I couldn't get my mind off this week at The Oval.

We had our meeting and agreed a format for our workshops after the season had finished. I left Lane 4 and headed for the team hotel near Tower Bridge. It was Monday afternoon; 11am Thursday morning seemed an age away.

The joy of Trent Bridge had long receded. Its only meaning was the lead that it now gave us in the series. But considering the way the series had gone, there was likely to be a result in the last Test, unless the weather played a major part. A loss would mean a drawn Ashes series and the Aussies retaining the little urn. We couldn't bank on a draw, and certainly we couldn't play for one. We had to approach this Test as we had done every other one; positively and to win it. Winning at Trent Bridge and Edgbaston would mean nothing if we cocked it up at The Oval.

We had come a long way in those few weeks. We had grown as a team. We had become closer and more confident as a unit. We had a belief now that we could beat this Australian machine. We were almost there. All of us in that team had wanted to be England cricketers. All of us had wanted to be Ashes winners. The last time we had held them I was still at school.

The nation's attention had been captured and the newspapers, radio stations and TV channels were full of cricket. For the last few weeks I had done everything I could to avoid all the media. Edgbaston week had taught me a lesson and since then I had been a good student. I must admit I did have a little look at the back pages the morning after hitting the winning runs at Trent Bridge but otherwise had avoided everything.

Going into the last and most important week of the summer the media attention was like nothing I had ever experienced. Everywhere you turned, Ashes fever had struck. Even the weather forecasts from morning TV were coming from The Oval. I ignored the papers. I turned the TV over when reference was made to it. The radio in the car certainly didn't go on. James Blunt, the music sensation of 2005, had kept me company in the car on long motorway journeys all summer.

I really enjoyed our practice days that week. Somehow I felt more relaxed at the ground. The boys were going through exactly what I was and I felt stronger with them around. Most of us had played a lot of cricket together, but we had become closer during this series. The scraps we had endured and the battles we had won had taught us to respect and appreciate each other more. Everyone had played a part.

For the first time during the series I also managed to spend some valuable time with Merlin, our magnificent leg-spin bowling machine. It pretty much replicated the flight and spin of Shane Warne. Many of the boys had gained a lot from facing it in the nets. He was a big, heavy machine and had his own trailer that carried him around the country.

I had wanted to use him many times before this summer but at every Test venue, after each of the batters had had a few goes, Merlin broke down. He got injured.

So, as I finished most of my preparation on the Tuesday and saw that Merlin was still going strong, in a net on the edge of the square, I seized my opportunity. Andrew Strauss was still in there so I stood and waited. And waited. And waited. In the end I got pretty fed up with hanging around and thought that any minute Merlin would probably break down again. So I shouted down the net towards Straussy "Any danger mate?" Straussy didn't take it very well. But it did the trick and after a couple more balls he wandered out of the net. He didn't say anything but I could tell I might have upset him slightly. We didn't fall out about it. He was just uptight about the Test, as I was. That's why I wanted a proper go with the magical Merlin.

I hadn't had the best run against Warne, and I sensed that with this Test more than any other, I might have an important role in batting out time and scoring valuable runs down the order. From my experience, there are two key things when playing the best spinners in the world. The first is spending time at the crease, which sounds obvious, but the longer you are in, the more time you have to get used to variations in pace, flight, line and so on. The trouble is, the better the spinner, the harder it is to survive. The second thing, and this works hand in hand with the first, is a solid defensive technique against the spinning ball. Having confidence in your ability to defend gives you time. It also reduces the likelihood of playing an aggressive shot out of panic, as a result of the pressure created by men around the bat and the spinning ball. Merlin was a brilliant resource for us, and my only regret is that I didn't get to use it earlier in the series.

Fletch was a brilliant technical batting coach, and he was a great help to me in those days before the match. He explained to me how you extend forward against spin, that it's to do with the positioning of your back foot; rather than the foot being flat on its side, he got me to extend out from the front of the foot, so I could really get out to the ball, and thus the bat could be fully extended beyond the front pad. Facing Merlin, and leaning on Fletch's expertise, gave me a shot of confidence going into the match.

I felt good in the build-up. I was nervous, of course, who wouldn't be? My mind drifted back and forwards constantly, but I tried as much as I could to stay in the moment. The building blocks which had got me through my career would surely get me through, as long as I got my mind in the right place. In fact, I felt as ready as I had in the whole series.

The team meeting that Wednesday evening was a good one. The only worry for us was losing Simon Jones. We had played the same XI for four Tests. More than that, Simon had bowled beautifully, taking five-wicket hauls at Old Trafford and Trent Bridge. He particularly bowled well with the reverse swinging ball. It gave our attack great variation for all conditions.

Vaughany finished the meeting by announcing the team and in his normal composed manner gave us our final pre-Test team talk of the year. He didn't say much. Just that this was what we had all worked so hard for. Not just this year, but all our professional careers. And as usual he finished with "Enjoy it, lads".

Paul Collingwood came in for Simon and no-one in the team had any worries about his selection. Paul had been around the England set-up for years. He had played Test cricket and loads of ODIs. We all knew that in tough situations Colly would always be up for it.

He could play as well. We also knew he could bowl a few overs if required but the overs weren't a problem for us. As a bowling attack any one of us would have bowled all day to get us through that match.

This was it now. No going back.

The Oval, September 8, 2005. It was busy, very busy. The atmosphere carried us through the warm-ups and before we knew it the coin was going up for the toss. Vaughany won it and remembered his lines. We were to bat first. Time for the talk to stop.

The wicket was a good one, a typical Oval Test wicket. It had good pace and tennis ball bounce. Winning the toss was a perfect start. We knew we had to capitalise and get a big first innings score. We could bat for five days if we wanted to.

Try as we might to ignore it, everyone also had an eye on the weather. The forecast wasn't great for London that week. It may have crossed my mind that it wouldn't be too bad if a monsoon struck London for those five days.

As Straussy and Tres walked out on that Thursday, Jerusalem playing over the loudspeaker, the weather was set fair. Every one of us found our seats, sat down, and prayed for a strong start. We got it.

After our lefties powered us to 82 in quick time, back came the Australians again. Or, more precisely, back came Warne. In the eighteenth over of the day the man did his thing, having Trescothick well caught by Hayden at slip. The dressing room went quiet for a while. And it was about to get quieter.

We thought we'd managed to survive Warne this series, and that he couldn't possibly surprise us anymore. Well, bang on cue, he set about the most awesome piece of bowling on a good first day pitch that I have ever seen from a spin bowler.

Warne's spell took our feet from under us. With Trescothick, Vaughan, Bell and Pietersen in the shed and all falling to him, we were suddenly 131-4. At this rate just batting out the first day would be a good effort.

Straussy and Fred set about steadying things, but we never really relaxed again in that dressing room for the rest of that day. We knew it wasn't going to be an easy ride. Warnie had reminded us of that. He had our full attention now.

Fred had been a star this summer. He'd had success with bat and ball against the best team in the world and he now carried a reputation as the best all-rounder in the game. He did it again for us here, making 72 in a stand of 143 with Strauss.

Not long after Straussy got to a fabulous hundred, Warne picked him up too, his fifth of the day. I passed Straussy on the steps, the crowd having risen as one to acclaim his knock. But there was also huge applause for Warne and his fifth wicket; all game, it was that kind of atmosphere.

I kept my head down and got out to the middle. I wasn't trying to hide away but I just wanted to ignore what was going on around me. The applause, the singing, the Aussies. I just needed to focus on the ball. I went out with the idea of just batting balls for the first period. One ball at a time and nothing too expansive. I figured that there was certainly no hurry. The Aussies had attacking fields and I would pick up some runs along the way. The longer I batted the more time was taken out of the game. I knew also that the longer I batted the easier it would get out in the middle. Everyone who had had some success against Warne that summer said that time against him had made a massive difference. Both in being able to read his variations and picking his flight. So far I hadn't managed much time against Warne, let alone runs. So that was my aim.

By the close of day one I had managed to survive. We were 319-7 and I was 5 not out.

At Trent Bridge I'd got into a fantastic mental state to bat. At The Oval I'd managed it again. My aim on the second morning was to get back to that place. I focused on the process, on playing one ball at a time. Not on what had happened the previous ball, nor what was going to happen the next ball – the unplayable delivery, the quick bouncer. Just one ball at a time.

After Geraint went early with the score on 325, Hoggy, my partner at Trent Bridge, joined me and played in typically stubborn style. We kept the Aussies out, kept the board ticking, and used up overs, batting together for more than 10 overs. It might seem negative to be thinking about time out of the game, but it gave us a focus. After Hoggy went, Harmy came in and made it look easy, scoring 20 at a run a ball. We got us up to 373 before I was given out LBW to Warne, a shocking decision! I was out for 32 and had batted for two hours. I'd done my bit.

Langer and Hayden had struggled all series to put together a meaningful partnership. They have one of the best records in history as an opening pair but we had restricted them across four Tests to a best of 56. Well, that day they were back at their best.

They cruised past the century partnership, with Langer playing me more positively than he had done before, hitting me for two sixes in my first over and outscoring Hayden with ease. Then, unbelievably, the Aussies were offered the light and they took it. Rain had been forecast for later in the day and during the afternoon the cloud level had dropped over The Oval. With it the light also worsened, but not to an unplayable level as far we were concerned. We were amazed, but we didn't need to be out there, so got off the pitch as quick as we could.

The Australians were 112-0 and looking comfortable. There was plenty of time left in the game but the forecast wasn't great and we just thought they would take every opportunity that came their way to be out there. We didn't get back on for the rest of that second day. We were 251 runs ahead and three days of cricket away from winning the Ashes. It was almost impossible to sleep. Scenario after scenario went through my mind. I'd have felt better just staying all night at the ground.

The first session of day three was interrupted by rain. The Australians only managed to add 45 runs. After the interval Langer got to his hundred and the Aussies seemed to cruise to 185-0. We had bowled well and had some good shouts for LBWs but nothing had come our way. We needed a breakthrough and thankfully Harmy got us one by dismissing Langer for 105. After the wicket the rain came again and we took an early tea. After tea I had Ponting caught at silly point but Billy Bowden gave it not out. He owed me two now in my eyes after giving me out LBW to a ball that probably wouldn't have hit a fifth stump, and now giving the Australian captain not out. I wasn't happy. We were desperate to stem the flow.

Fred got Ponting for 35 in the end, but by then Hayden had passed the hundred mark. The Aussies finished the day on 277-2 with Hayden and Damien Martyn at the crease. We still had a lead of 96 runs. Just two days left. Two days from the Ashes. Two days, we knew, was a long time against this Australian team. The monsoon hadn't come and we would have to do it the hard way. We all convinced ourselves it would be better that way. To leave no doubts about how we would win these Ashes back.

If Fred had performed well in the game so far he was about to take it to a different level on the Sunday. The man bowled unchanged for 18 overs from the Pavilion End, only the close of the Australian innings bringing his efforts to an end. He finished with 5-78, figures that still didn't seem to do that spell justice. At the other end Hoggy was rewarded for his hard work throughout the series and finished with 4-97.

The light on that fourth day had been bad again at times, even as a fielder it was difficult, but this time the Aussies stayed on. They'd needed to push on, but Fred and Hoggy held them at bay. Brett Lee was the last man out to give Hoggy his fourth. I took the catch in front of an ecstatic Oval crowd and ran my way along the boundary geeing the locals up even more.

Somehow we had taken a six-run lead into our second innings, when at one stage we were staring at a heavy deficit. The day belonged to Fred, his five-wicket haul being a monumental effort, and all we had to do now was bat, and bat and bat. Not for the first time in the series we had fought back. Fred had led that charge with a look in his eye, not necessarily of a man possessed, but of total focus and determination. With about a day and a half remaining there was plenty of work still to do, but Fred's effort stirred us all for one final push.

With the clouds closing in on The Oval, we started our second innings. Everyone sat on the balcony. It was quiet, focused. We all prayed for an easy ride. But we knew it wouldn't be that way. In our fourth over, Warne had Strauss caught at bat-pad off a ball that exploded from the rough. With that moment, any thoughts of an easy ride home disappeared.

The weather and bad light did come to our aid, as we went off and on a couple of times. Even in such a tight situation, the Aussies made light of the moment and all donned sunglasses during one short spell of bad light. At the end of day four we finished 34-1.

That evening, eight of us went out to dinner with our wives. Nothing fancy, just Pizza Express. It was good to be with my teammates. As I looked up and down the table I felt proud of every one of them. We had been through one hell of a summer and worked our bollocks off to get into this position. We deserved to win this series now. But we still had to negotiate one more day. All of us drifted off in our own thoughts at one time or another over dinner. I thought of how many we needed to be safe. How long we needed to bat for. Would I be required? I hoped not. Tomorrow we could win the Ashes. How am I supposed to get to sleep?

On our walk back across Tower Bridge Stine told me that she and the kids were staying down to watch the final day. The kids had school but I knew they would understand, considering the circumstances. I still resisted it at first because I just thought it would be tempting fate to change plans at this late stage. Resistance was futile, however. Stine said they were staying. We would all be together.

29

September 12, 2005

I had at least managed to get some sleep. It hadn't been quality, but that was nothing new. I got dressed while the family stayed in bed. The kids looked so peaceful. They didn't have a care in the world. They'd actually managed to get a day off school. They didn't have a clue what lay before their father that day. I'd prepared for this moment since I was close to Anders' age, and he was just five years old. My whole journey through life and cricket had led me to this point. How could so much depend on this one day? I knew that the next time I would come back to this room it would be decided. It was difficult to comprehend that so much depended on the next few hours. Eventually I said my goodbyes, took a deep breath and shut the door behind me. No going back now. "Just relax, come on, just relax," I remember saying to myself.

Breakfast was a quiet affair. I knew everyone must be feeling the same way as I did, but we didn't talk about it. We were all tense, but particularly our batters. They had the bulk of the work to do today. If one of them got a big score we would surely be safe. I hoped again that it would be an easy ride and I wouldn't have to bat, but we had a habit of making these situations difficult.

The crowds flocked to the ground and many were there before we were. The weather was set fair; no more help from the gods. We would have to do this ourselves.

Before we started warm-ups we got together as a team. Fletch led proceedings, and he was visibly nervous. His voice was a little broken. In all the years I had played under Fletch I had never seen him like this. He was rock solid as a man and kept his emotions very much on a level in good and bad situations. If anything this actually relaxed me a little. Seeing Fletch so nervous made how I felt just seem normal. I don't remember anything he said. I was wrapped up in my own thoughts and already thinking about how I would bat if required.

I remember having a good net and some throw-downs with Phil Neale. I felt good about my batting, particularly after my runs in the first innings. I also felt that I still had more to do in this match.

Everything, for a while, looked fine. We started solidly. I briefly wondered if perhaps I wouldn't be needed after all. That feeling lasted no more than 45 minutes.

Glenn McGrath had endured an up-and-down series, missing those Tests at Edgbaston and Trent Bridge, and had looked under par so far. But the champion, on his last day of Test cricket in England, would still have his say, producing a good one to Michael Vaughan, who nicked behind to Adam Gilchrist. Vaughany had played well for his 45 but we were now 67-2.

Next ball, Ian Bell's first, was again on the button. Belly nicked it to Warne at slip, and it meant a pair in the match for the youngest member of our team. England 67-3. McGrath had produced a bit of magic and all the dressing room went quiet. Enter Kevin Pietersen.

If nerves were jangling after McGrath's double, the next ball caused time to stand still all around the ground. A well-directed bouncer from McGrath clipped Kev's shoulder and the ball was caught behind the stumps. From the viewing area you couldn't tell with the naked eye whether Kev had gloved it or not and the Aussies appealed ferociously. Fortunately Billy Bowden gave it not out, the correct decision, and we could all breathe again. In the next over, bowled by Warne, KP survived another sharp chance when he nicked a ball that turned, and a deflection off Gilchrist took it away from Hayden at slip. Not long before lunch, one of the biggest moments of the series happened as Kev drove and nicked a ball from Brett Lee that headed, at head height straight to Warne at slip. Warne was a terrific slip fielder and had a great pair of hands.

Almost in slow motion the moment unfolded in front of us. The ball went in... and came out... and fell to the floor.

At this point, I just couldn't watch any more. I just couldn't take it. I'm normally a big watcher when we are batting. Some of the lads like to sit inside the dressing room and read or listen to music. Some manage to get some shut eye but I always like to be out in the viewing area watching the game live. Today was different. Every ball seemed to be taking more and more out of me physically and mentally, and I wasn't even batting. I had to get away, and Hoggy felt the same. We went out the back into the players' dining room with a pack of cards. I never play cards at cricket. I never really play cards, full stop. But I needed a distraction. There were no TVs in the dining room and the only contact we had with the game was the crowd noise. That was plenty bad enough.

What we couldn't know from our position was that Kev had decided to go on the attack. After the Warne drop and a couple of near misses Kev had wandered down to Tres and told him that he had had enough of blocking it and would whack it instead.

Soon after, Tres got trapped on the crease by Warne for 33. Someone came and told us in the dining room. I can't remember who it was but I asked them to tell me if – OK, when – we lost another. I would need to start getting ready to bat.

After a short period the door opened again. We had already guessed from the noise of the crowd. Fred was out. Caught and bowled by Warne. I got up and moved back into the dressing room to put on my box, thigh pad and whites. Colly had gone out to join Kev, Geraint Jones was next in and I was due to follow him. I passed Freddie who was sitting in his seat with his pads still on. He looked devastated. I felt so much for him. Fred had been through the ringer, and done everything for us on the field the previous day to bowl Australia out. That stuff with me is important. Seeing him there, it brought it into focus that we couldn't let this fucking day get away from us.

I felt cold and was shaking a little from nerves. They weren't unusual sensations, but this was different. We might never get another opportunity like this in our lives. Surely we couldn't throw it away. But the game and the Ashes were slipping through our fingers. Kev and Paul Collingwood managed to get us to lunch without losing another wicket: 127-5, a lead of just 133, and plenty of overs left in the day.

I didn't eat much at lunch. I just felt sick. I kept wandering through the dressing room, picking up my bat occasionally and practising a few straight bat shots and a couple of leaves as I watched the clock tick slowly through the lunch break. Only two sessions left now.

I'd missed Kev's onslaught before lunch but I was now sat with all my pads on in the coaches' office. At the Pavilion End, as Brett Lee ran in faster and faster and bowled quicker and quicker, Kev took everything on. It was incredible. A man in his fifth Test match, under this amount of pressure, standing up to the Aussies and coming back at them.

It must have been fantastic for the crowd to watch, though not so fantastic if you are waiting to come in. Don't get me wrong, it was the right thing to do; we had to keep scoring runs and not just try to survive. But my heart seemed to be constantly in my mouth.

At the other end Paul Collingwood was justifying his selection by acting as the perfect foil for Kev's aggression. He played solidly and ate up valuable time and overs out of the day. The two of them put on 60 of which Colly made 10 from 51 deliveries, but he had done more than a decent job when Warne eventually got the better of him. We were 186-6 when Jones joined Kev.

I was still sat in the coaches' office with the door open so I could see the cricket from my chair. I was still shaking and just hoped that it would stop when another wicket fell. Nigel Stockhill, our fitness man, came in and asked if I needed anything. I asked for water. When he returned I asked Nigel to sit with me for a while and have a chat.

"What about?" he asked. "Anything," I said. "How's the missus?" I knew Nigel had just started a new relationship, and anything would do.

We didn't get that long. With the score at 199 we lost Geraint. Bowled by Tait. Seven wickets down, a lead of 205, and more than 55 overs still to be played. We knew the Aussies would, and could, chase almost anything. We had to get a few more yet or at least take a lot more time out of the game.

In the office I put on my gloves and helmet. I didn't want to be fumbling with my equipment when I was on my way down the steps. The closer I got to the middle the more I got my 'cricket head' on. Tait was bowling quickly. From the screens up in the dressing room I could see the ball was reversing slightly. I had to keep my front pad out of the way to avoid LBWs and look to play straight. Anything wide I would leave. Anything short I would look to get under. Generally I would try and get into a good position early, line it up and keep my weight going forward. The skiddy straight ball was the danger ball.

To Warne I certainly wouldn't sweep. I would look to keep my front pad out of the way to straight balls and play with my bat, take my time to get in and watch the ball harder than I'd ever watched it before. I would play the line and if it turned, hold that line and not follow the ball. If I got a good one, then so be it. But I wouldn't get myself out.

Kev came and greeted me. I was OK now. I just wanted to get the first ball out of the way. Get into it. After a couple of overs we decided to start breaking the innings down into balls first, and then overs. With each delivery that passed we encouraged each other to do another one.

"Brilliant Kev, keep going Kev," I would shout down the other end.

"Great work, George," Kev would shout after every ball I survived. George was a reference to George Clooney, who wasn't someone I'd often been compared to, but the lads were ribbing me one day in the dressing room about my grey hair, so I just said that it was the 'in thing', the George Clooney look. It stuck with Kev, and every ball he now reminded me about it.

The Aussies were loud and confident, convinced they would roll us over soon and chase down whatever was set. They threw absolutely everything at us. Warne bowled beautifully. Lee bowled the speed of light. We survived. And with it, our confidence in the situation grew. We started to count down bigger blocks of deliveries. We went from six balls to 12, to 18 to 24. Four overs at a time.

Meanwhile Kev continued along on his extraordinary way, and I'd be watching him play shots that we're basically superhuman. The way he just pushed forward and gently stroked the world's greatest leg spinner of all time back over his head for six with hardly any effort. Or the ball that he pulled flat off Lee at 96mph to the longest part of the ground. I simply had the best seat in the house for the greatest Ashes innings of all time.

Afterwards people asked me a lot, 'When did you know you had done it, when did you realise you had won the Ashes?'. The truth is, I probably didn't really comprehend it until just before I got out. I was doing the sums in my head as we went along, the lead we had against how many overs were left. Even when it got ridiculous, up above 10 an over, I wouldn't discount the Aussies. I had got in such a zone while I was batting with Kev that I shut any thoughts of getting bowled out, and the Aussies batting again, out of my head.

It was great being there with Kev when he got his hundred. That one partnership will go with me to my grave and I will always feel a special bond to Kev because of it. He was eventually out for 158 from 187 balls. He received the most amazing ovation and a personal and touching send-off from Shane Warne. After the show, Hoggy strolled out to join me and helped me along to my fifty.

Brett Lee continued to tear in with the second new ball. The light deteriorated slightly and I got into the umpires' ears about getting us off. It didn't work. It now started to dawn on me that we had actually done it. I wanted to stay out there and keep batting until the end but I also wanted to get up to the dressing room and my mates. That's when I guess my concentration slipped and I got out. Bowled round my legs by Warne for 59. I was gutted to get out and started to make my way off with my head down. Halfway off I had a look up and noticed that everyone was standing for me. It was amazing. I thought I'd better make the most of it and slowed down a little. The closer I got to the dressing room the bigger I felt my grin get. At the top of the steps my teammates waited for me. Fred was one of the first to give me a huge bear hug, followed by Kev. It was great to see everyone smiling again after how the dressing room looked earlier in the day. I just felt wonderful.

Harmy was out soon after to give Warne his second six-wicket haul of the game and as a team we prepared excitedly to go out to field one last time in this Ashes series. We all wore our blue England caps as we made our way out for one last huddle. For every one of those four balls we were out in the middle for, we all just smiled at each other. Almost in disbelief that we'd actually done it. After the fourth ball the light was offered and the Aussies took it. It was basically over. Not officially, that happened about 20 minutes later when the umpires returned to the middle, decided the light would not improve and removed the bails.

As players and management we got into a circle and cheered and jumped with joy together. I always imagined I might cry at this moment, but didn't, I was too happy. It was over, we had done it. All our boyhood dreams had been realised. The toughest and possibly greatest series of all time was over.

We made our way down the steps one more time to be presented as Ashes winners. We did a lap of honour and almost drowned ourselves in champagne. The crowd was amazing, and among them were Mum, Dad, Stine, Anders and Tilly. They had been through hell that summer with me, it was beautiful that we could all be there together.

Between us 12 boys who played that wonderful summer, a bond had developed that will stay with us forever. It had taken everything we had, mentally and physically, and at times I bet we all thought we couldn't take any more.

What got us through? Each other is my answer. Because when it gets tough, real tough, when you think you have nothing left to give, if you are playing for that man next to you, if you are playing for your mates, you find that little bit extra, you bowl that extra over, you bat that hour longer. You don't let your mates down.

Don't get me wrong. We also won that magical series because we had some excellent cricketers and played some brilliant cricket. But it was the whole and not the individual that got us across the line.

Then, as you might recall, we had a little drink.

30

The day after the 20 years before

When the laps of honour, the champagne spraying and all the media had finished, the celebrations could really begin. Although we'd wasted a lot of bubbly on the Oval outfield there was still plenty in the dressing room to go around. More arrived by the minute from well-wishers and supporters, some by the case load. Straussy broke open a box of Cuban cigars he had been given and one by one we all coughed and spluttered as we lit up and inhaled too much of it.

Once the cameras had left the dressing room we were asked for just five minutes of calm and quiet while the plans for the following day were given to us. I'd almost forgotten, amongst everything else that was going on, about the 'open top bus ride' that was being planned. David Clarke from the ECB ran us through proceedings and it all sounded very exciting. The families would be with us on the bus as well.

Afterwards we wandered around the dressing room, a drink in one hand and cigar in the other. We laughed and smiled and hugged each other and the underlying theme was that none of us could believe that we'd actually done it. The series, at times, had felt as though it would never end. I was the first to come clean and say that I hadn't slept well for weeks. One by one, almost to a man, everyone said the same. It's strange that this was the first time we'd talked about it. We had all just got on with it.

Most of the Aussies came in for a beer and congratulated us. It was great to be able to talk about what was probably the greatest ever Ashes series with the guys you had been battling with for the past few weeks.

We also wandered into their dressing room for a chat. I managed to get my head clear enough to remember that I had been awarded a testimonial the following year. I'd had 24 small bats sent to The Oval, 12 to be signed by us and 12 by Australia. Boxed up and framed they looked magnificent and I still have one today that I will keep forever. They made good auction items during my year.

Eventually, at about 10.30pm we left The Oval for the last time. Outside the ground some supporters still waited for us for pictures and autographs. They would have been lucky if the signatures were still legible when they got their little bits of history home. We'd all had a few, but the night was still young.

Back at the hotel we agreed that we would have a quick change and meet back in the lobby. A club had been lined up by Kev.

In our room the kids were already in bed and asleep. Stine was out with the rest of the girls and a babysitter was watching Anders and Tilly. I remembered leaving this room that morning with such different feelings. Joy and happiness had replaced fear and worry.

We made it to the nightclub and were treated like heroes. It was busy and loud. It wasn't the sort of place we could chat easily and we kept losing each other. I just wanted to be with my teammates and enjoy what we'd done together. We obviously attracted a lot of attention from people who just wanted to talk to us. We appreciated the support, and the drinks, of course. But I just wanted to have a drink with my mates, the mates who had got me through this summer.

I stuck it out until about 3am and got a car back to the hotel with Tres. Outside there were loads of cameras. I was a bit drunk but more emotionally shattered as I made my way back to the room. I crept in and the kids were fast asleep. Stine also seemed to be. I went over to the bed the kids were sharing. I bent over them and kissed both of them.

"We did it kids, we did it, we won the Ashes." The drink must have started taking effect.

I kissed them both again and told them I loved them. Stine woke and rolled over.

"What you doing, you'll wake them up," she said.

She wasn't angry. She was smiling. She could see I was a bit drunk. She wouldn't have expected anything else, but Stine didn't really need me waking the kids in the middle of the night.

"We did it," I said to Stine.

"I know you did. I love you. Now come to bed."

I must have been asleep shortly after hitting the pillow. I hoped to get my best night's sleep in weeks.

About three hours later I was awake again. For a change it wasn't the worries of the cricket that woke me. I also felt amazingly fresh considering I'd had such little sleep and so much alcohol. The adrenaline was still pumping through my veins. I didn't want to go back to sleep. I was afraid that if I did I might oversleep and miss the bus ride and our big day out in London. The rest of the family were still asleep and so I made every effort to wake them and get them out of bed and dressed.

In my head I kept saying the same words over and over. "We've done it…we have actually done it." Stine was not best impressed when she realised what the time was. "Go back to sleep," she said with her eyes still closed.

"I can't! Come on, we need to get up and have breakfast. We don't want to be late for the bus."

Eventually, probably about 7am, Stine had enough of my nagging and got up. The kids had started to wake and we began the process of getting showered, bathed and dressed. I was just so excited I felt like a little boy again, wanting to go and see my mates.

We were close to being first down for breakfast. Gradually more of the boys and the wives joined us. It was obvious that everyone was just so happy and excited about the day. There were newspapers everywhere, and we were all over them. Front pages, back pages, middle pages, everywhere.

There were a couple of obvious candidates missing at breakfast. I then remembered that when I'd woken up earlier and put the TV on, I was a bit surprised to see a live BBC report coming from the reception of our hotel. The reporter talked a lot about Andrew Flintoff and Steve Harmison. They hadn't come to the nightclub with the rest of us. The reporter went on to say that Fred and Harmy had spent most of the night in the hotel bar, and that they might even still be in there!

Apparently they had only just gone up when we arrived at breakfast. We all knew that Fred would be in a right state. Fred could drink as much as the best of them but he never hid it particularly well the following day. But if anyone deserved it, he did. He'd had a fantastic summer and put in performance after performance for the team at crucial times. He had worked damn hard for that night on the booze.

Later that morning we all met in reception ready to get on the coach to take us to Mansion House where, after a reception, we would get on the open top bus.

Fred was last to appear out of the hotel doors and onto the coach. He was still pissed. He hadn't got to the hangover stage yet as most of us had. Fred's wife Rachael had a tough job getting him dressed and out of the room that morning. He looked unsteady on his feet as he came up the coach steps. He had a quite brilliant, Cheshire cat grin across his face.

There were a lot of people outside the hotel that Tuesday morning. Mostly city workers just coming to have a look and take pictures on their phones. Lots of press guys were there also. Some had made it inside the hotel lobby to do interviews, others waited outside for pictures of the team and particularly of Fred as rumours of his all-night antics had spread pretty quickly.

The coach took us on the short trip to Mansion House. We enjoyed our first glass of bubbly of the day with each other and representatives of the city. I remember chewing on the first glass a bit but by the time I had finished my second the bubbles had started to settle my hangover.

The reception at Mansion House was fine but we were all in a pretty shabby state, we just wanted to get on the bus with our families, have a laugh and enjoy the day with some more bubbly.

We had talked about the open top bus ride earlier that morning and we all wondered how many people might turn out to greet us. None of us expected very many. A few old ladies and a couple of dogs, we thought.

As we turned up Victoria Street towards Trafalgar Square, enjoying another toast to the Ashes and patting each other on the back one more time, we couldn't believe the scenes that greeted us on the streets. The crowds were probably five deep on either side of the road. Others were hanging out of their office windows and taking pictures. We were amazed. Straussy and I just turned from the scenes towards each other and grinned and giggled like little boys. Anders and Tilly just sat and stared at the people. Tilly could only just see over the side of the open top. We had never done an open top sight-seeing tour of London as a family before, and this wasn't a bad way to start.

We sat about halfway down the bus on the left hand side as it moved along. The Strausses were in front of us. Occasionally I would get up and have a wander, look out of the other side and wave a bit, or go and get some more bubbly. Up front, Fred, Kev and Vaughany stood. It was a miracle actually that Fred was still able to stand. Gary Pratt, our supersub fielder, was also up front and I think spent most of his time holding Fred up. Kev stood tall, big hair with a white stripe and took the applause he deserved for such an amazing innings the day before.

Vaughany was calm, maybe a little pissed, and waving at the crowds. Vaughany had got most of us on that bus through the summer, Fred and Kev included. He had grown into a fantastic captain. Tactically he had always been ahead of the game in 2005 and his man-management skills were just superb. Every one of us that summer had struggled mentally or physically to get through the series at some point. After Lord's particularly, when we had all struggled and I'd had my run-in with the media, Vaughany had settled the ship and got us re-focused and, more importantly, positive before Edgbaston.

At times he had struggled with his own game, but he never let it show. He just got his head down and worked harder in the nets. He never changed in the dressing room. All he asked of us as a team was that we gave everything to what we did that summer. We would all make mistakes, play shit shots or bowl bad balls, but so long as we learned from them and didn't make the same mistake twice Vaughany didn't have a problem. Michael is a fantastic communicator and very rarely flies off the handle and even when he does give you a bit of a bollocking, he almost makes you feel good about it! His leadership was one of the standout factors of that summer. His even temperament and laid-back manner, at least on the outside, was a great foil for the rollercoaster of emotions that the rest of us seemed to be going through.

I think as a leader there was always a bit of the thespian in him. The best leaders have a go-to style, and Vaughany's was open, expressive, attacking, and about having a laugh. But he was so much more than that when he had to be. That whole thing about what style of leader you are – that's not really the right question. That leads people to think there's a fixed position of leadership. The reality is that you've got to be able to adapt, depending on what's in front of you. You've got to be whatever the room needs, and all summer he read that room beautifully.

The other key was his relationship with Duncan. The two of them communicated very well. They didn't always agree but you wouldn't expect them to. Outwardly they were always united, and, more importantly, massively supportive of everyone in that dressing room.

Duncan kept a pretty low profile on that bus ride. Never far from his lovely wife Marina and, as always, immaculately turned out. He stood proud of his team. For once he forgave us our shabby, drunken appearance. We were all in our team uniform, but most of us had seen better days. In the past our ties might have been straighter and our shirts less creased but Fletch knew as well as anyone how hard the summer had been and enjoyed our celebrations with us.

There's two sides to Fletch. There's the very old-school 'respect' side – even down to how you address your elders. But then there was this other side, which people rarely saw, which was someone with a very dry, funny sense of humour, who was really fun to be around and to share a glass of something with. He rarely revealed that side, but when he did, as on that day, you could see that he really enjoyed the guys in those moments.

A great strength of both Vaughan and Fletcher was how they managed to keep their emotions so level through good and bad times. When we lost they wouldn't curse and go off at us, they would debrief, re-plan and re-focus. When we won, likewise, they wouldn't start doing cartwheels around the dressing room and be bigging up our egos, they would look ahead to how we could still improve and find a new challenge. Fletch was technically brilliant as a coach and will always remain a student of the game, looking for new ways to improve and make the game slicker. Vaughan and Fletcher were the true driving force behind that summer.

If we were shocked by the numbers lining the streets, we were all totally speechless as we entered Trafalgar Square. It was just a mass of people. There didn't appear to be even an inch of free space. A stage had been erected in front of the National Gallery and we pulled up behind it on the bus. Tilly had fallen asleep, which was quite amazing considering the noise. We made our way down the steps of the bus and waited to be announced. By this point I was gagging to go to the toilet and couldn't wait any longer. There wasn't a toilet on the bus but our team coach had made its way ahead of us to Trafalgar, ready to take us to Downing Street, and I made a dash for it. The introductions started. In batting order I heard each of the names before me in the line-up announced. The announcer got to my name and I was still in the toilet. I thought I'd missed my big moment. I still got a great cheer but I wasn't there. I was still in the loo.

When I finished I dashed out and onto the stage to join my mates. I got another great reception and waved at the crowd. Near the front was the unmistakable colour of the Spanish flag, with 'Gilo is our King' written across it. It was brilliant.

We all did interviews with David Gower and at the end had a good sing-a-long. As we stood in a line, arms around shoulders, Hoggy turned to me and said it was 'Band of Brothers' sort of stuff. Those scenes that day will stay with me for the rest of my life. I turned and saw Stine and the kids on the bus, Tilly was awake again now. Both Anders and she looked a little frightened by the numbers of people and the noise.

After just one more rendition of Jerusalem we were cheered off the stage. We all said our goodbyes to our families. As we headed for Downing Street to meet the Prime Minister the families would be taken to a private reception for lunch before returning to the hotel. Stine had already told me that she would go home that afternoon with the kids. As a team we still had a long day ahead of us. After Downing Street we would be heading to Lord's for another reception and Stine had given me her blessing to go out and celebrate again with the team. She knew what this meant to all of us. I told her as I left that I would see her before the end of the week!

As we arrived at Downing Street we faced our biggest setback of the day. No alcohol.

After a few words the situation was sorted out. After all we couldn't stop drinking now. The hangovers would start kicking in again and most of us would be asleep before we even reached Lord's!

Tony Blair came out and had a chat with everyone. Cherie wandered around and spent some time talking to Kev behind me. I was impressed with him until she left and he turned to me and said, "Who was that?"

Now, I don't honestly know whether or not the reports that someone was sick in the Downing Street gardens were true. Fred was an obvious suspect but, surprisingly to me, the following day in the papers so was I. Well, I can confirm that it wasn't me and I would be very surprised if it was Fred. I've seen him drink incredible amounts of alcohol in the past and not throw up. He spent most of his time sitting in the corner of the garden on the Blair children's swings minding his own business and talking to Harmy.

As the time came to leave Downing Street we all filed outside for the moment Blair had invited us for, his photo opportunity. As we all shuffled out onto the pavement, across the road there must have stood 30 cameramen. Tony Blair stood in front of me. As if to try and be funny, or simply make conversation, he said, "Well I wonder what this lot want?" As quick as anything and clear for all to hear Matthew Hoggard responded. "A photo, knobhead!"

That was our cue to leave Downing Street before we got thrown out, and we headed for Lord's.

When we arrived we walked across the outfield towards the Pavilion. This had been the scene of our humiliation in the first Test. Now we were Ashes champions.

The reception in the Long Room involved the official handover of the little Ashes urn back to the MCC from the England captain. Of course the urn never really left Lord's because it is too fragile. The reception also involved more champagne and small talk with MCC hierarchy.

"How do you feel?" some would ask.

We felt like replying, "Well, how do you think? Yesterday we won the Ashes and we've basically been on the piss since!" But generally I settled for "Over the moon."

From Lord's, we headed back to the Grange Hotel. On the coach Freddie finally gave in, or his body did anyway. He fell unconscious on the back seat. His best mate, Harmy, who was pretty pissed like the rest of us, saw his opportunity. Fred likes to be a prankster in the dressing room and loves to take the piss out of everyone. Armed with a black marker pen Harmy set about writing all sorts across Fred's face. He finished with TWAT right across his forehead. As we got close to the hotel we woke Fred up but were horrified to see the large numbers of cameramen waiting for us. Fred didn't have a clue what was going on. He was completely out of it. Harmy got Fred under his arm, head down, and smuggled him into the hotel and up to his room.

We agreed as we got in the lift that we would meet in the bar downstairs after a quick shower and change. But as I got into my room I realised how exhausted I was. The room was quiet and empty without Stine and the kids in it. It was the first time that day that I'd experienced this sort of peace. The bed looked incredibly inviting. As I undressed out of my England blazer and tie I became unsure of what move to make next. I had two options. To get into bed and sleep, which is what my body needed, or get in the shower, get dressed and go downstairs to the bar. I thought about bed briefly, but shower it was. After all, you don't win the Ashes every day. Stine had given me her blessing as well, so the bar it was. I had to be at Edgbaston the following night with Belly for some press work but I would be able to have a lie-in and work my way up slowly to Edgbaston after lunch.

Most of us made it down to the bar. Not surprisingly Fred and Harmy didn't. It was a quiet affair for the first half hour or so, until the alcohol started to take effect again and we all got what was probably our fourth or fifth wind. We had some bar snacks and then decided as the hotel was pretty quiet to get out and have a drink at somewhere with a bit of atmosphere. I don't remember what the first bar we went to was called. A couple of the Aussie boys were in there and they chatted and joked with us at the bar.

As a group we were instantly recognisable from the scenes in London and on the telly earlier that day. Everyone wanted to know where Freddie was and whether or not he was still drinking.

Later in the evening we decided we would go off to a nightclub. Someone got our names on the door at Boujis, which actually wasn't very difficult because I think anyone would have had us that night, and we enjoyed free drinks in the VIP area.

We were joined by some guys we'd never met before and continued to drink as the clock past midnight. Ben Goldsmith and James Rothschild were two of the guys that joined us. We had a great time and I still keep in touch with those lads today, and they both helped me out a lot in my benefit year.

When I actually took notice, I realised that all our lads had gone home apart from me and KP. We stayed a little longer and were introduced to Mickey Rourke. We must have looked a right state at that point.

It was about 3am by the time we left. I was helped up the steps and onto the street because I was just so 'tired'. As we got onto the pavement we were greeted by hundreds of camera flashes. It was difficult to see where we were heading as we dived towards and into our waiting car, blinded by the lights. The following day the *Evening Standard* published a full-page photo of me and Kev coming out of the club with the headline ASHES STARS STILL UNDECLARED AFTER 32 HOUR PARTY. Not bad.

I don't remember getting to bed. I woke about 8:30am with my clothes still on and my mobile phone ringing, wishing that I'd remembered to turn it off. It was Radio West Midlands. My throat was dry and I struggled to speak at first. They of course wanted to know 'how it felt' to win the Ashes and what the celebrations were like. The chat then moved on to Freddie and I was asked if I thought it set a bad example to children. I palmed it off and explained again what a tough summer it had been and that Freddie deserved to have that one big night on the drink for how he had performed for England. I didn't really have a leg to stand on anyway as I'd only got in just a few hours earlier after almost 32 hours on the booze. Fred had been tucked up fast asleep when KP and I got in that morning.

My head actually felt OK. I just felt so happy. The adrenaline must have still been flowing. We hadn't held the Ashes since I was in my early teens. It was a fantastic feeling and for one of the only times in my career I sat back and felt proud of myself. I couldn't get the smile off my face.

After a late breakfast and half a ton of coffee I started my way back up to the Midlands. I'd had loads of messages and took the time in the car to ring a few people back. I made one particular phone call of thanks to someone that, although they didn't stand on that stage with us at Trafalgar Square, had played a huge role in England winning those Ashes. I dialled Nasser Hussain. He didn't answer. I left a message to say thank you and well done for the part he'd played in this success. His partnership with Fletcher had started to turn things around for the England cricket team. I thought it important he get some praise. I know that one other person rang Nasser that day. It was Duncan Fletcher.

Back at Edgbaston, introduced to the crowd by Charles Colvile, I was still grinning stupidly. I couldn't help it. After I'd completed my media commitments I headed up to a friend's box to watch the game and enjoy a glass of red wine with Stine who had come to join me at Edgbaston. As the long night game came to an end, so did my resistance. I hit the wall big time. Stine drove me home and I slept like a log. It had been the most amazing week of twists and turns, highs, lows and not to mention quite a few bottles of bubbly. And it ended with us achieving a dream.

31

The hips don't lie

By the middle of the Ashes series my right hip was starting to feel heavy and 'full' again. There was no way I wasn't going to get through the Ashes series, of course, but once the dust had settled, it was decided that we needed to be more proactive in terms of treatment on my hip ahead of the Pakistan tour, starting late October.

It was agreed that I would receive an injection in my hip to try to resolve the issue. This took place in Oxford. I was given a sedative, but despite this, I was acutely aware that this massive needle was making its way into my hip joint. Once the doctors finished with me, I was asked to wait three hours before driving home in case I experienced an adverse reaction. While this was frustrating, I made good use of the time. I had been awarded a testimonial year for 2006 from Warwickshire, which was timely, and I spent the entire three hours calling and messaging potential sponsors, prize donors, and individuals who might be able to organise and run events for me.

Testimonial years, at that time, were awarded to players who had served at least a decade as capped players at the Bears. Back then, being awarded a testimonial year was immensely important to county professionals, generally fostering more loyalty and longevity. It seems less significant today and certainly requires more effort to organise now than it did. Clearly, having just won the Ashes, most people I contacted were very pleased to speak with me, but it was equally important to me that I handled this myself. I didn't want to take the support for granted, and I genuinely felt privileged to have been awarded a testimonial by the club. By this point, I had also engaged a secretary for the year, Ali Prosser, who was invaluable, organising events and rallying support when I needed it.

By this time, we had already enjoyed our fair share of celebrations, pats on the back, and nights out on the town. Before we headed off to Pakistan, we had one more trip lined up for us and our wives, organised by Red Bull. They had sponsored a few of the boys over the summer and provided energy drinks for the dressing room whenever we needed them. To thank us and to say well done, they arranged the most incredible few days for us.

We met at Biggin Hill Airport in Kent, previously a Royal Air Force station and now a commercial airport, and we were flown on a private jet to Salzburg. We were taken to Red Bull's private hangar, Hangar 7, which not only houses a fantastic museum full of planes and helicopters but also features a café, bar, and Michelin-starred restaurant. Once we had finished lunch and had a look around the museum, we were asked to come outside. As we stood there, a vintage DC6 aircraft, fully decked in Red Bull's colours, was rolled out of a hangar next door in front of us, and it was to be our ride for the next leg of our journey to Venice. Inside, the plane was adorned with huge plush seats and a large sofa that wrapped around the tail end, and we were served by Red Bull girls. It was the most amazing experience, and as we flew over the Alps, it felt as if you could reach out and touch the mountains. Once in Venice, we checked into our hotel, were taken out for drinks and dinner, followed by more drinks, and the next morning we were flown back by private jet directly to Biggin Hill.

Soon after that, we had to get our heads around the tour of Pakistan. I had thoroughly enjoyed my first tour of Pakistan, but this one was very different straight away. For a start, so much had changed since the attacks on 9/11 and our security was presidential level; roads cleared of traffic, no stopping at all, and guns everywhere. There was an edge to proceedings; it would later transpire that in 2008, the Islamabad hotel we stayed in, the Marriott, a place which was often frequented by Americans, was blown up in a terrorist attack.

When the cricket got underway, as soon as I got into a heavier workload my hip started to flare up. The discomfort was different from anything I'd felt before and went deeper into my right buttock and down my right leg. I could continue to bowl, but it was sore and took me a while to get going. In the field it again felt heavy and I was laboured when chasing anything to the boundary.

I got through the warm-up matches, just about. I had a bit of a moment at Rawalpindi in the first of the practice matches. Having had a curry the previous night, I was feeling a little dodgy standing at about fifth slip to Liam Plunkett when a ball came to me. I crouched down to stop it and, well, it would be fair to say I lost control. I ran from the field immediately, got cleaned up, went back to the hotel, and spent the rest of the day in bed and on the toilet. The way I'd run off the pitch, some of the media thought I'd broken a finger fielding the ball, but it was only my pride that was broken. It was also in Rawalpindi where a number of aftershocks hit our hotel, waking us in the night, a result of the devastating Kashmir earthquake that struck in early October. A few of us went to the hospital to visit those who had been injured in the disaster, many of whom were kids who had lost their families. It was harrowing in the extreme to see these children suffering so much.

The first Test in Multan was a match we shouldn't have lost. We had a lead of over 140 runs on first innings, and we only needed 198 to win batting last in the match but were skittled for just 175. In the second innings I pretty much had all three stumps knocked out by a Shoaib Akhtar yorker. The only saving grace was that I got my front foot out of the way; otherwise, I'd have been stretchered off too.

The second Test in Faisalabad ended in a draw, and this time I survived against Shoaib and was not out when everyone shook hands. I was really starting to struggle physically, and my hip was becoming not only performance-affecting but also a distraction. I particularly felt it during our second innings in the field. Inzamam scored two centuries in the match but the biggest moment was perhaps when a gas canister attached to one of the concession stalls blew up and for a moment everyone thought a bomb had gone off in the ground.

A couple of our lads even started packing their bags. During the commotion Shahid Afridi did a couple of pirouettes on a length to try and rough the pitch, clearly forgetting that the fixed cameras would still be on the pitch! Once everything had calmed down (and our players had unpacked), play got under way again and, later, Afridi was suspended by the ICC. Despite the huge noise and the rattling of the windows that came with the explosion of the canister, one of our security guys, a former SAS soldier, told us that a real bomb would have been 10 times that noise.

At the end of the match, it was agreed that we needed a surgical opinion on my hip and that I wouldn't play in the third Test. I hung around for a few days and performed my duties as 12th man before returning to the UK to prepare for surgery – when you see a surgeon for an opinion, you normally end up having surgery. I had no idea then that the next first-class game I would play would be over a year away. I had surgery in the first week of December. The following week, those players who were in the country, mostly Test specialists, attended the Sports Personality of the Year show in London. Fred, who was in Pakistan, won the main award for his heroics against Australia, and those of us there enjoyed the night, and celebrated us also picking up the team award.

I was looking forward to getting things moving and preparing myself for the tour of India that was scheduled for after Christmas. This had been the plan as I left Pakistan, and Fletch had consistently asked, if I had the operation, whether I'd be ready in time for that tour. That was key for him. As it turned out progress was dreadfully slow, and I was still having a lot of discomfort in my hip. It was soon clear that I had no chance of being fit for the India series. I was gutted, and I also didn't like giving up my place in the team. Monty Panesar was selected for the tour to replace me.

I returned to the Wellington Hospital and had an injection into the joint under general anaesthetic to try and settle it. After that, I began weeks of rehab, in the pool, in the gym, and in the pilates studio. In the pool, I was doing about two hours of running around in the deep end, five days a week, to get the joint moving while trying to strengthen the muscles around it. I'd go straight from there to the gym and do a session, and then at least three days a week I would head over to Malvern for pilates. It was exhausting. In an attempt to get fit, the reality was that I was probably over-training as well. I looked pale and gaunt and my progress was at best slow. All the while, my hip remained sore and uncomfortable.

It also felt much weaker than my left side. After further conversations with the England medical team, I was referred to Jerry Gilmore, a specialist in groin injuries, in Harley Street. We wanted to know whether anything else was going on, apart from the hip. He performed a rather uncomfortable test on me, where he poked his little finger underneath my scrotum and to the side. I almost jumped off the bed from the shooting pain I felt. That was all he did, and he was convinced immediately from his experience that I had a sportsman's hernia, also known as Gilmore's groin. As strange as it sounds, I was delighted with the news as I thought this might help explain why I was making such slow progress and that this might actually be the underlying issue and the main cause of my symptoms. I remembered that one day while I was running in the pool, I felt something pull in my groin. We hadn't been sure at first what had happened and assumed it was just scar tissue breaking down around the hip. However, after that incident, in certain positions and while performing certain exercises, my hip became uncomfortable. I was now thinking that it was this all along which had been holding me back. I hoped, maybe naively, that once this was sorted, I would be able to return to full training.

I had the operation a few days later in London, and within a couple of weeks, I was fully engaged in my rehabilitation. Once I was cleared from a groin perspective, about six weeks post-op, we tried to build more intensity into my training to really test my right hip out. Unfortunately, the pain I had been feeling in my hip remained, and while I'd clearly had a hernia injury, it wasn't the underlying cause of my symptoms.

It was a hammer blow. We were now entering May, and our summer of cricket was well underway, but I was nowhere near being fit enough to return to the field. I was now not only starting to worry about my availability during the summer, but also the Ashes series that following winter.

Pressure was starting to ramp up from the media, and questions were being asked. The same applied to Simon Jones, who hadn't played since the Ashes Test at Trent Bridge. Under this pressure, the ECB began looking further afield for second opinions on both of us. As a result, I was booked on a flight to Denver for an appointment with Dr Marc Philippon, a globally renowned orthopaedic surgeon, specialising in hip disorders. The England team doctor travelled with me, and while I was only scheduled for a consultation, I again prepared myself for surgery. Philippon operated out of the Steadman Hawkins clinic in the beautiful ski town of Vail, a two-hour drive west of Denver up in the Rocky Mountains. We arrived in Denver late in the evening, stayed the night in a hotel near the airport and made our way up to Vail early the next morning. We had just sat down with a coffee when our team doctor got a message to say that I shouldn't eat or drink anything as they might get me into surgery that same day.

We made our way to the hospital and began a set of scans and tests ahead of a meeting with Philippon. The process took hours, but eventually, once I'd been poked, prodded and had a number of needles in me, we went to see him. He was clear in his own mind what needed to be done and told me that, if we agreed, he'd get me on his list that afternoon. I don't think I really had an option, I wasn't making progress, and in front of me I had one of the best in his field. Later that afternoon, I was wheeled into surgery.

I spent the next week in Vail making daily visits to the hospital for treatment from a flat we rented in town. I was completely non-weight-bearing on my right side and would remain so for the next eight weeks. The intensity of care was completely different in Vail from anything I'd ever received, and although I wasn't allowed to put my foot down, there was a concerted effort to keep the joint moving, including being put in a continuous passive motion [CPM] machine for hours every day which moved my leg for me when I was lying down, even when I was asleep. This made getting any meaningful sleep very difficult. I also had several sessions a day of ice on my hip and, at the clinic, would be put on an exercise bike, with no resistance, to keep things moving.

After that first week we returned to the UK. It was boiling hot at home. The ECB medical team also had a CPM machine delivered to our house, and I continued with that day and night for the next two weeks. During that first eight weeks of being non-weight-bearing, which was really tough, I decided I'd also try to lose some weight. I wasn't big by any means but I knew that if I shed some extra pounds it could only further ease pressure on my hip. Given I wasn't able to do anything particularly strenuous and wasn't able to even put my foot down, to lose weight my diet consisted almost entirely of protein. I had virtually no carbs at all. As a result, in just two weeks, I lost over a stone.

Once I was able to put weight through my leg again, we began building my workloads, and my programme was very carefully managed. I did far fewer hours this time round than I had after my first hip operation, and while I continued with pilates, I was no longer running in the pool every day and my gym sessions were far more controlled. Thankfully, I made good progress and as well as my hip feeling completely different this time round, I was also in much better physical condition. As a result I made huge strides in that first three months and I was in better physical shape – leaner and stronger – than I'd been for years, possibly ever.

At the three-month stage, I was booked on another flight to Denver for a check-up. Simon Jones travelled with me as he'd also had surgery in Vail, and we were accompanied by one of the ECB's physios. It was a brilliant week. I passed all my tests, and it was nice to be fully mobile and enjoy Vail and Denver. We went to a baseball match and managed to get a behind-the-scenes look at batting practice before the game. We were also able to enjoy a couple of pints and a hot dog, which was a nice break from the strict regime at home. I was buoyed when I returned home by the fact that I had been given the all clear to start bowling again. Having been genuinely concerned that I might never play again, I now had a realistic chance of getting on the plane for the Ashes.

On September 12, exactly a year on from that magical final day at The Oval, I was named in the Ashes tour party. I hadn't played for about 10 months at that point, and it was unlikely I would have any other opportunity to play before the Ashes tour began. But at that moment, it didn't matter to me. I just wanted to play again. Had my surgery in Vail not been successful, I was acutely aware that I would have likely been finished.

Ahead of the Ashes, I joined the team on the Champions Trophy trip to India to continue my preparation outdoors and in the warmth. Unfortunately we finished bottom of our group and were eliminated from the competition before the knockout stages, so we returned home for a couple of days. In the first few days of November, we made our way back to Heathrow and headed for Australia for one of the most anticipated Ashes series of all time. I left feeling excited and relieved, considering the year I'd had, and as a squad, we had high hopes that we could replicate our performance from the previous year.

As our plane left the runway, I had no idea that this trip would be my last with England and that by the time I returned home, I would not only have played my last Test but also my last competitive cricket, full stop. Worse still, I would return to a crisis that threatened our family and eclipsed any challenge we'd ever faced before.

32

Perspective

It was around 8pm in Perth when my phone rang. I was sat on the end of my bed with my head in my hands and the phone broke the unusual quiet in my room. I'd just finished in the shower and would normally be listening to music or have the TV on. Tonight was different. I didn't feel like music or watching TV. In fact I didn't feel like much. My mood was low. I'd been left out of the team for the third Test, we were 2-0 down in the series, and I was waiting for Stine to call.

While I was pissed off with being dropped, I was more worried about her. She had been having terrible headaches and had recently started to struggle with other worrying symptoms. She was also due to fly out in a few days with the kids, and I couldn't wait to see them all. She had rung me the previous evening and told me that the doctors were a little concerned about her symptoms and weren't happy about her flying without having further investigations. When she'd called I'd felt incredibly guilty, sitting there feeling sorry for myself about a cricket match. Apparently Stine had been suffering for weeks, often to the extent that she wasn't able to get out of bed or take the kids to school. But she didn't want to bother me with it on tour, so didn't tell me. The doctor managed to arrange an MRI scan for Stine at short notice, and we were now waiting for the results.

We had just completed the second day of the Test match in Perth and after losing the toss, we were actually doing OK. Australia made only 244 in their first innings and in reply we'd made 215. In their second innings Australia had made a better start and were 119-1, but given the result of the first two Tests everyone was pretty happy. I was still reeling from being left out. Monty had replaced me in the team but I had no complaints. We had been beaten comprehensively in the first Test at Brisbane, then at Adelaide in the second Test we had handed the match and virtually the series to the Australians on a careless last day.

Since Brisbane questions were being asked as to why I was in the team ahead of Monty. He had certainly had an amazing English summer and helped the team to a series victory over Pakistan while I was injured. Along with his cricketing performances his eccentric ways and bizarre celebrations had captured the hearts of fans in England. As far as I was concerned, when we left for the Ashes in November, Monty was the man firmly in possession of the spin bowler's position. I had everything to do. I hadn't played a first-class match since the end of 2005.

When Monty was selected as the only spinner to play South Australia in Adelaide, the week before the first Test, I was convinced that he would get the nod. We were told that this was 99.9 per cent our Test team for Brisbane. That was fine with me; as I said, Monty was in possession and I had to fight my way back in. I spent the week working hard in the nets with our bowling coach Kevin Shine and assistant coach Matt Maynard to try and get my game up to speed.

But in Adelaide, Monty didn't bowl well and suddenly there was a concern. If Monty isn't bowling well he offers very little else to the team. He had improved his batting a lot, but he wasn't going to get you a lot of runs. If he plays, he plays as a 'strike bowler' and if he wasn't doing that job his place had to be in jeopardy. I suddenly found myself back in contention for the first Test. Most of the British media were writing that I had bowled as well as Monty on tour to date and might easily get the nod for Brisbane. Senior players were coming to me and saying that Monty might have bowled me back into the side. They would be proved right.

The first Test in Brisbane was my first first-class game in 12 months. I felt I bowled pretty well and got some useful runs but we were outplayed and lost the game heavily. A terrible start to our Ashes campaign. Questions started to be asked as to why Monty wasn't playing in the team and, as is always the case with the Ashes, the media were looking for things or people to blame. My selection in the team ahead of Monty was one of them. Many of those critics hadn't been at Adelaide to watch Monty bowl himself out of the team. He hadn't started the tour at all well, and while my selection for the Gabba was still a bit of a surprise to me, I could totally understand it. As could the majority of the team.

Heading into Adelaide I knew I would be under a huge amount of pressure. I now felt like I was playing not only against the Australians, but also against my critics in the media. It was, of course, nothing that I hadn't felt before. I also knew that part of the media's job was to challenge what we are doing and, in particular, whether we were picking the right people to win games of cricket. I had no problem with that.

But the last 12 months had taken it out of me. After three separate operations, followed by three lots of rehabilitation, I'd spent months working my backside off, mostly on my own, with only one goal in mind: to play for England again. I was proud that I'd managed to achieve this, but part of me now questioned whether it had really been worth it.

I hold my hands up and admit that at Adelaide I could have bowled better. But I wasn't to blame for losing that Test. We froze on the last morning with the bat and dug ourselves a huge hole. We were eventually dismissed for 129 from 73 overs. Shane Warne bowled 32 of them and finished with 4-49. The Aussies cruised to their target of 168.

Leaving Monty out was identified as one of the key reasons we were 2-0 down in the series and why we lost at Adelaide. That was rubbish. Yes, I had only taken one wicket in the first innings in 42 overs, but everyone looked past the fact it had taken Warne 53 overs to do the same thing. We played Warne timidly in the second innings and dug our own grave. There were many reasons why we lost that Test, and the series, but leaving Monty out, in my mind, wasn't a significant one.

More worrying to me was my bowling. I was struggling to really drive through on my right hip. I had no reason to think that there was anything else going on in the joint, but it was as though my body just wouldn't allow me to spend enough time on it to drive through and get pace on the ball. That hip took all of the weight through my delivery stride, and was fundamental to everything that happened on release. Ultimately, I probably wasn't ready from a cricketing perspective. As much as we'd tried to get my bowling workloads up, I had missed a year's worth of cricket and that takes time to catch up.

After the debacle that was the final couple of days at Adelaide, I knew I was going to get dropped. As it turned out, the Adelaide Test of 2006 was to be my last match for England, and my last first-class game anywhere.

Monty took five wickets on the first day in Perth and I was genuinely pleased for him; it was an exceptional effort to get a five-wicket haul against that Aussie team. I have always considered myself a team man first, and my worries were always secondary to the needs of the team. As a non-player part of my role was to do 12th man duties. Basically fetching and carrying drinks for the boys, and making sure they had everything else they needed. I knew that with each Monty wicket the cameras would turn to me looking for a reaction. But I was on point, I did my job and I was first to give Monty a pat on the back when the team came back in. I was also pleased for the team. Australia is the toughest place on earth if you aren't competing, and after two days we were still in it.

I had spoken to Phil Neale and Duncan Fletcher about Stine earlier in the day and they'd both been very supportive. Phil had even reserved a flight for me back to the UK, just in case. I'd spoken with Stine while I was at the ground at the end of play to see if there was any news. She was at the hairdressers! I couldn't believe it. Here I was, halfway round the world and worried sick while she was getting her hair done. Stine had convinced herself that everything was going to be fine and she wanted to get her hair done before flying out to Australia.

So when, at 8pm that night, the phone rang back at the hotel, I was quick to get off my bed and pick it up. The next few moments are still a bit of a blur. It was Stine. I only just had a chance to say hello. She was crying.

"What is it, Stine, what's wrong?"

"Well, I won't be coming to see you." She was in pieces at the other end of the phone. "I have a brain tumour."

Those five words cut through me, and I don't remember anything else that was said. I just knew I had to get home. I got onto the phone again to Phil Neale, and broke down as I spoke to him.

33

Real battles

On Saturday December 16, 2006, in the early hours of a Perth morning, I officially left the Ashes tour party. After 12 months of battling injury, this was a tour I'd worked my backside off to get on, and I now left without my teammates, in civilian clothing, feeling sick to my stomach and emotionally shattered. A good number of the team I'd arrived in Australia with wouldn't know of my departure. By the time they would become aware, I would be flying across the seas heading for home in the UK. It had been less than 12 hours since I'd put the phone down. How the world changes in such a short space of time. The time it takes your wife to tell you she has a brain tumour.

But for a few of the guys I had given the news to the previous evening, my leaving was a secret. Nasser Hussain was the only member of the press that knew what was going on. He had approached me in the hotel on the Friday evening and told me he knew something must be going on, that he didn't want to know the specifics, but whatever it was he hoped everything was OK. I gave him the news I had received only a couple of hours earlier. I knew I could trust him to keep it under his hat; I considered Nas a mate and always enjoyed his leadership and playing with him. I didn't see any point in keeping it from him.

I only managed a couple of hours' sleep that Friday night. I got packed up and left the hotel with Phil Neale and one of our security guards about 4:30am. Before we got to the airport I managed to speak to Stine at home to see if there had been any more news and to give her my travel plans. All she knew was that the tumour was a big one – the size of an orange, the doctor had told her – but that they were pretty sure it wasn't malignant, and that they could operate to remove it. She sounded a lot clearer and brighter than when I had spoken to her earlier. The immediate shock had passed – for her at least – and our local GP had come round and given her a rundown of what she had going on in her head. I told her I would be home on Saturday evening.

Check in at Perth airport was easy. I was taking only one suitcase out with me. Not the four bags and over 100kg I had come in with. I wouldn't be needing my cricket equipment for a while.

I made my way through security. I remember feeling really alone. I'd spent the last four weeks in the very public eye of an Ashes campaign and now I slipped on my own through immigration and out of Australia, under the radar. Soon after 7am I was flying away from the Western Australian coast and from the country that had held such high hopes for me just weeks earlier. My trip would take me via Dubai back to Birmingham, only half an hour from Stine and home in Droitwich. The hope was that we would manage to keep this whole thing under wraps until I got home. It wasn't people finding out that bothered me, they would do that at some stage anyway. It also wasn't about any hassle that I might get on my way home. It worried me that as soon as the media found out that they would be hassling Stine at home and on the phone. It was the last thing she needed and I didn't even know if she'd told the children anything yet.

My mind raced on that flight to Dubai. It probably not being malignant was fantastic news… but we didn't know for sure at that point. Even with a very limited knowledge of brain tumours I knew this was really serious. If it *definitely* wasn't malignant then Stine still had this massive lump growing inside her head. It would have to come out. What would that entail? What were the risks? What were the chances she might not make it through the operation? All these things went through my head.

As cricketers we work a lot on playing the percentages. I wanted to know *now* what our percentages were. I wanted to speak to whoever would be taking care of Stine *now*. In reality, the percentages would matter little. I would have no control over what would happen to Stine. I wouldn't be able to make some sort of risk assessment and play the situation accordingly. I felt hopeless. I didn't get much sleep on that leg of my trip. I just wanted to be at home. I hated Australia at this point for keeping me away from my family when they really needed me.

When I arrived in Dubai, I'd managed to get the bulk of my trip home out of the way; I turned my mobile phone on in preparation to call home. Immediately I realised that the news about Stine had broken. My phone beeped and buzzed non-stop for a couple of minutes as message after message came in. One of them was from our press officer in Australia that said news had leaked and they had released a short statement to say that I'd had to return home due to a serious illness in the family. I had some great messages from friends and family. I felt like crying as I stood in the airport as the seriousness of Stine's illness hit me again and again with each text. I rang home and told her that it was common knowledge now. She already knew that of course, as the phone at home had already started to ring. She had also seen it on the TV.

Stine told me that she hadn't told the children anything yet. She also said that friends of ours were going to have the kids on Saturday night just in case things at home got a bit emotional. Anders and Tilly at this point were still expecting to be flying out to Australia on Sunday. They had really been looking forward to it.

Our friends, Andy and Barb, said they would make lunch for us at theirs on Sunday. Stine had an appointment to see her surgeon at 11am that day, and while I was desperate to see the kids, it was a good idea to talk things through without the kids around. We had to work out how best to tell them that Mummy was very ill. Stine would be having another scan that Saturday afternoon, which should clarify the cancer situation and give us more idea of exactly what we were facing, though I wouldn't be getting any news until I got home. I would be in the skies somewhere between Dubai and Birmingham.

Stine had somehow sounded quite upbeat. For the first time in weeks she had managed a good night's sleep. The doctors had given her some strong tablets to shrink the size of the tumour and decrease the pressure in her head, which had had an immediate effect and she had slept right through the night. She had put up with terrible headaches every night for at least a couple of months now. Even if the tablets hadn't cured the very real problem of the tumour they had at least allowed her some respite.

Her relaxed and positive manner must have had an effect on me because I managed to get a few hours' sleep myself. It might have just been exhaustion. But I did feel happier that Stine was up for whatever was coming our way. We still didn't really know how bad it might be, but I knew that whatever happened we had to be ready to take this on and I had to be strong for Stine. She had always been there for me. I had to now be totally there for whatever she might need to beat this.

On arrival at Birmingham Airport I collected my luggage and made my way out to meet my chauffeur. After receiving the news that Stine's tumour had got out to the press I expected that there may be some interest at the airport. Thankfully I was able to clear the airport with very little difficulty and head for home. But if I'd thought that the press were on their best behaviour and were respecting our privacy then I was mistaken. In the car I rang home and Stine told me that a couple of guys had been sniffing around the house and the neighbours looking for a story. I thought it was totally out of order to knock on our front door and hassle Stine. Fair enough if they wanted to get something from me but I just thought it was terrible to bother her when the shock of the news was still so fresh.

Stine did have some fantastic news for me though. After another scan, the doctors were now sure, because of the nature of the tumour, that she didn't have a malignant growth. They told her that they thought the lump could have been growing for up to 20 years. It had got to the point where it couldn't get any bigger because there wasn't any space for the brain to move out of the way. It was on the verge of bursting. The pressure in Stine's head was causing the terrible headaches and of late the symptoms of semi-paralysis on Stine's right side.

Luckily, when I arrived home there was no-one outside the house. I'm not sure I would have been too polite if someone had stuck a camera in my face as I arrived at the door.

Stine looked fine. I didn't know what to expect really. Whether she should look like she was dying or terribly ill. She looked amazingly relaxed. Just seeing her like that had an immediate impact on me. I felt better for seeing her. The only visible signs that she was ill, or that something was wrong, were on the left side of her forehead. I probably wouldn't have noticed if I'd been with Stine every day but having been away I could notice the difference. The skin across the left side of Stine's forehead seemed to be pulled really tight and stretched compared to the right side. It was almost as though she had had botox on one side of her head. The pressure of the tumour on the side of her head was stretching everything to its limit.

We went into the lounge and sat on the sofa. We didn't cry. We just sat and talked for an hour about what the doctors had said, how the kids were and where we would go from here. When we'd finished we both realised we were quite hungry. We didn't want to cook so I said I'd go down to town and get a take-away curry. Stine said she wanted to come with me; she didn't want to be alone again. When we got down to Droitwich we decided that, as we didn't have the kids at home and the curry house didn't look very busy, we would eat in. As we tucked into our food a gentleman at the table next to us turned to me and asked if I'd be going back to Australia. I looked at Stine and looked back at him and said that I wasn't really sure at the moment because my wife was very ill. It felt a strange thing to say as we sat there stuffing our faces and talking quite calmly, I'm sure he must have thought that we were having everyone on.

We both slept pretty well that Saturday night. Stine's tablets had continued their good work and I was exhausted from the trip back from Australia. We awoke with a positive attitude that Sunday and I felt so buoyed by Stine's positivity. We knew a lot lay ahead, most of it unknown, but we looked forward to meeting with the surgeon and finding out more about the operation, the treatment and the rehabilitation.

On the way to the Priory Hospital in Birmingham we stopped off to see my parents who had recently moved to Bromsgrove, about halfway between home and Birmingham.

I hadn't seen them for weeks while I'd been on tour. They had been a great help to Stine with the kids while she had endured these terrible headaches. We stayed for a cup of tea and a chat. I knew something was bothering them – and I also knew what it was. They were due to travel out to Australia to see me play cricket and have a couple of weeks' holiday. Obviously they now wondered whether they should go at all. They of course wouldn't see me play cricket, that was the last thing on my mind now. But I wanted them to go. They had been looking forward to the trip for months. They would be here until just after Christmas anyway by which time Stine's operation would hopefully be over and she may even be home. Stine's parents would be coming over before the New Year as well so we should have some help with things. It was the second time that this had happened to Mum and Dad. On my previous Ashes trip I had come home about a week before they departed when Steve Harmison broke my arm in the nets. I told them they should go and they looked relieved that I'd given my blessing.

When we arrived at the hospital we were shown to a private room and waited for the surgeon. When Professor Cruickshank arrived we almost immediately felt better about what was going to happen. He had a very relaxed and calm way about him. He dressed smartly, but not over the top, and this put me at ease because it generally shows that the man has a focus and confidence in what he does. He's not pretending to be something he's not. We see it a lot in and around cricket and I hate it. Sure, it's nice that people dress nicely and look after themselves but in this case wearing an Armani suit wouldn't have made me feel more comfortable about this man operating on my wife's brain. Quite the opposite in fact.

From a large brown envelope the professor pulled out Stine's brain scans. As cricketers, scans are part of life. Generally it's difficult, or near impossible, to see what is going on in them. Knees, hips and ankles are such small, tight joints that abnormalities are very difficult to spot for us mere mortals. We just get told something is wrong, get on the bed, and get it sorted. When Cruickshank put up one of Stine's scans to the light of the window, I was knocked back by what I saw. This cloudy large mass in Stine's head was huge. We had been told it was big, but to see it now taking up so much space where Stine's brain should be sitting was like being hit by a thunderbolt.

Cruickshank explained that the tumour was sitting at the top and on the left side of the head. It wasn't malignant and most importantly it was operable. He said that it was a slow growing tumour called a meningioma and explained that as the tumour had grown the brain had made space for it by moving out of the way. The tumour had got too big now and the brain couldn't move out of the way any longer. This was creating a huge amount of pressure in Stine's head. The surgeon also told us, most shockingly, how lucky Stine had been to spot the lump now. He told us that if she had travelled to Australia, as she had been due to, she could have been in serious trouble. The pressure at altitude could have been one push too far for the tumour and Stine may well have had a massive fit and died. It was a shock to hear. Stine would have been travelling alone with Anders and Tilly. That one flight could have ruined all our lives.

Cruickshank told us that in terms of tumours he had to deal with, this was a pretty good one. He could obviously see we were uptight and was trying to put us at ease. Stine's lump was operable and benign; other patients the professor saw weren't so lucky. Nevertheless, it wasn't easy to know exactly what the extent of the tumour was until he got into Stine's head. One thing he was worried about was that the tumour appeared to have a tail, much like that of a comet, and this would have to come out as well. He thought the tail may be running inside the main vein that lay between the two sides of the brain and could be tricky to remove, but reiterated that everything should be OK. I asked about the percentages.

"They are good," he said. "I have to deal with a lot worse than this."

We then had to discuss when to do it. He gave us the option. Stine could either go in on the Wednesday, the last Wednesday before Christmas, or wait until the following week after Christmas. I guess he just thought that Stine might want this week and Christmas with the kids and get her head around taking this thing on next week. Stine asked me what I thought. My opinion was that if it was me I would want it out as soon as possible so I could get on with the rehab, getting well again, and the rest of my life. Christmas at home with the kids was a discussion point but Stine, in my mind, wouldn't be there totally anyway. How could she be, with surgery looming. Stine agreed that she wanted to get on with it. The professor told us to go away and think about it and let him know on Monday morning.

On the way to our friends' place for lunch and the kids, Stine decided that Wednesday would be the day. She was so brave as she spoke about it. So matter of fact. "I have a tumour, let's get on with it."

Tilly and Anders, who were upstairs at Andy and Barb's playing Playstation with their son William, were pretty shocked to see Daddy behind them when they turned around.

"We're going to Australia today, Daddy, are you coming with us?" Tilly shouted at me excitedly. Stine and I looked at each other and thought that maybe now was a good time to let them know what was going on.

It was difficult to know exactly what to say but this is something like how it went.

"We aren't going to Australia any more, kids. Daddy has had to come home because Mummy has to go into hospital to have an operation. Remember when Mummy had to go in last year to hospital and the doctors made her better? Well, Mummy has something in her head that the doctors need to take out. They will make Mummy better and then she will come home. Do you understand?"

Both Anders and Tilly said OK, and didn't seem that bothered about not going to Australia.

"The good news is that Father Christmas will be able to bring you lots more presents now you are staying at home. He wouldn't be able to take them all to Australia, would he?"

We enjoyed a fabulous Sunday lunch and a glass of wine. We talked about what the surgeon had told us. Stine talked about how she had found out and I talked about Australia and getting home. It was good to be with friends, rather than bottling it all up inside. After dinner we went home as a family again. It was great to see the kids after being away so long.

We all got to bed early that Sunday night. I slept pretty well but got the feeling Stine didn't. I don't think the headaches had returned but she obviously had a lot to think about.

On the Monday we rang the surgeon's secretary and told her that we wanted to do it on Wednesday. That afternoon we went back to the hospital to get a pre-op chest X-ray done and have some bloods taken and tested.

As the day wore on, the decision to do the operation that Wednesday seemed a better and better idea. Stine didn't have headaches but she was becoming exhausted very quickly, another symptom of what was going on in her head. On the Tuesday Stine had wanted to go to Birmingham, an idea that I wasn't too keen on, to get some things to take into hospital, including new pyjamas, but she was so tired that she just couldn't face the trip.

We decided that we would pop in on the Wednesday morning before going to the hospital. We dropped the kids at Mum and Dad's. Stine found it difficult to say goodbye. The kids of course didn't know the severity of the situation and they didn't need to. They didn't need to know that this might be the last kiss or cuddle they ever got from Mummy. We knew it, and it was hard enough for us to take. The percentages were in our favour but this was brain surgery, a lot could happen.

In Birmingham, Stine managed somehow to get what she needed. She was absolutely shattered when we got to the car and made our short trip to the Priory in Edgbaston from the City Centre. We checked in about 1pm, Stine's surgery was scheduled for that evening. It was terrible waiting. The longer Stine sat there the more nervous she became. And the more she worried, the more the worst kinds of thoughts entered her head.

"I am going to make it, aren't I?" she said. "I'm not going to die today, am I?"

What could I say? I didn't know. I had no control at all over what was about to happen. I hated it. I felt I should be able to protect my family from trouble, from danger. All I could say was "No" and "Don't be silly babe; you are going to be fine". I didn't know whether I was trying to convince Stine or myself.

The anaesthetist came and saw us during the afternoon and explained the operation to us again. Professor Hutton was very thorough in his explanation and very honest about the risks. We did feel a little at ease knowing that not one but two professors would be taking care of Stine. Hutton also explained how things would happen when Stine came round in intensive care. He told us that with this operation the type of anaesthetic used meant that Stine would be awake almost immediately afterwards. This was to allow the doctors to get a good idea on the patient's condition straight away. Messing with the brain was a tricky thing to do so they wanted to check as soon as possible that her arms and legs were moving and speech was unaffected.

Just before 5.30pm, Stine was wheeled out of her room and taken down to theatre. I went with her and said my goodbyes at the operating room doors. I told her I loved her and that I would see her later. I wanted to be with her all the way through it. I knew that the docs wouldn't let that happen. So I went back to the room that now felt empty without the bed and Stine on it.

During the first hour I managed to read the magazines I had brought with me. During the second I managed to watch a bit of TV. Professor Hutton had told us that the operation should take two to three hours, but there were no guarantees. They wouldn't know how long it would take until they got inside Stine's head and got down to work removing the tumour.

At almost 8pm the door opened. I jumped up waiting for news. A nurse came in and I felt relaxed immediately by her expression. She explained that she had come from theatre and was heading home. The professor had asked her to come up and let me know that everything was going OK but they would need two more hours to finish the job.

It was great to get some news of what was going on. There was obviously a bit more going on inside than originally thought.

Although the news was good to have, from that moment I couldn't focus on anything but the clock. The football was on the telly, but I wasn't really watching it. I called Mum and Dad and Stine's parents to tell them what I had been told and that I would call again when it was over.

One hour passed. 9pm. No news.

Another hour. As the clock hit 10pm I thought the door would open at any minute. The four hours were up. Surely someone would come and tell me soon that everything was alright. I spent the next hour waiting for that door to open. Thinking that every step I heard come down the corridor was my messenger coming to tell me that everything was OK. Those footsteps were never for me. At 11 I was starting to get worried. I had told our parents that I would call when I had news. But I didn't have any. I knew they would be worried. So was I now.

As 11:30pm came and went I spent every minute thinking that the worst was happening downstairs. I had tried not to think worst case scenarios since I had been given the news in Perth, but now I couldn't do anything else. I wondered how I would tell Stine's parents that I couldn't save their little girl. How would I ever tell

Anders and Tilly that they would never see Mummy again, that they would never have another cuddle.

I had almost convinced myself that the next time the door opened it would be Professor Cruickshank to tell me that Stine hadn't made it. I didn't want the door to open, I just wanted Stine back.

At midnight the door opened. Professor Cruickshank walked in. He must have seen how worried I had become. The professor said the words that I'd convinced myself I would never hear.

"It's OK. Stine is OK."

The end of the beginning

Stine's operation proved to be far more complicated than they had initially anticipated. The following day, I met with her surgeon and anaesthetist, who explained what had transpired once they opened Stine's skull. Cruickshank's primary challenge was a tail connected to the tumour that ran directly between the two hemispheres of her brain. It took hours to remove this portion of the tumour, and during that time, Professor Hutton, Stine's anaesthetist, had to manage her blood pressure carefully to prevent excessive bleeding while ensuring her survival. She lost over half of her total blood volume during the operation.

Stine came home on Boxing Day against the advice of her surgeon and unsurprisingly her recovery was slow. Several times, we rushed back to the hospital because of worrying symptoms Stine developed, including issues with her sight, swelling of her head or face, and loss of feeling in parts of her body. She also suffered several fits caused by the scar tissue from the operation, which was terrifying for all of us, particularly for Stine.

In hindsight, we didn't manage any of this well with Anders and Tilly, who were only six and four at the time. We thought we were doing the best thing by not sharing too much information with them, but that decision came back to bite us, as both of them struggled emotionally and at school for some time afterwards. Tilly still struggles to this day with anything related to illness, particularly if it affects those closest to us. Since then, I have always promised to be as honest as I can be when it comes to Stine's health, and over the last two decades, we have had to have some really difficult conversations.

In Australia, the team continued to struggle in the Ashes, and we were thrashed 5-0. While I kept an eye on what was happening, I had enough on my plate at home to worry about watching cricket through the night. You realise in those moments what is truly important. The kids and I had come so very close to losing Stine and everything else, including cricket, had just become so insignificant. I felt for my teammates. It had been a disastrous tour, which is not uncommon when it comes to Ashes series away from home, but it also felt like the end of a cycle. One which had started in 2000 with Nas and Fletch, had been taken up by Vaughany in 2003, culminating ultimately in arguably the greatest Test series of all time – and one that I'd been involved in almost the entire time.

I had very little communication from the team, which didn't really surprise me given the intensity of an Ashes series. To be fair, the medical team, led by Nick Peirce, did check in with me quite regularly to ask about Stine's progress. I also heard from the ECB head office a couple of times. Once, soon after Stine's operation, I was told that I wouldn't be receiving the rest of my tour fee as I'd left halfway through the series, which felt rather insensitive at the time, though of course I really didn't give a damn. Later, I received a call informing me that I wouldn't be on the long list for the World Cup in the Caribbean in March, meaning there was no chance of making the final 15. This was the first time I began to think that my time with the England team might be over. I had been distracted by far more important matters but that call was probably my first indication of the team moving on without me.

As February arrived, I hadn't engaged in any cricket activities at all since returning home in December. Between the school run, caring for Stine, shopping, cleaning, cooking, and everything else that needed doing, I managed to maintain my gym programme and stayed as physically fit and lean as I was when I left for Australia.

The gym served as a great distraction and outlet for me, providing an escape from everything else. My mum and dad were, of course, a tremendous help, as were Stine's parents, Marit and Kjell, who visited for a couple of weeks from Norway. Stine's mum is a wonderful cook, and her dad, who is sadly no longer with us, was exceptionally skilled and could build, make, or repair just about anything. In fact, he nearly single-handedly constructed two family homes during his time. He was also a lovely man and one of the calmest individuals I have ever known.

As we got into March, and with Stine making better progress, we agreed that I should return to cricket, and I rejoined the Bears for the 2007 pre-season preparation. I had spent a considerable amount of time at Edgbaston and in the dressing room during the summer of 2006, for rehab and physio sessions following my hip operations.

Every time I walked in, you could feel how poor the environment was. There was a lot of discontent among the playing group, and many of the senior players in particular. On the field the team had underperformed, and from the outside looking in it felt like we'd lost much of the discipline and work ethic that had been the hallmark of so many Bears teams over the years. The culture was poor and there seemed a complete disconnect between the team management and players. As a result, we spent much of the 2007 pre-season talking about how we should operate as a team, what we stood for and what our behaviours, on and off the field, should look like. I enjoyed being back in the thick of it and had got my head around the strong likelihood that I'd be spending the entire season with Warwickshire.

In the middle of March, with Stine's blessing, I headed off with the Warwickshire squad for a pre-season tour of Grenada. The tour started off really well personally and, although there continued to be some signs that the underlying issues with culture may still be lingering, it was great to be back outside and in the sun playing. It was also nice being able to play the role of senior player in that environment and give something back to the Bears, having spent the majority of the last few years with England.

Then, one day in the gym, while doing what seemed the most innocuous of exercises – simple box jumps – I felt something go in my hip. I stopped what I was doing immediately but over the next few days the discomfort didn't ease at all, and it became obvious again that I had an issue. I played very little part in the rest of that tour, and at one point it looked like I might fly straight to Colorado from Grenada to see Marc Philippon. In the end, I went home first, for further scans and meetings with the ECB medical team. Despite it looking less and less likely that I would play for England that summer, I was still a centrally contracted player and, ultimately, the ECB had responsibility for me and my treatment.

Before long, I found myself back on a plane heading to Denver for another visit to Vail to see Philippon. Like my first visit, as soon as I arrived in Vail, it was clear that I would go under the knife. When I came round from the operation, Philippon told me that he had discovered a new injury near the site of the previous one. I was already finding the prospect of another lengthy rehab incredibly daunting. Last time, I had a clear goal in mind – getting to the Ashes. This time I didn't have a clue what lay ahead for me and whether, even if I got through the gruelling months of physio and training, I'd be able to perform again at the required level, without risk of further injury. I knew there was every chance I could be back in this same position again, and that was unsustainable from everyone's point of view.

I had a long conversation with Philippon and sought his perspective, given his expertise, on the risks associated with my return to professional sport. He was quite clear that, in his opinion, there was an increased risk considering I had now undergone two major operations on the same hip. His advice, all things considered, was that I should retire from the game. This wasn't a decision I would take lightly or quickly, and I wanted to discuss it with Stine when I returned to the UK.

Once home, after embarking on another lengthy rehabilitation period and speaking to Stine and others close to me, we came to a decision. For nearly two years I had spent most of my time doing rehab or physio, and in the gym or on crutches. I had played just two first-class matches during the Ashes, and I was becoming both unemployable and uninsurable. I also didn't want to further risk my long-term physical health by continuing to play. On August 9, 2007, I travelled to The Oval, where England were playing India, and announced my retirement, did some interviews with the written press, and that was it. It was over.

I had no idea what I was going to do. I had known nothing else but playing cricket for my entire working life. It was over the next couple of weeks that the reality started to kick in. Cricket wasn't just my job, it was my life, my identity, my friends, it was why I got out of bed. Over the previous two years, I'd started to think there was a possibility that retirement may be the eventual outcome of everything that was going on. But it was still like a sledgehammer when it happened. Stine's illness had given me perspective, and still does to this day, but I now struggled to see my purpose. It was my first experience of feeling like the circus was leaving town without me, and no one was looking back to see where I was. I had done some radio work for *Test Match Special* during the summer, and a little bit of summarising for Sky, but, apart from them being very competitive markets for ex-players, I really didn't enjoy it that much. It didn't give me the buzz that I got from playing or working within a team.

On August 27, after spending the day at Edgbaston with TMS covering the ODI between England and India, I wandered into the committee room at the end of the day for a drink while the crowds dispersed and traffic eased. While I was there, Dennis Amiss, the Warwickshire and England legend and former CEO of the club, pulled me aside for a quiet chat. "We think you can do the job," he said. "What job?" "The director of cricket; we think you can take over."

I was shocked. Despite their best intentions earlier in the year to turn the culture around, the team had continued to decline, and by the end of the summer, would be relegated in both white-ball and red-ball competitions. At that point, they were well on their way, which I was aware of, but I'd never considered going into coaching at that time or taking on a role at the club. I think I made it pretty clear to Dennis then that I wasn't interested and thought he had the wrong man. However, he'd planted a seed, and over the next few days, that seed began to grow.

I went home and spoke to Stine about what Dennis had said and then in my own head began thinking about what the team needed and what I would do if I were in charge. I felt lucky that I'd had a great education in cricket, in high performance, in good – and bad – cultures, and in coaching from some of the very best players and coaches in the game over a 15-year professional career.

I also had the benefit of seeing what really good looked like at the Bears having been involved through some of the glory years of the Nineties. Colin Povey, the club's CEO, asked to see me at Edgbaston. Our conversation got onto the team and my future, and he asked me whether I might consider a role as part of the coaching team, perhaps as bowling coach. Strangely, and I honestly have no idea why I said it, but I replied: "If I'm going to do it, I'll do the whole thing, not just bowling coach."

Over the next two weeks, Colin and I began to talk increasingly about what it might look like. Simultaneously, the team edged closer to double relegation. At that point, nothing was agreed, and I certainly hadn't been given the job. But the more these conversations continued, the more I came to realise that I actually wanted it. In the end, the inevitable happened: the team was relegated, the coach Mark Greatbatch was sacked, and just a couple of days after the season ended, I was appointed Warwickshire's new director of cricket. I had been retired for just five weeks.

Initially, I wasn't exactly sure what I was doing; I simply didn't know what I didn't know, as I had no first-hand experience of leading in such environments. What I did know was that the successful teams I had played for had certain elements that ran through most high-performing teams. They are disciplined, they work incredibly hard, they are professional, they are generally fitter than their opposition, and they feature highly skilled players. There are many other factors, but that was my starting point. My attitude towards standards of work rate, discipline, and fitness shocked a few at first, I think, but I believed they were the foundations we needed to establish before we even thought about winning anything.

That marked the beginning of an incredible journey with the team over the next five years, elevating us from one of the worst and least respected teams in the country in 2007 to county champions in 2012. We narrowly missed out on the double that year on the last ball of the season in the Lord's final.

Thirteen years later, I remain in the game, having held almost every position in the sport, and now as CEO at Worcestershire. During this period, I attended university and completed a Master's degree, became a Level 4 coach, and, perhaps most proudly, with Stine, founded the Giles Trust Brain Tumour Fund, which focuses on research and treatment of this dreadful disease that remains the biggest cancer killer among people under 40.

I have come to love being told that I can't do something or that I'm not good enough. Writing this book myself was yet another challenge and, if you are reading these words, it will be another one overcome. I am now 33 years in the game and counting, but this book focuses on the first part of that journey, which was at times incredibly challenging, but also so rewarding and enjoyable. It culminated, of course, in that one amazing summer, when those Test matches I played against the back wall of our house with a stump and a tennis ball, simulating series against the Australians and the great West Indies teams, became reality.

At times, I found cricket hard. The scrutiny, the pressure, the very low lows, and there have been many periods since my retirement when I reflected negatively on my playing career. I understand better now that I have actually learnt the most through those tougher times and adversity: the losses, being dropped, being told I wouldn't make it or wasn't good enough, the self-doubt and anxiety, the time away from my family and, in the worst moments, the feelings of worthlessness and of walking down the street hoping no one would notice me for fear of ridicule. It's only with experience that one realises that, while painful, that's the part that fosters real learning and development. Failure and adversity in life are inevitable, and if I could offer any advice, it would be to be comfortable with that; it's normal, that's life. It's how you respond to each of these setbacks that's important.

In Māori culture, 'Whakapapa' operates on the principles that every community has a past, present, and future, and that each individual member of this community or family is linked, arm in arm, with all those who have come before, back to the beginning of time, as well as with all those who will come after. It provides communities with a sense of identity, connection, and belonging, along with a better understanding of their place in the world. It suggests that over time the sun travels along this line, and each of us has a certain amount of time in the sunlight, that time will inevitably come to an end, and it is everyone's responsibility to do their utmost for all those who went before, as well as for those who are yet to come.

Owen Eastwood discusses this beautifully in his book *Belonging*. When I reflect on my time in the sun, I do so with a tremendous sense of pride. I feel privileged to have played alongside and against some of the game's greats on some of the finest grounds, in some of the greatest matches in history, witnessing first-hand some of the very best performances. These are things I could never have dreamed of as that young boy on Ripley village green in the early Eighties. I feel proud to have stood in that line and comfortable that I did everything I could to honour both those who came before me and those who are yet to come.

In 2007, my time in the sun as a player came to an end; the team moved on. That is just the way of things. I had never imagined that the sun would come round again on an off-field career in cricket leadership, coaching and administration. But I guess that's a story for another day.

Ashley Giles in numbers

Test matches for England

Batting & Fielding

Team	M	I	NO	R	HS	Ave	100	50	Ct	St
England	54	81	13	1421	59	20.89	0	4	33	

Bowling

Team	Balls	Mdns	Runs	Wkts	BB	Ave	5wl	10wM
England	12180	397	5806	143	5-57	40.6	5	0

Test matches for England season by season

Batting & Fielding

Season		M	I	NO	R	HS	Ave	100	50	Ct	St
1998	England	1	2	1	17	16*	17	0	0	0	
2000-01	Sri Lanka	3	6	2	15	5	3.75	0	0	2	
2000-01	Pakistan	3	3	1	56	37*	28	0	0	3	
2001	England	1	2	0	7	7	3.5	0	0	0	
2001-02	India	2	3	0	43	28	14.33	0	0	0	
2001-02	New Zealand	3	4	1	39	21*	13	0	0	4	
2002	England	5	6	0	130	45	21.66	0	0	2	
2002-03	Australia	1	2	0	17	13	8.5	0	0	2	
2003	England	6	8	0	218	52	27.25	0	2	2	
2003-04	Sri Lanka	3	5	1	74	18	18.5	0	0	0	
2003-04	West Indies	3	3	0	75	37	25	0	0	2	
2003-04	Bangladesh	2	2	0	25	19	12.5	0	0	0	
2004	England	7	9	2	219	52	31.28	0	1	3	
2004-05	South Africa	5	8	1	188	39	26.85	0	0	5	
2005	England	5	10	2	155	59	19.37	0	1	5	
2005-06	Pakistan	2	4	1	69	26	23	0	0	2	
2006-07	Australia	2	4	1	74	27*	24.66	0	0	1	

Bowling

Season		Balls	Mdns	Runs	Wkts	BB	Ave	5wI	10wM
1998	England	216	7	106	1	1-106	106	0	0
2000-01	Sri Lanka	1092	55	410	17	5-75	24.11	1	0
2000-01	Pakistan	727	30	309	7	4-11	44.14	0	0
2001	England	150	0	108	1	1-108	108	0	0
2001-02	India	651	46	198	6	5-67	33	1	0
2001-02	New Zealand	600	20	236	6	4-103	39.33	0	0
2002	England	1221	34	544	11	4-62	49.45	0	0
2002-03	Australia	320	5	191	6	4-101	31.83	0	0
2003	England	1056	26	569	9	2-45	63.22	0	0
2003-04	Sri Lanka	1185	49	539	18	5-116	29.94	1	0
2003-04	West Indies	186	2	137	2	2-67	68.5	0	0
2003-04	Bangladesh	234	7	112	1	1-52	112	0	0
2004	England	1801	62	811	31	5-57	26.16	2	0
2004-05	South Africa	839	18	449	11	3-105	40.81	0	0
2005	England	960	18	578	10	3-78	57.8	0	0
2005-06	Pakistan	450	9	247	3	2-85	82.33	0	0
2006-07	Australia	492	9	262	3	1-46	87.33	0	0

Test matches for England against each opponent

Batting & Fielding

Opponent	M	I	NO	R	HS	Ave	100	50	Ct	St
Australia	9	18	3	253	59	16.86	0	1	8	
Bangladesh	2	2	0	25	19	12.5	0	0	0	
India	5	7	0	128	31	18.28	0	0	1	
New Zealand	6	8	3	152	45*	30.4	0	0	4	
Pakistan	5	7	2	125	37*	25	0	0	5	
South Africa	10	16	2	321	41	22.92	0	0	6	
Sri Lanka	8	13	3	134	45	13.4	0	0	3	
West Indies	7	8	0	181	52	22.62	0	1	5	
Zimbabwe	2	2	0	102	52	51	0	2	1	

Bowling

Opponent	Balls	Mdns	Runs	Wkts	BB	Ave	5wl	10wM
Australia	1922	32	1139	20	4-101	56.95	0	0
Bangladesh	234	7	112	1	1-52	112	0	0
India	1407	69	552	11	5-67	50.18	1	0
New Zealand	1284	41	538	15	4-46	35.86	0	0
Pakistan	1542	64	657	20	5-75	32.85	1	0
South Africa	1907	40	1057	19	3-105	55.63	0	0
Sri Lanka	2377	90	1038	31	5-116	33.48	1	0
West Indies	1303	43	646	24	5-57	26.91	2	0
Zimbabwe	204	11	67	2	1-15	33.5	0	0

ODIs for England

Batting & Fielding

Team	M	I	NO	R	HS	Ave	100	50	Ct	St
England	62	35	13	385	41	17.5	0	0	22	

Bowling

Team	Balls	Mdns	Runs	Wkts	BB	Ave	4wl	5wl	SR	Econ
England	2856	17	2069	55	5-57	37.61	0	1	51.92	4.34

ODIs for England season by season

Batting & Fielding

Season		M	I	NO	R	HS	Ave	100	50	Ct	St
1997	England	1	0							0	
1998	England	1	1	0	2	2	2	0	0	0	
1998-99	Australia	2	1	1	10	10*		0	0	1	
1998-99	Bangladesh	1	1	1	5	5*		0	0	0	
2000-01	Pakistan	3	2	0	14	11	7	0	0	0	
2000-01	Sri Lanka	1	1	0	7	7	7	0	0	0	
2001-02	India	3	2	0	18	18	9	0	0	2	
2001-02	New Zealand	5	3	1	35	21*	17.5	0	0	1	
2002	England	4	1	1	2	2*		0	0	0	
2002-03	Sri Lanka	1	1	1	2	2*		0	0	0	
2002-03	South Africa	2	2	0	19	17	9.5	0	0	4	
2003	England	8	4	3	24	20*	24	0	0	1	
2003-04	Bangladesh	2	0							2	
2003-04	Sri Lanka	1	1	0	21	21	21	0	0	0	
2004	England	9	6	2	93	39	23.25	0	0	5	
2004-05	South Africa	7	4	0	79	41	19.75	0	0	3	
2004-05	Zimbabwe	3	1	1	3	3*		0	0	1	
2005	England	8	4	2	51	25*	25.5	0	0	2	

Bowling

Season		Balls	Mdns	Runs	Wkts	BB	Ave	4wl	5wl	SR	Econ
1997	England	54	0	48	0						5.33
1998	England	54	0	37	2	2-37	18.5	0	0	27	4.11
1998-99	Bangladesh	60	1	41	1	1-41	41	0	0	60	4.1
1998-99	Australia	60	0	71	2	1-31	35.5	0	0	30	7.1
2000-01	Pakistan	168	1	118	3	2-45	39.33	0	0	56	4.21
2000-01	Sri Lanka	30	0	21	0						4.2
2001-02	India	156	0	145	7	5-57	20.71	0	1	22.28	5.57
2001-02	New Zealand	222	2	155	2	2-32	77.5	0	0	111	4.18
2002	England	180	1	157	5	3-39	31.4	0	0	36	5.23
2002-03	Sri Lanka	24	0	31	0						7.75
2002-03	South Africa	60	0	42	2	2-42	21	0	0	30	4.2
2003	England	378	2	257	3	2-3	85.66	0	0	126	4.07
2003-04	Sri Lanka										
2003-04	Bangladesh	114	3	61	4	3-29	15.25	0	0	28.5	3.21
2004	England	354	3	214	9	3-26	23.77	0	0	39.33	3.62
2004-05	South Africa	378	0	278	7	3-18	39.71	0	0	54	4.41
2004-05	Zimbabwe	162	2	93	5	2-12	18.6	0	0	32.4	3.44
2005	England	402	2	300	3	1-28	100	0	0	134	4.4

ODIs for England against each opponent

Batting & Fielding

Opponent	M	I	NO	R	HS	Ave	100	50	Ct	St
Australia	10	5	2	53	25*	17.66	0	0	5	
Bangladesh	4	0							2	
India	10	5	2	61	39	20.33	0	0	5	
New Zealand	6	4	1	35	21*	11.66	0	0	2	
Pakistan	7	4	0	34	17	8.5	0	0	1	
South Africa	13	8	3	106	41	21.2	0	0	4	
Sri Lanka	5	4	2	38	21	19	0	0	2	
West Indies	2	2	1	31	31	31	0	0	0	
Zimbabwe	5	3	2	27	23	27	0	0	1	

Bowling

Opponent	Balls	Mdns	Runs	Wkts	BB	Ave	4wl	5wl	SR	Econ
Australia	486	2	390	6	2-42	65	0	0	81	4.81
Bangladesh	234	3	141	5	3-29	28.2	0	0	46.8	3.61
India	510	2	397	17	5-57	23.35	0	1	30	4.67
New Zealand	222	2	155	2	2-32	77.5	0	0	111	4.18
Pakistan	312	1	204	4	2-45	51	0	0	78	3.92
South Africa	672	3	477	12	3-18	39.75	0	0	56	4.25
Sri Lanka	96	0	84	2	1-2	42	0	0	48	5.25
West Indies	60	1	43	0						4.3
Zimbabwe	264	3	178	7	2-12	25.42	0	0	37.71	4.04

First-class matches

Batting & Fielding

Team	M	I	NO	R	HS	Ave	100	50	Ct	St
England	54	81	13	1421	59	20.89	0	4	33	
England A	9	10	1	221	46	24.55	0	0	4	
England XI	14	18	2	326	49	20.37	0	0	6	
First-Class Counties Select XI	1	1	0	81	81	81	0	1	2	
Warwickshire	100	139	30	3297	128*	30.24	3	17	35	

Bowling

Team	Balls	Mdns	Runs	Wkts	BB	Ave	5wl	10wM
England	12180	397	5806	143	5-57	40.6	5	0
England A	2062	118	670	31	5-43	21.61	1	0
England XI	2086	86	954	41	4-37	23.26	0	0
First-Class Counties Select XI	168	10	68	1	1-55	68	0	0
Warwickshire	20808	997	8460	323	8-90	26.19	20	3

First-class matches season by season

Batting & Fielding

Season		M	I	NO	R	HS	Ave	100	50	Ct	St
1993	England	2	4	1	53	23	17.66	0	0	0	
1995	England	6	5	0	84	32	16.8	0	0	0	
1996	England	17	27	9	600	106*	33.33	1	4	11	
1996-97	Australia	3	4	0	66	29	16.5	0	0	0	
1997	England	16	20	4	624	97	39	0	5	4	
1997-98	Sri Lanka	5	6	1	155	46	31	0	0	3	
1997-98	Kenya	1	0							1	
1998	England	14	21	5	489	83	30.56	0	3	7	
1999	England	16	23	5	375	123*	20.83	1	0	6	
2000	England	13	14	3	444	128*	40.36	1	1	4	
2000-01	Pakistan	6	6	1	147	39	29.4	0	0	5	
2000-01	Sri Lanka	5	9	2	57	17	8.14	0	0	2	
2001	England	4	7	2	72	40*	14.4	0	0	4	
2001-02	New Zealand	4	5	1	65	26	16.25	0	0	6	
2001-02	India	3	5	1	55	28	13.75	0	0	0	
2002	England	9	12	0	264	68	22	0	1	3	
2002-03	Australia	3	4	1	24	13	8	0	0	2	
2003	England	12	18	1	556	96	32.7	0	4	2	
2003-04	Bangladesh	2	2	0	25	19	12.5	0	0	0	
2003-04	Sri Lanka	4	6	1	104	30	20.8	0	0	0	
2003-04	West Indies	5	5	0	99	37	19.8	0	0	3	
2004	England	8	10	2	289	70	36.12	0	2	3	
2004-05	South Africa	6	10	1	212	39	23.55	0	0	6	
2005	England	9	16	3	274	62	21.07	0	2	5	
2005-06	Pakistan	3	6	1	139	49	27.8	0	0	2	
2006-07	Australia	2	4	1	74	27*	24.66	0	0	1	

Bowling

Season		Balls	Mdns	Runs	Wkts	BB	Ave	5wI	10wM
1993	England	249	6	128	3	1-27	42.66	0	0
1995	England	881	46	354	16	5-23	22.12	1	0
1996	England	3801	192	1615	64	6-45	25.23	3	0
1996-97	Australia	554	28	199	6	3-28	33.16	0	0
1997	England	3037	155	1225	38	4-54	32.23	0	0
1997-98	Sri Lanka	1478	89	458	23	5-43	19.91	1	0
1997-98	Kenya	30	1	13	2	2-13	6.5	0	0
1998	England	2757	154	1025	36	5-48	28.47	1	0
1999	England	2686	145	938	39	5-28	24.05	2	0
2000	England	3160	163	1200	52	8-90	23.07	5	2
2000-01	Pakistan	1467	74	553	25	5-75	22.12	1	0
2000-01	Sri Lanka	1105	41	521	13	4-11	40.07	0	0
2001	England	929	41	429	12	5-46	35.75	1	0
2001-02	New Zealand	753	49	246	7	5-67	35.14	1	0
2001-02	India	811	32	304	7	4-103	43.42	0	0
2002	England	2515	67	1222	36	7-142	33.94	3	1
2002-03	Australia	728	16	410	13	4-101	31.53	0	0
2003	England	2249	62	1146	22	5-115	52.09	1	0
2003-04	Bangladesh	1323	59	595	22	5-116	27.04	1	0
2003-04	Sri Lanka	522	18	245	11	3-23	22.27	0	0
2003-04	West Indies	234	7	112	1	1-52	112	0	0
2004	England	2173	79	939	35	5-57	26.82	2	0
2004-05	South Africa	899	20	494	13	3-105	38	0	0
2005	England	1943	44	1023	34	6-44	30.08	3	0
2005-06	Pakistan	528	11	302	6	3-14	50.33	0	0
2006-07	Australia	492	9	262	3	1-46	87.33	0	0

First-class matches against each opponent

Batting & Fielding

Opponent	M	I	NO	R	HS	Ave	100	50	Ct	St
Australia	9	18	3	253	59	16.86	0	1	8	
Bangladesh	2	2	0	25	19	12.5	0	0	0	
Cambridge University	1	1	0	17	17	17	0	0	0	
Canterbury	1	1	0	26	26	26	0	0	2	
Carib Beer XI	1	1	0	22	22	22	0	0	1	
Derbyshire	4	6	1	118	67*	23.6	0	1	2	
Durham	3	5	2	39	13	13	0	0	0	
Essex	6	9	0	170	63	18.88	0	1	1	
Glamorgan	8	8	2	111	29	18.5	0	0	2	
Gloucestershire	7	11	1	149	37	14.9	0	0	3	
Hampshire	6	8	3	166	75	33.2	0	1	3	
India	5	7	0	128	31	18.28	0	0	1	
India A	1	2	1	12	10*	12	0	0	0	
Kent	6	8	1	219	68	31.28	0	2	5	
Kenya	1	0							1	
Lancashire	4	5	1	209	106*	52.25	1	1	1	
Leicestershire	4	7	3	93	34*	23.25	0	0	1	
Middlesex	7	9	2	310	96	44.28	0	2	3	
New Zealand	6	8	3	152	45*	30.4	0	0	4	
NW Frontier Prov Gov XI	1	1	0	24	24	24	0	0	0	
Northamptonshire	4	6	1	189	73*	37.8	0	1	1	
Nottinghamshire	7	10	1	297	94	33	0	1	1	
Oxford University	2	2	2	192	123*		1	1	1	
Oxford UCCE	1	2	1	1	1	1	0	0	0	
Pakistan	5	7	2	125	37*	25	0	0	5	
Pakistan A	2	3	0	151	81	50.33	0	1	2	
PCB Patron's XI	1	1	0	39	39	39	0	0	0	
Pakistan Cricket Board XI	1	1	0	28	28	28	0	0	2	
Pakistanis	1	1	0	28	28	28	0	0	0	
Queensland	2	2	1	27	20	27	0	0	0	
Somerset	4	7	0	143	97	20.42	0	1	3	
South Africa	10	16	2	321	41	22.92	0	0	6	
South Africa A	1	2	0	24	22	12	0	0	1	
South Australia	1	2	0	17	17	8.5	0	0	0	
Sri Lanka	8	13	3	134	45	13.4	0	0	3	
Sri Lanka A	3	4	1	115	46	38.33	0	0	2	
Sri Lanka Board Pres XI	4	5	0	78	30	15.6	0	0	1	
Sri Lanka Colts XI	1	1	0	34	34	34	0	0	0	
Surrey	6	10	1	224	70	24.88	0	2	0	
Sussex	8	10	4	322	128*	53.66	1	1	1	
UWI Vice-Chancellor's XI	1	1	0	2	2	2	0	0	0	
Victoria	1	1	0	29	29	29	0	0	0	
West Indies	7	8	0	181	52	22.62	0	1	5	
Western Australia	1	1	0	0	0	0	0	0	0	
Worcestershire	6	6	1	134	83	26.8	0	1	3	
Yorkshire	4	8	3	166	83	33.2	0	1	4	
Zimbabwe	2	2	0	102	52	51	0	2	1	

Bowling

Opponent	Balls	Mdns	Runs	Wkts	BB	Ave	5wI	10wM
Australia	1922	32	1139	20	4-101	56.95	0	0
Bangladesh	234	7	112	1	1-52	112	0	0
Cambridge University	114	7	44	4	2-10	11	0	0
Canterbury	211	12	68	1	1-40	68	0	0
Carib Beer XI	204	9	59	4	2-25	14.75	0	0
Derbyshire	914	56	304	14	4-62	21.71	0	0
Durham	582	24	220	13	6-45	16.92	1	0
Essex	1288	70	535	19	5-115	28.15	1	0
Glamorgan	1784	82	732	30	6-44	24.4	3	0
Gloucestershire	1425	69	583	22	4-60	26.5	0	0
Hampshire	1562	75	640	24	5-48	26.66	1	0
India	1407	69	552	11	5-67	50.18	1	0
India A	102	3	48	1	1-48	48	0	0
Kent	1361	48	635	28	7-142	22.67	3	1
Kenya	30	1	13	2	2-13	6.5	0	0
Lancashire	658	29	303	8	4-165	37.87	0	0
Leicestershire	698	27	356	6	5-126	59.33	1	0
Middlesex	1970	80	822	20	6-91	41.1	1	0
New Zealand	1284	41	538	15	4-46	35.86	0	0
NW Frontier Prov Gov XI	114	6	65	2	2-33	32.5	0	0
Northamptonshire	1021	56	394	24	8-90	16.41	3	2
Nottinghamshire	1161	37	506	8	5-70	63.25	1	0
Oxford University	450	31	125	10	5-28	12.5	1	0
Oxford UCCE	245	19	80	6	5-46	13.33	1	0
Pakistan	1542	64	657	20	5-75	32.85	1	0
Pakistan A	246	12	123	4	3-14	30.75	0	0
PCB Patron's XI	207	11	63	4	3-38	15.75	0	0
Pakistan Cricket Board XI	54	2	15	2	2-13	7.5	0	0
Pakistanis	180	16	41	5	3-39	8.2	0	0
Queensland	336	11	156	3	3-124	52	0	0
Somerset	589	21	312	12	4-69	26	0	0
South Africa	1907	40	1057	19	3-105	55.63	0	0
South Africa A	60	2	45	2	2-40	22.5	0	0
South Australia	278	14	120	5	3-28	24	0	0
Sri Lanka	2377	90	1038	31	5-116	33.48	1	0
Sri Lanka A	921	53	264	13	5-43	20.3	1	0
Sri Lanka Board Pres XI	809	36	395	17	4-37	23.23	0	0
Sri Lanka Colts XI	264	21	67	3	2-47	22.33	0	0
Surrey	1074	41	513	12	4-134	42.75	0	0
Sussex	1579	99	554	25	6-58	22.16	2	0
UWI Vice-Chancellor's XI	132	7	49	5	3-23	9.8	0	0
Victoria	180	10	47	1	1-32	47	0	0
West Indies	1303	43	646	24	5-57	26.91	2	0
Western Australia	168	4	95	4	3-42	23.75	0	0
Worcestershire	1298	73	408	23	5-23	17.73	1	0
Yorkshire	855	37	353	10	4-54	35.3	0	0
Zimbabwe	204	11	67	2	1-15	33.5	0	0